Praise for *Journey to the Heart of Aikido*

"An extraordinary contribution . . . this intimate and penetrating look into the development of Aikido reveals a sacred world of power, vision, and harmony. Linda Holiday has deftly crafted a historical narrative that allows us to see the inspiration of the founder of Aikido, embodied in one of his direct students. As the Aikido community evolves, this book will be a guidepost along the way. It's a classic."

— **Richard Strozzi-Heckler**, PhD, author of *The Leadership Dojo* and *In Search of the Warrior Spirit;* chief instructor, Two Rock Aikido; co-founder, Tamalpais Aikido

"Through his teachings, Anno Sensei guides us with a benevolent smile and the deepest humility to 'the heart of Aikido.' His reflections on all aspects of practice are very rich. *Journey to the Heart of Aikido* is also a beautiful testimonial to fidelity: that of student to teacher, and teacher to O-Sensei."

— **Christian Tissier**, Aikido seventh dan, shihan, Paris, France

"Today there are few instructors who can speak from personal experience about the founder of Aikido. I read with great interest Motomichi Anno Sensei's portrait of the founder, and his impressions of O-Sensei's instruction and personal character, interwoven with his own reflections on a lifetime of practice. Linda Holiday's experiences practicing Aikido at the Kumano Juku Dojo in the 1970s also make for a truly fascinating story."

— **Hiroshi Ikeda**, Aikido seventh dan, shihan; chief instructor, Boulder Aikikai

"The teachings of Aikido are truly universal, and thus this book is for everyone. Anno Sensei's lifelong journey along the path of love and harmony is an inspiration to us all. I praise Linda Holiday for her dedication in bringing this treasure to the world, as I know it will help guide countless readers on their path to personal and global peace."

— **Brant Secunda**, shaman and healer in the Huichol tradition; author of *Fit Soul, Fit Body: 9 Keys to a Healthier, Happier You*

"*Journey to the Heart of Aikido* offers a portrait of the founder born of Anno Sensei's deep love and close contact with O-Sensei. He retells many wonderful stories and shares profoundly important teachings received directly from the founder. This is an invaluable resource for all Aikidoists and for other martial artists as well . . . a book I am planning to read many times over, to let its rich wisdom sink in."

— **Robert Frager**, PhD, Aikido seventh dan; founder, Sofia University; president, Western Aikido Association

"Linda Holiday writes with devotion and a pure heart. *Journey to the Heart of Aikido* inspires greatness through humility, dedication, and self-responsibility. Through Linda's personal story and the teachings of Anno Sensei, I feel that I have been introduced to the living flame of the lineage of Aikido burning bright."

— **Tami Simon,** founder and publisher, Sounds True

"For over forty years I have endeavored to understand how O-Sensei was able to manifest *love* in response to aggression, both on and off the Aikido mat. This book is a gift for all who wish to develop greater spiritual understanding of Aikido, its universal application, our potential to embody the principles, and the amazing abilities of its founder."

— **Wendy Palmer,** author of *The Practice of Freedom: Aikido Principles as a Spiritual Guide*

"A truly exceptional and vibrant Aikido book. Reading *Journey to the Heart of Aikido* is like traveling through time and space to meet with the founder of Aikido and step into his world of sincere physical and spiritual determination and practice, inspired by the sacred nature in Kumano. This book is a treasure."

— **Jan Nevelius,** Aikido sixth dan, shihan, Vanadis Aikido Dojo, Sweden

"Brilliant, illuminating. . . *Journey to the Heart of Aikido* is aptly named. Linda Holiday opens our eyes to the light that shines on the path."

— **Frank Doran,** Aikido seventh dan, shihan; chief instructor, Aikido West Dojo

"Those who read this book will not only be rewarded with a deep understanding of what Aikido is, they will be entertained and moved by Anno Sensei's personal and ongoing journey to go deeper into Aikido's essence."

— **Mary Heiny,** Aikido sixth dan, Seattle, Washington

"The flow of universal knowledge from O-Sensei through Anno Sensei to Linda Holiday. . . Read this book and enjoy that inspired journey."

— **Robert Nadeau,** Aikido seventh dan, shihan, direct student of O-Sensei

"This is a long-awaited account of Aikido's development in Kumano's mysterious mountains. The simplicity with which Aikido's positive message is articulated here may stir many people looking for meaning in life to seek an answer in the practice of Aikido. It may well help us all to transform the ravages of a materialistic world."

— **Susan Perry,** PhD, Aikido sixth dan; author of *Remembering O-Sensei*

"Linda Holiday's clear, poetic translation of Anno Sensei's teachings provides a wonderful resource for those of us wishing to better understand the words of Aikido founder Morihei Ueshiba. Anno Sensei's humility, compassion, and wisdom are ever apparent."

— **Darrell Bluhm,** Aikido sixth dan, shihan; chief instructor, Siskiyou Aikikai, Oregon

"*Journey to the Heart of Aikido* resonates with the truth of the Oneness of us all. Even readers unfamiliar with the art of Aikido will feel and recognize it. The most important thing for our world community is recognizing and valuing the connection that we have with all beings—a connection that the founder of Aikido talked about, and that Motomichi Anno teaches from his own heart."

— **Danielle Smith,** Aikido sixth dan; chief instructor, Aikido of Monterey

"What a great story. Well told, tender in places, with a genuine warmth and depth . . . and so inspiring. It is a tale of humanity, not just a martial art. It will reach out and touch everyone."

— **Hans Goto,** Aikido seventh dan; founder and chief instructor, Bay Marin Aikido

JOURNEY
to the HEART
of AIKIDO

The Teachings of
Motomichi Anno Sensei

LINDA HOLIDAY

BLUE SNAKE BOOKS
BERKELEY, CALIFORNIA

Published by Blue Snake Books, an imprint of North Atlantic Books
Berkeley, California

Cover photo of Anno Sensei © Beau Saunders, 2012.
  Cover photo of Nachi Falls © Akhenaton Lichterowicz, 2011.
Front cover image collage by Scott Evans
Book design by Brad Greene
Photo archiving, restoration, and editing by Beau Saunders
Printed in the United States of America

Journey to the Heart of Aikido: The Teachings of Motomichi Anno Sensei is sponsored and published by the Society for the Study of Native Arts and Sciences (dba North Atlantic Books), an educational nonprofit based in Berkeley, California, that collaborates with partners to develop cross-cultural perspectives, nurture holistic views of art, science, the humanities, and healing, and seed personal and global transformation by publishing work on the relationship of body, spirit, and nature.

North Atlantic Books' publications are available through most bookstores. For further information, call 800-733-3000 or visit our websites at www.northatlanticbooks.com and www.bluesnakebooks.com.

PLEASE NOTE: The creators and publishers of this book disclaim any liabilities for loss in connection with following any of the practices, exercises, and advice contained herein. To reduce the chance of injury or any other harm, the reader should consult a professional before undertaking this or any other martial arts, movement, meditative arts, health, or exercise program. The instructions and advice printed in this book are not in any way intended as a substitute for medical, mental, or emotional counseling with a licensed physician or healthcare provider.

Library of Congress Cataloging-in-Publication Data
Holiday, Linda, 1952-
    Journey to the heart of aikido : the teachings of Motomichi Anno sensei / Linda Holiday.
        pages cm
    ISBN 978-1-58394-659-6
  1. Aikido—Philosophy. 2. Aikido—Training. 3. Anno, Motomichi. I. Title.
    GV1114.35.H64 2013
    796.815'4—dc23

2013008239

3 4 5 6 7 8 9 SHERIDAN 21 20 19 18 17

Printed on recycled paper

North Atlantic Books is committed to the protection of our environment. We partner with FSC-certified printers using soy-based inks and print on recycled paper whenever possible.

CONTENTS

FOREWORD by MOTOMICHI ANNO SENSEI

Aikido is a path, both extremely old and extremely new, which shows us how to live as human beings.

"*Aiki* is love," declared the founder of Aikido, Morihei Ueshiba O-Sensei. "Aikido is the form and heart of *kami* [divine spirit]." By this, I believe the founder taught that all existence, all things in the universe, form a vast, unified world of harmonious connections.

The purpose of Aikido is not to create opponents or to engage in win-lose competitions with others. It is a way to develop the heart: to cultivate, together with others, a heart of harmony, a heart of love, and a heart of gratitude. The true purpose of Aikido is to make a contribution to the world with this spirit.

As cultures around the world have become increasingly materialistic, people's values have radically changed. The spirit of harmony, love, and gratitude, essential to us as human beings, has been swept aside in the focus on material affluence, and there is a growing sense of unease and confusion.

Now more than ever, I feel there is a need to reflect on our way of life and reconnect with the fundamentals of our humanity. By recognizing that our own lives depend upon living in harmony with all things in nature, I believe we will reach a new understanding of the importance of the world of the heart.

The author and translator of this book, Linda Holiday, first came to Kumano in 1973. Kumano has been a sacred place in Japan since ancient times, and it was the birthplace of Aikido's founder. Drawn to Aikido, Linda became a student at the Kumano Juku Dojo, established by the founder of Aikido and headed by the late Michio Hikitsuchi Sensei.

In the remote countryside of Kumano, barely able at first to speak Japanese, Linda committed herself to the path of Aikido and threw body and soul into intensive training. Such dedication can truly be described as a journey to the heart of Aikido. For her tireless efforts and devotion to the path, I offer my deepest gratitude and respect.

It is my hope that this book will present the philosophy of Aikido in a way that makes it accessible to many people. My sincere wish is that the book will inspire you to a deeper understanding of the heart of Aikido—the heart of harmony, love, and gratitude—and illuminate the future with the light of new hope.

—MOTOMICHI ANNO
JANUARY 2013

TRANSLATED FROM THE JAPANESE BY LINDA HOLIDAY

まえがき

合気道は　最も古く　最も新しい　人間として生きる道です

合気は愛なり　と合気道開祖植芝盛平大先生が　喝破されました
さらに　合気道は　神の姿　神の心である　と教えて下さいました
その意味は　宇宙万有すべてのものが　大和合した営みの世界であることを
お説きくだされたと受け止めています

合気道は　相手を作り　相手と勝ち負けの競い合いが　目的ではありません
相手と共に　和の心　愛の心　感謝の心　こころを養成する道です
この精神を以って　社会に貢献することが　本来の目的です

今日の社会は物質文明が主体となり　人間の価値観が大きく変わってしまった
人間として一番大切な精神　和と愛と感謝の心が　ものの豊かさに押し流され
世界は不安と混迷の現状です

今一度　人間としての生き方を　根本から問い直すことが必要です
自然のすべてのものと共に　調和して生かされている自分を知ることによって
心の世界の大切さが解ってくると信じます

作者と翻訳者　リンダ　ホリディ氏は　1973 年に熊野に訪れました
熊野は日本の古い歴史のある聖なるところ　開祖の出生地です
リンダ氏は合気道に魅力を感じ　開祖の残した　熊野塾道場で
故引土道雄道場長のもとに入門しました

当時　言葉も通じない彼女は　熊野の奥地で　合気道一筋　必死の修行に
打ち込まれました　　その姿は　まさに　合気道の心への旅
この言葉につきると思います　　今日にいたる　幾多の努力と労苦に対し
衷心より感謝と敬意をおくります

本書は　合気道の理念をだれにでも解りやすく書かれていると希望します
本書によって　合気道の心　和と愛と感謝の心を　もう一度見直して頂くことで
明日の世界に　新しい希望の光が輝いてくることを祈ります

2013 年1月　　　　　　　　　　　　　　　　　　　　庵野素岐

Aikido, "The Way of Harmony"; brushed by
Morihei Ueshiba O-Sensei, founder of Aikido.

INTRODUCTION
An INVITATION to the JOURNEY
Linda Holiday

The founder of Aikido, Morihei Ueshiba O-Sensei, presented a profound paradox.

During his long life (1883–1969), the founder of this new martial art inspired thousands of people with his powerful techniques and his message of transcendent spirituality. Called simply O-Sensei, "Great Teacher," he was known as an invincible martial artist, yet he proclaimed, "The essence of *budo* [the martial way] is love." While demonstrating nonviolent control of all would-be attackers, O-Sensei taught that his effectiveness derived from the principles of harmony, purification, and love.

Countless students were attracted by the power of O-Sensei's martial art and by his uplifting spiritual message. They were drawn to the inexplicable yet palpable unity of apparent opposites, which he manifested daily on the Aikido mat. O-Sensei described his Aikido as the art of loving attack and peaceful reconciliation. "Attacker" and "defender" joined together in a startling, seamless harmony that rendered violence harmless. People traveled from all over the world to experience this phenomenon firsthand. The paradox O-Sensei presented was resolved, during his lifetime, by his personal presence.

Since the founder's passing in 1969, his art has spread rapidly throughout the world. More than a million and a half people in ninety countries now practice Aikido, known as "The Way of Harmony" or "The Art of Peace." Aikido has proven to have wide appeal as a nonviolent martial art, a model of successful conflict resolution, and a multifaceted mental, physical, and spiritual discipline promoting health and harmony. People who undertake the practice of Aikido are

xi

understandably enthusiastic about its many pleasures and benefits. Yet how many of this growing number of Aikido students and teachers are fully exploring the profound spiritual message embodied by its founder?

As the lifetime of Aikido's founder recedes into the shadows of the previous century, there is a new challenge to be met. O-Sensei's personal students—the first generation of Aikido teachers, who dedicated their lives to passing on what they had absorbed directly from its founder—are rapidly decreasing in number. Without the personal presence of O-Sensei or his direct students, how will Aikido continue to revitalize its essence in new generations, as the path of spiritual evolution envisioned by its founder? There is a possibility that Aikido may gradually devolve back into the combat techniques that constituted only the beginning of O-Sensei's art, and lose the spiritual essence he so treasured.

The aim of *Journey to the Heart of Aikido* is to increase the accessibility of the founder's spiritual teachings around the world. It brings into print for the first time the wise and compassionate voice of Motomichi Anno Sensei, eighth-degree black belt, master-teacher *(shihan)* of Aikido, and a direct student of the founder. Born and raised in the Kumano region of Japan, the founder's homeland, Anno Sensei was profoundly moved by the experience of learning directly from O-Sensei during the final fifteen years of the founder's life. Since 1954, Anno Sensei has trained and taught Aikido at the Kumano Juku Dojo, headed by the late Michio Hikitsuchi Sensei, who was a close personal disciple of the founder. In 2004, fifty years after stepping onto the mat, Anno Sensei succeeded Hikitsuchi Sensei as the chief instructor of this historic dojo. Now in his eighties, Anno Sensei has devoted his life to offering the heart teachings of Aikido to students in Japan, Europe, and the United States. *Journey to the Heart of Aikido* brings Anno Sensei's story, his early studies with O-Sensei, and his teachings on the spiritual philosophy of Aikido to readers worldwide.

I began my own study of Aikido more than four decades ago, as a young American woman in the early years of Aikido in the United States. I traveled to Japan to undertake intensive training in 1973, just four years after the passing of Aikido's founder. Studying under O-Sensei's direct students in Japan was a life-changing experience for me. While living and training in the mystical Kumano region of Japan, I first met Anno Sensei, who became my lifelong Aikido mentor and teacher. Since returning to the United States in the late 1970s, I have dedicated myself to Aikido training and transmission in the West, as director and chief instructor of a major Aikido school in California and through seminars in the United States and Europe.

I feel very fortunate to have had the opportunity to bring Anno Sensei from Japan to the United States numerous times, and to introduce his deep, encouraging wisdom to others. Since 1999, I have facilitated Anno Sensei's visits to the United States and served as his interpreter and interviewer. Much of the content in *Journey to the Heart of Aikido* has been drawn from classes, conversations, and interviews with Anno Sensei since he began teaching in the United States. I am grateful to Anno Sensei for allowing me the opportunity to transcribe, translate, and edit this material, which has deepened my own practice and my appreciation of the profound teachings of Aikido. *Journey to the Heart of Aikido: The Teachings of Motomichi Anno Sensei* is the result of many years of study, translation, teaching, and collaboration with this generous and inspiring teacher.

I should tell you that Motomichi Anno Sensei does not like to call himself a teacher. He prefers to emphasize an open-ended, mutual learning process, often remarking, "We are all brothers and sisters walking the path together." While he speaks with simple eloquence about the philosophy of Aikido, Anno Sensei also emphasizes a rigorous practice of physical techniques, utilizing them as tools to develop understanding. His presence on the mat is vibrant and expansive. But he consistently points away from himself, away from the ego, and calls our attention to the ongoing process of purification exemplified by the founder of Aikido.

It is our hope that *Journey to the Heart of Aikido* will be a valuable resource for the global Aikido community, and a source of inspiration for all who are interested in Asian wisdom and spiritual practice. These teachings of the heart of Aikido speak powerfully to Aikido students and teachers of all levels, as well as to people who have not participated in Aikido before and may never undertake its physical practice. This is not a book of technique, nor is it an advertisement for any particular "style" of Aikido. Through focusing on the essential message of the founder of the art, we hope to strengthen a sense of worldwide common purpose, inquiry, and practice.

~

Journey to the Heart of Aikido: The Teachings of Motomichi Anno Sensei consists of two complementary parts. In Part One, The Journey, I weave together personal narrative and historical information, inviting you into a deep connection with the world of Aikido and its living lineage. Chapter 1 tells the story of my personal journey on the Aikido path, which drew me from California to Japan in 1973. Come along with me as I meet Anno Sensei and others in the remote Kumano area of Japan and undergo the traditional rigors of training there. In Chapter 2, I introduce you to Motomichi Anno as a child in rural, war-torn Japan, and describe the evolution of his life in Aikido. His fateful meeting with the founder of Aikido in 1954 set Anno Sensei's life on a new course, and ultimately led him to become an international teacher of peace. Anno Sensei's story is braided together with stories of O-Sensei, Hikitsuchi Sensei, and others, providing a new window into the postwar development of Aikido in Japan and its subsequent international expansion.

In Part Two, The Heart of Aikido: Teachings of Motomichi Anno Sensei, the book shifts from narrative to deep reflections on the heart of Aikido, direct from a master-teacher who studied with the founder. In Chapter 3, Anno Sensei communicates what it was like for him to study personally with O-Sensei, and shares his memories of O-Sensei's teachings and presence. In Chapter 4, he explores the basic spiritual principles that are the foundation of Aikido practice, and gives thoughtful answers to questions posed by Western students. In Chapter 5, Anno Sensei explains how the principles of Aikido can be expressed and cultivated in the physical training of Aikido. Chapter 6 introduces the traditional practices of breathing and purification in Aikido and applies the concept of *misogi* (purification) to other parts of life. In Chapter 7, Anno Sensei explores the meaning of terms O-Sensei used to "express the inexpressible," such as *kami* and the Floating Bridge of Heaven, and offers an essential understanding of interdependence and gratitude. In the final chapter, Anno Sensei articulates the value of Aikido's spiritual philosophy and pragmatic practice to a global community urgently in need of peace. It is an empowering vision, communicated sincerely from one heart to another.

$\sim$

My own motivations in writing *Journey to the Heart of Aikido* are simple ones: gratitude and service. I believe the best way to repay the generosity of Motomichi Anno Sensei, and all of the Aikido teachers who have shared their inspiration with me, is to pass it on. I dedicate *Journey to the Heart of Aikido* to the hope that the integrated spiritual practice of Aikido will play a positive role in the evolving future of humankind.

Step forward with us on the *Journey to the Heart of Aikido*. It is a work of love, an offering of the heart.

—LINDA HOLIDAY
SANTA CRUZ, CALIFORNIA

Motomichi Anno Sensei at the Kumano Juku Dojo in Shingu, Japan, 2012. The calligraphy, "Aikido," was brushed by the founder of Aikido.

Oyunohara, an ancient sacred site in the mountains of Kumano, Japan.

Nachi Falls, in Kumano. The highest waterfall in Japan, it has been a place of pilgrimage and purification for over a thousand years.

The founder of Aikido, Morihei Ueshiba O-Sensei (1883–1969).

PART I

The JOURNEY

How beautiful!
The sacred form of
Heaven and earth
Created as
One family

—A "Poem of the Way"[1]
by Morihei Ueshiba O-Sensei,
founder of Aikido

Michi, "The Path"; calligraphy brushed
by Motomichi Anno Sensei.

~1~

STEPS on the PATH

"There are no strangers, and no national boundaries, in the spirit."[2]

—MORIHEI UESHIBA O-SENSEI, FOUNDER OF AIKIDO

Reunion

On a clear summer day in 1999, Motomichi Anno Sensei steps through the door of my new Aikido dojo for the first time, fresh from Japan. He is nearly seventy years old, his short black hair sprinkled with white and his face deeply creased with smile lines, but he is essentially unchanged from the robust teacher I first met in Japan almost thirty years before. The same electricity is in the air around him, the same inviting light in his eyes. Although he has journeyed here from the other side of the planet, he seems to feel naturally at home.

With familiar warmth, Anno Sensei connects directly, heart to heart, with my students. They experience firsthand the flowing movement, startling humility, and joyful presence of the teacher whose practice has inspired me since 1973. The aura of peace surrounding him has only deepened over the years. Listening to Anno Sensei, my students immediately learn the Japanese word *kokoro:* heart. He speaks to them candidly of his personal experiences with the founder of Aikido, O-Sensei, just as he first did to my eager ears a quarter of a century ago, in the remote countryside of western Japan.

"O-Sensei taught us that the essence of Aikido is love," Anno Sensei tells them. "It is the path of peace. The goal of Aikido is to bring people together in friendship and harmony."

When Anno Sensei teaches, a subtle illumination occurs. It seems that people begin to shine from the inside. He invites us to remember the original teachings of the founder, O-Sensei, and to make a commitment to explore the heart of Aikido as "brothers and sisters walking the path together." The words are simple, but the experience of hearts opening is real.

Pouring out their questions, people ask Anno Sensei what kind of person O-Sensei was, and how it is possible for the spirit of love to be cultivated through training in martial art techniques. They ask Anno Sensei how they can pursue a lifelong practice of Aikido with inspiration and integrity. They want to know what kind of obstacles Anno Sensei has encountered in his own training, and how he has overcome them. I translate for hours every day, Japanese and English cascading through me in a rapidly alternating current, until I am no longer able to tell which language I am speaking.

"O-Sensei told us to study English," Anno Sensei reminisces ruefully in Japanese, as I interpret his words for a group of students gathered around him. "He predicted that Aikido would spread throughout the world as a path of peace, and his personal students would need to be able to talk with other people about it. At that time, it was hard for me to imagine how such a thing would ever come to be. World War II was not long over, and I was training in Shingu, where everyone spoke Japanese. So I didn't take up the study of English. But look! O-Sensei's vision of Aikido spreading throughout the world has come true."

As Anno Sensei speaks, it feels as if everything I have done over the last three decades has led to this moment. Those thirty years of perseverance in Aikido, several years of intensive training in Japan, and my study of Japanese language and culture now enable me to facilitate this unique transmission. More than twenty years of develop-

Linda Holiday interprets for Motomichi Anno Sensei during a class at her dojo, Aikido of Santa Cruz, California.

ing a large, lively Aikido community here in Santa Cruz, California, and the recent, long-awaited acquisition of our own spacious dojo building have made it possible for these crowds of eager students to study closely with my own teacher, who brings the personal message of the founder right into the room. The inspiration is flowing like a stream from O-Sensei, through Anno Sensei, through me, and through all the people gathered here, transcending differences of language and culture. I can feel the waves spreading into the future.

In the years that follow, the heart-teachings of Aikido continue to stream through Anno Sensei in classes, interviews, and discussions, forming the spontaneous, natural legacy of a rare teacher. I begin to dream of preserving these unrepeatable moments and making them available to all. With a tape recorder and a video camera, I try to capture what is pouring out so freely, as Anno Sensei conveys the heart of what he learned from O-Sensei. Finally, I approach Anno Sensei to ask if I might put together a book from the material generated through his connection with me and the other Western students. In his elder years, Anno Sensei's humility has become even more pronounced, and

I'm not sure what his response will be. His immediate "Yes" takes my breath away.

"But I'm not a writer," Anno Sensei reminds me. "You'll need to write the book, in English."

"I will write the book," I promise Anno Sensei. "I'll tell the story."

First Steps on the Aikido Path

When I initially encountered Aikido as a student at the University of California, Santa Cruz, in 1970, I had no idea it would become my life's passion and profession. In fact, I first took up the study of Aikido because I thought I would be bad at it.

The arts college required all first-year students to take a class in something we had never studied before, or for which we believed we would have no talent. "Aikido" seemed to fit the assignment, so I signed up. Although academic success had given me faith in my intellectual strength, I lacked physical confidence and had no history in athletics. Despite my nervousness in the unfamiliar environment on the Aikido mat, I was captivated from my very first class by the connection of mind and body in Aikido.

What fascinated me was the visceral experience that the mind, or *ki* as we called it, could lend strength to my body in perceivable ways. As instructed, I meditated on the *tanden,* the center point just below the navel, and visualized ki energy coursing through my limbs. Even as a beginning student, my body felt newly alive and more substantial, with the strength of harmony rather than physical force. The self-defense techniques of Aikido seemed to double as lessons in the power of the mind. I applied myself to the techniques and exercises my instructors shared with us, and although my physical progress was slow, I was an enthusiastic student.

At that time, Aikido was not known to the general public. Our university Aikido class was one of only five fledgling Aikido clubs in all of northern California, and there were no more than a handful of black belts in the region. Luckily, two of these rare resources teamed up to teach us in Santa Cruz. Robert Frager, a professor of psychology and religious studies, had studied in Tokyo under the founder of Aikido, O-Sensei. Upon returning to the United States, Frager Sensei started the first Aikido club in Berkeley, and then again in Santa Cruz, when he transferred to the newly established University of California campus there. His lighthearted, spiritual approach allayed my apprehension about practicing a martial art. He alternated classes with Frank Doran, a police officer with crystal-clear technique and a dignified presence, who soon became a highly regarded, professional Aikido teacher leading many international seminars. The next year, the program expanded to include an energetic black belt instructor by the name of Stanley Pranin, who later founded the internationally known periodical *Aikido Journal*. But in 1970, our classes were held just twice a week on folding mats in the middle of the gym, a casual and

The founder of Aikido at his residence in Iwama, Japan, with Aikido student Robert Frager, 1965.

decidedly un-Japanese environment. Frager Sensei had a few eight-millimeter silent films of O-Sensei, which he would occasionally show us. We gathered around the noisy projector to watch the small, grainy, black and white figures swirling mysteriously on the screen. I couldn't understand what I saw of O-Sensei's quick techniques, yet his demonstrations stirred in me an unexpected desire.

Although Frager Sensei told us that the founder of Aikido was no longer living, I didn't fully grasp the fact that O-Sensei had passed away only one year before—and that Aikido training was still ongoing and available in Japan. I would have been astonished to know that by attending these Aikido classes in Santa Cruz, I was taking the first steps of a life-changing journey that would lead me to Japan, to study with Aikido teachers who had been among O-Sensei's closest students. At the time I began my Aikido training, I was an eighteen-year-old woman, fresh from the music festivals and antiwar demonstrations of counterculture California. I wasn't looking for a teacher. I wasn't sure anyone knew any more than I did. But the Aikido training opened doors I never knew existed. The second year, I started going to all the Aikido classes there were—three or four times a week. Gradually, my academic studies paled in comparison to the mind-body epiphanies I seemed to experience every time I stepped on the mat. After two years at the university, I took a leave of absence. I borrowed money from my Aikido classmate Dick Revoir, and off we went to Japan for what I assumed would be a few months' adventure.

Off to Japan

My first glimpse of Japan from the air revealed a pretty, green land of forested mountains and rice paddies, dotted with blue-tiled roofs. But our plane headed northeast toward the massive smog-covered metropolis of Tokyo. We staggered off the plane at Haneda Airport wearing the hiking boots and down jackets that unmistakably identified us as young Americans trekking the world. At the airport, we made a reservation for a few nights at a Japanese-style inn, and rode the monorail train into the city to search for it.

It seemed as if everyone we saw on the streets was short, slim, black-haired, and rather quiet. At five-foot-six, I could see right over the heads of the Japanese crowds in the train stations, and my pale skin and long blond hair made me even more conspicuous. With our handful of Japanese words, and no ability to read the writing on the signs, Dick and I laboriously navigated Tokyo's train system and arrived at our Japanese inn. I still remember how long it took us to unlace our big boots and slide into the delicate indoor slippers provided for us, while the proprietress waited patiently. Then she shrieked when I ignorantly wore the slippers right onto the woven straw tatami mats in our room, instead of leaving them properly lined up in the doorway. A long education in the intricacies of Japanese etiquette began that night.

The next morning Dick and I struggled to find our way through the crowded maze of Tokyo streets to the Aikikai Hombu Dojo—the world headquarters of Aikido, where our teacher Robert Frager had trained with the founder, O-Sensei. Eventually we found ourselves in front of a recently built, five-story concrete building on a quiet side street of the intensely populated Shinjuku district of Tokyo. We stepped through the glass doors, registered at the office, and with excitement and trepidation, began our Aikido training in Japan.

It was just four years since the founder of Aikido had passed away, and at the Aikikai Hombu Dojo, the first generation of Aikido *shihan* master-teachers were still active and teaching. These included O-Sensei's son Kisshomaru Ueshiba, who presided with quiet dignity as the second hereditary *Doshu* ("Head of the Way"); Koichi Tohei, the soon-to-be-founder of the Ki Society; Kisaburo Osawa and Seigo Yamaguchi, whose smooth, effortless technique amazed us; Morihiro Saito, who came in from the town of Iwama to teach two rousing classes on Sunday mornings; Sadateru Arikawa, Shigenobu Okumura, and Hiroshi Tada, who filled the dojo with quiet electricity; and Mitsugi Saotome, a cheerful sensei with powerful ki who later moved to the United States, where I was glad to have the opportunity to study under him again, years later.

But as they say in Japan, "Time is like an arrow." Most of these marvelous teachers have since passed away or retired, leaving the instruction of students in the dedicated hands of the founder's

Top left: Kisshomaru Ueshiba (1921–1999), the second Aikido Doshu; son and successor of the founder of Aikido.

Bottom left: Moriteru Ueshiba (b. 1951), the third and current Aikido Doshu; grandson of the founder of Aikido. He prepares to offer a formal demonstration of Aikido at Oyunohara, in Kumano, Japan, 2008.

Right: Moriteru Ueshiba, the third Doshu, offers a demonstration of Aikido at the Kumano Hongu Shrine, 2012.

grandson and third Doshu, Moriteru Ueshiba, and the current generation of Aikido teachers. When I arrived at Hombu Dojo in 1973, though, I was dazzled by the sophisticated technique and energetic presence of all the instructors who had studied closely with O-Sensei. Aikido teachers and students poured into the dojo from all parts of Tokyo, filling the mat with vigorous marvels numerous times each day. I felt as if I had been suddenly transported to a magical kingdom where all things were possible.

The reality was much more complex and arduous. The canvas-covered tatami mats I trained on felt as hard as cement, and the techniques of safe falling and rolling that had taken me so long to learn in California were no match for the energetic throws of Tokyo black belts. Bruises blossomed all over my body. Doggedly I went to class after class, soaking my body afterward in the scalding waters of the public baths. Despite the physical discomfort, I felt inexplicably energized by the training. Words of the founder that I had heard from my teachers in Santa Cruz reverberated in my mind: "Aikido is not a technique to fight with or defeat an enemy. It is the way to harmonize the world and make humanity one family."[3] My bumpy rolls started to become smoother, and my stamina increased. When I had a tough day or a rough training partner, the philosophy of O-Sensei challenged me to look within: "Aikido is not for correcting others; it is for correcting your own mind."[4]

At the time I first arrived in Japan, an American woman by the name of Mary Heiny had been training with never-say-die determination at the Aikikai Hombu Dojo in Tokyo for six years. Mary Heiny Sensei is now a well-known Aikido teacher in the West, but in 1973 she was a rarity—a foreign woman with a second-degree black belt, devoted and vigorous in her Aikido practice. Equally impressive was her fluency in the Japanese language and her intensive study of all things Japanese, including traditional kimono, koto music, and natural healing systems. At that time there were few women training in Aikido, but with sheer persistence Mary had broken through the gender barriers and established herself as a serious student of the art. She disregarded patronizing attitudes and persevered in her training regardless of any obstacles that she encountered. She was an eye-opening role model for me, and a generous friend.

With five classes a day, many different instructors, and an urban anonymity to the Tokyo environment, it was easy to feel lost in the crowds of students at Hombu Dojo, especially as an inexperienced foreign student who did not yet speak Japanese. However, in the early 1970s there were already a dedicated group of international Aikido students who trained regularly there and had a noticeable presence. The French students seemed the most numerous, and there were a number of Americans, in addition to Mary Heiny, who also helped me adjust to the rigors of training.

Mary Heiny at the Aikikai Hombu Dojo in Tokyo, with Michio Hikitsuchi Sensei, former chief instructor of the Kumano Juku Dojo in Shingu; early 1970s.

As I visited with these American expatriates, over tea in their tiny Tokyo apartments, a few of them spoke quietly about another Aikido dojo, deep in the countryside of Japan, in the distant Kumano region. They described it as a mysterious place, remote, and filled with the spirit of the founder, O-Sensei. Mary Heiny had been introduced to the head instructor there, in the town of Shingu, and she trained at his dojo when she could get time off from her work in Tokyo. Just the year before, she had taken a small group of foreign Aikido students to Shingu for a few days' visit. Mary was about to travel there again with a friend, but the friend was suddenly unable to go. Unexpectedly, Mary offered Dick and me the opportunity to go with her. Fate stretched out its hand and I followed.

Kumano: O-Sensei's Homeland

The Kumano region of Japan is the homeland of Aikido's founder, Morihei Ueshiba O-Sensei. Located on the southern part of the Kii Peninsula, the largest peninsula in Japan, Kumano is a lush, beautiful land of steep mountains and rocky coastlines. The name Kumano originated in prehistoric times and conveys a sense of mystery and sacredness. Although the area is remote, it is known throughout Japan as a place of deep spirituality. Mountain ascetics, called *yamabushi*, have practiced a mystical amalgam of Buddhism and native Shinto in the rugged mountains of Kumano for more than a thousand years. One of O-Sensei's childhood heroes was Kobo Daishi (Kukai), the founder of the esoteric sect of Shingon ("True Word") Buddhism. In 819 CE, Kobo Daishi established a monastic retreat on Mount Koya in the mountains of the Kii Peninsula; it has been the headquarters of Shingon Buddhism ever since.

Beginning in the Heian Period (794–1192 CE), emperors and commoners alike made sacred pilgrimages to Kumano from all over Japan. The pilgrims were so numerous that they were said to resemble columns of ants. The Kumano area was associated with the Buddhist "Pure Land." In the sixteenth and seventeenth centuries, Buddhist missionary nuns called *Kumano Bikuni* traveled from Kumano to other areas of Japan proselytizing for the Kumano faith. This was a form of Buddhist-Shinto syncretic worship that was welcoming to spiritual pilgrims regardless of gender, unlike some of the Buddhist institutions that did not allow the participation of women. The stunningly beautiful land of Kumano was seen as a sacred mandala representing the Buddhist *Taizokai*—the Womb World—which complemented the *Kongokai*, or Diamond World, associated with an area north of Kumano.[5] The network of pilgrimage paths winding through mountains and river gorges—the *Kumano Kodo*, or "Ancient Paths of Kumano"—was designated by UNESCO in 2004 as a World Heritage Site.[6] It is still used by ascetic practitioners for spiritual training.

Morihei Ueshiba O-Sensei, Aikido's founder, was born in Kumano, in the coastal town of Tanabe. Throughout his life, he returned to Kumano frequently to make pilgrimages to the three Grand Shrines of Kumano, located in Shingu, Nachi, and Hongu. His own parents had undertaken the arduous pilgrimage from Tanabe through the steep mountains to the Kumano Hongu Shrine, to pray for the birth of a son (in addition to their three daughters); after O-Sensei was born, he was

Morihei Ueshiba on a pilgrimage to Nachi Falls in Kumano, c.1925.
(Image provided courtesy of Moriteru Ueshiba, Aikido Doshu.)

considered to be a child of the *kami* (sacred spirits; deities) of Kumano. Later in life, O-Sensei said, "My spirit was nurtured by Kumano, and part of me is always there."[7]

O-Sensei taught his *budo* (martial art) in the Kumano area before World War II. After the war ended, O-Sensei came again to Shingu, bringing his newly named art of "Aikido," which can be translated as "The Way of Harmony." At O-Sensei's request, his students in Shingu constructed one of the first postwar Aikido dojos in Japan, the Kumano Juku Dojo, only a block away from one of his favorite pilgrimage destinations, the Kumano Hayatama Shrine. O-Sensei considered the dojo in Shingu to be one of his personal dojos, and he often made the long journey down from Tokyo and Iwama, where he lived, to teach there.

On our first day in Shingu, Mary Heiny introduced Dick and me to the dojo's chief instructor, Michio Hikitsuchi Sensei, who had been a close personal student of the founder of Aikido. I was in awe of Hikitsuchi Sensei. His presence on the mat was stern and powerful, though his body was slight, and there was a subtle magnetic energy ever present around him that drew me in and generated a feeling of closeness. His one-story, traditional dojo in Shingu, with its large Shinto altar and O-Sensei's own calligraphy hanging on the wooden walls, looked like it was straight out of the samurai era. Hikitsuchi Sensei's techniques seemed sharp as a sword and filled with light. Outside of class, Hikitsuchi Sensei smiled at us and spoke warmly of his years studying with O-Sensei. He urged us to dedicate ourselves to spiritual training in Aikido. Then he surprised us by inviting us to study with him, in Shingu. We were to become the first non-Japanese students ever to live in Shingu and train full-time in the Kumano Juku Dojo.

Elated and excited, I said yes. Dick and I arranged to move to Shingu after a trip around Japan with Mary Heiny. A few weeks later, I moved from Tokyo to Shingu and spent the first week there by myself, waiting for Dick to arrive. I stayed in a youth hostel around the corner

Michio Hikitsuchi
Sensei teaches class at
the Kumano Juku Dojo
in Shingu, 1970s.

from the dojo while I attended classes morning and night. The atmosphere in the dojo had a dreamlike intensity, and the unbelievably fast-paced training exhausted me. I recall literally crawling up the wooden stairs to my second-story room at the hostel, in the evening after class. My intensive training in Shingu had begun.

Training in Shingu

A small coastal city of 40,000 people, Shingu sat in an idyllic environment of mountains, rivers, and farmlands, with *torii* gates marking sacred Shinto shrines on what seemed like every street of the town. It was the most exotic place I had ever seen. Paradoxically, right from the beginning I felt a mysterious sense of being at home in Shingu. I was happy to say sayonara to the smog and urban streets of Tokyo. The tall Japanese *sugi* trees in the Kumano mountains recalled the California redwoods of my childhood. Reverence for the beauty of nature, central to the traditional faith of the Kumano region, was familiar to me. But it was more than that. Hikitsuchi Sensei and the other members of the dojo invited us young Californians into their homes and hearts like welcome members of the human family. And there was a palpable, vibrant energy in the Aikido dojo that resonated inside me. I felt instinctively that I had come to the right place.

When my friend Dick joined me in Shingu, he brought with him one of our Aikido friends from Santa Cruz, Jack Wada. A quiet, intense young American of Japanese descent, Jack had just arrived in Tokyo, and fortunately had been included in the invitation to live and train in Shingu. The three of us rented rooms in the second story of a house near the mouth of the Kumano River. We lived on the floor, Japanese-style, sitting on the woven straw tatami mats and sleeping under traditional futon quilts of cotton batting. Every morning we rode our one-speed bikes ten minutes across town to the dojo, where we spent most of our time.

In 1973, Hikitsuchi Sensei was a fiercely intent man in his fifties who burned with the message of Aikido and the mantle of leadership he had received from the founder. He was about my height, five-foot-six, and as thin and sharp as a samurai's sword. When he would lay his delicate, long-fingered hand lightly on mine, I found that I was unable to move. He clearly delighted in this—the power of ki, of Aikido. A strict teacher, he demanded the best of his students, and frequently challenged us to do more than we thought we could. It was also clear that Hikitsuchi Sensei had paid close attention to O-Sensei's lectures on spiritual matters. Unlike most Aikido instructors I had encountered, he often

Michio Hikitsuchi Sensei lectures on Aikido during a class in the Kumano Juku Dojo in the 1970s. The calligraphy on the wall, brushed by the founder of Aikido, reads *Take Musu Aiki*. This is a term the founder used to refer to the creative principle of harmony (Aiki) at the highest levels of his art.

quoted the founder's long discourses word for word, elaborating on the meaning of the spiritual terms. Hikitsuchi Sensei's devotion to the teachings of the founder of Aikido was both austere and contagious.

"An Aikidoist must be constantly aware," Hikitsuchi Sensei told us over and over. "You must not have a single moment of inattention!" The first class of the day started at 6:30 A.M., and the evening class ended at 9 P.M. We trained in every class, shared meals, served tea to guests, participated in chanting ceremonies, chopped firewood, cleaned the dojo, simply did whatever needed to be done. Hikitsuchi Sensei constantly reminded us to approach all of our activities as *shugyo:* intensive spiritual training. *Shugyo* has the further meaning of embracing hardship and challenge in order to grow. When we had to do something particularly onerous, someone was sure to joke, "That's your *shugyo!*"

"Make a total commitment—*inochi gake de keiko o suru*—train as if your life depended on it!" Hikitsuchi Sensei would frequently exhort us all. On the nights when he launched into a lecture on the spirit of O-Sensei's Aikido, the atmosphere in the old wooden dojo became so charged with ki that it felt as if we were inside a vibrating rocket on a launch pad. "Aikido is not a sport! Aikido is true *budo!*" he would exclaim. "To do Aikido, you must harmonize with the movement of the universe, and reach a state of spiritual oneness in which you have no opponents!" We would listen with all our might, and then leap up and train with the intense desire to manifest O-Sensei's vision of harmony through our own bodies.

A *Gaijin* Woman

People often ask what it was like for me, an American woman, to be a student in a traditional dojo in the Japanese countryside. I was frequently the only female on the mat, and my long strawberry-blond hair created quite a sensation. At that time in Japan, it was prescribed

that by age twenty-five, a woman would get married and stop partici-
pating in activities outside the home. I passed my twenty-first birth-
day during my first year of intensive training in Shingu. Japanese
acquaintances frequently asked me, "When are you getting married?"
and after a while I became bothered by the question's implications. I
had traveled halfway around the world to practice Aikido, not to fade
away into married life!

The Kumano Juku Dojo was small, and its population was almost
entirely male. The Japanese men in Shingu were clearly startled to meet
me. I must have looked unreal to them, like a movie star on the screen.
Sometimes, upon first meeting, a man would utter a spontaneous pro-
posal of marriage, which I learned to deflect reflexively, as if doing a
well-practiced Aikido maneuver. These proposals were annoying but
innocent, and easier to deal with than the occasional intrusive advances
of the more persistent men. I did my best to ignore the distractions and
obstacles presented by this focus on my gender.

My commitment to gender equality was put to the test every day in
physically rigorous training sessions. The pace was fast and continuous. After watching a brief instructional demonstration by the teacher
of the class, we would divide into pairs and alternately throw our partners and be thrown, with the selected technique, until the instructor
demonstrated again. The throws were powerful and the mats in Shingu
were even harder than the ones in Tokyo. I had no athletic training
and no natural talent; but I was young and determined to keep at it.
Little by little, my body came to enjoy the feeling of flying through
the air and springing up off the mat. When a technique went well, I
felt vividly alive. A powerful wave of energy would pass through me
as I threw my training partner, uniting us momentarily in a profound
harmony that was the physical and philosophical aim of Aikido. These
moments, and the inspiring examples of my teachers, kept me going.
Surprisingly, despite the gender distinctions ever present in Japanese
society, Hikitsuchi Sensei, Anno Sensei, and most of the other Shingu

teachers treated me as a serious student when I was on the mat—which is to say, the training was equally hard for me, and equally inspiring.

For instance, after class we students would frequently request to take *ukemi*—repeated falls—from Anno Sensei or one of the other high-level teachers. By dojo custom, once I had uttered the ritual words *Onegai shimasu* (I ask a favor), I was committed to attack the instructor repeatedly and be thrown continuously, until the instructor decided I had done enough. "Enough" was always much more than I had imagined.

At the beginning of each *ukemi* session I started out optimistically, with my best speed, commitment, and a sincere desire to receive from my teacher. It was amazing to feel each attack instantly and skillfully neutralized by the instructor. My energy and momentum would be swept up in a powerful blending movement that led to an effective resolution—a throw or a pin. When I was thrown by these masterful teachers, the *Aiki*—blending of ki—was clear and exhilarating. But sooner or later I would run out of gas, and that was when the real *shugyo* began. After being thrown many times, I would have to get myself together to stand up, attack, and take the fall again. And again. No matter how long it took me to get up, the teacher would wait for me. He knew I could find the strength to keep going—if I searched for it. He expected nothing less than everything I could give. I struggled each time to give it all. Finally, he would release me. The *ukemi* session would always end with a formal, though breathless, bow.

There was no discrimination in this strenuous practice. Whoever stepped up to it engaged in a humbling internal battle to find reserves of physical and spiritual strength. The next time I would find I could do a little more. I was drawn to the intensity of the practice, but every night I would dread the exhausting struggle that inevitably awaited me at the end. I would think, *Perhaps not this time.* Then when I saw one of the instructors waiting, more often than not I'd go over to him and say *Onegai shimasu* to begin the arduous process once again. It was a constant reminder of the Aikido principle of *agatsu:* "victory over oneself." Through my willingness to train every day and to dig deep in the after-class *ukemi* sessions, over time I earned the respect and friendship of my training partners, who were mostly Japanese men sincerely surprised to find themselves training with an American woman.

It often seemed that my identity as *gaijin* (foreigner) was even more shocking than my gender. For many people in the Kumano area, it was the first time in their lives they had ever encountered a person who was not Japanese. When I walked along the streets of Shingu, young children would scurry away, shouting, *"Gaijin! Gaijin!"* Adults would be visibly stunned at the sight of my pale skin and hair, and then reflexively blurt out the first lines they had learned from their English textbooks in school: "This is a pen!"

One time, strolling through a neighborhood by the river, I greeted a young girl with a well-practiced *Konban wa*—"Good evening." The girl replied in astonishment, "Why do you speak a human language?"

"Because I am human," I continued in Japanese.

"Chigau! No, you're not!" she insisted with innocent conviction. "My mother has black hair, and you don't!"

Mary Heiny and Linda Holiday, with Michio Hikitsuchi Sensei at the Kumano Juku Dojo, 1973.

"Touch me," I encouraged her, "and you'll see I'm a human being, too." The girl touched my arm and ran away.

In the decades since then, many foreign Aikido students from the United States and other countries have followed in our footsteps to train in Shingu. *Gaijin* are no longer a shocking spectacle on the streets. We three young people from Santa Cruz broke the ice, made friends in the dojo, and even made headlines in the local newspaper: "Blue-Eyed Foreigners Come to Study Aikido!"

Linda Holiday attempts an Aikido technique with Hikitsuchi Sensei during a class in the Kumano Juku Dojo, 1973. Jack Wada can be seen training behind them. This photograph accompanied an article in the local newspaper.

Hikitsuchi Sensei demonstrates an Aikido technique with Anno Sensei, in the Kumano Juku Dojo, 1973. Watching (left to right): Jack Wada, unknown student, Dick Revoir, Funatani-san, and Linda Holiday.

Mary Heiny herself moved to Shingu, later in the year, to undertake six months of intensive training with Hikitsuchi Sensei before returning to the United States to teach, as one of the pioneering American instructors of Aikido. She first spent a year teaching Aikido in Santa Cruz, where she took the initiative to set up a formal "Sister City" connection between the cities of Shingu and Santa Cruz, a relationship of Aikido and cross-cultural civic exchanges that has thrived ever since.

In 1973, Aikido was poised on the verge of a rapid international expansion that would, in a few short decades, grow to include more than a million and a half practitioners in over ninety countries. O-Sensei had envisioned Aikido spreading throughout the world, and it was beginning to happen. Hikitsuchi Sensei welcomed us, the first full-time international Aikido students in Shingu, as a sign that Aikido would play an important role in strengthening peace around the world. After he finished remodeling and enlarging the Kumano Juku Dojo in Shingu, Hikitsuchi Sensei put up a sign in English, high up on the front wall of the building, which read boldly, AIKIDO WORLD DOJO.

Deepening Our Connection with O-Sensei

Every day we young Americans trained with Hikitsuchi Sensei, Anno Sensei, and others for whom O-Sensei's touch was a living memory from four short years ago. To the people of Shingu, it was as if O-Sensei had just recently walked out the door. They carried O-Sensei's teachings deep within their bodies. They spoke of the founder frequently, with respect and a sense of loving familiarity.

Due to the fact that O-Sensei had passed away on April 26, 1969, the twenty-sixth day of every month was—and still is—a time of remembrance in Shingu. Formal Shinto ceremonies with soaring *Norito* chanting brought many people together at the dojo on the evening of the twenty-sixth. After a short training session, we would kneel in the traditional *seiza* position as ceremonial offerings were made. Hikitsuchi Sensei would speak at length about Aikido to the people in attendance. He often reminded us that after O-Sensei's passing, his long white beard was brought to Shingu for a formal enshrinement of O-Sensei's spirit in the dojo's sacred altar, acknowledging the close connection the founder had to the Kumano Juku Dojo. Hikitsuchi Sensei urged us all to dedicate ourselves to O-Sensei's teachings, make the most of our Aikido practice, and make a contribution to the world.

Michio Hikitsuchi Sensei, personal student of O-Sensei, prepares flower offerings at the founder's grave at Kozanji Temple in Tanabe, 1970s.

On the twenty-sixth of the month, Jack, Dick, I, and others would often accompany our teachers to O-Sensei's grave at Kozanji, the Shingon Buddhist temple in the nearby town of Tanabe. As new members of O-Sensei's Aikido clan, we learned to tend the Ueshiba family gravesite, to pull out even the tiniest weeds, to smooth with our hands the small field of stones, and to pour soothing water over the gravestones. We left fresh offerings of chrysanthemums, sticks of incense, and the traditional *manju* sweets that we were told O-Sensei had loved.

Hikitsuchi Sensei, in his formal black Western suit and a short, fresh haircut, would squat down to light the incense, and he would maintain that position while chanting the Buddhist sutras. As he balanced perfectly still, and we attempted to balance behind him, the ancient sounds flowed through him and seemed to form an invisible connection between all of us and the spirit of O-Sensei. After a while our knees would begin to ache, and in the summertime the gigantic Japanese mosquitoes would raise welts on our arms, adding an element of *shugyo* to our experience. But the feeling of familial connection was strong, and increased with each visit.

I was always moved at those times by the way Hikitsuchi Sensei and Anno Sensei would speak to O-Sensei, naturally, as if he were present and listening. They would let him know how things were going, and express their intention to do their best to carry on the Aikido path. In recent years, it has come to be my turn to take my own students to O-Sensei's grave in Tanabe. We pay our respects to Aikido's founder, tend the grave and make our offerings, and promise to renew the practice of Aikido on the mats of America.

Linda Holiday at the grave of the founder of Aikido in Tanabe, 2004.

Learning the Language of Aikido

I wonder how many hundreds of hours I spent sitting on my knees on the tatami mats that first year in Shingu, struggling to comprehend Hikitsuchi Sensei, Anno Sensei, and the other instructors as they spoke passionately about Aikido. Sometimes it seemed that every other word in their rapid stream of Japanese was "O-Sensei." How I wished I could open my pores and directly absorb what they were saying! I had learned a few basic Japanese words and phrases before arriving in Tokyo. But these were the tools of a tourist, and were clearly inadequate to the tremendous opportunity that now lay before me. A Romanized Japanese dictionary became my constant companion. I took notes on my teachers' lectures and drilled myself on patterns of Japanese grammar when I had time to myself. I bought a copy of a massive reference book, Nelson's *Japanese-English Character Dictionary,* and searched though it to decipher the cryptic characters my teachers wrote for me on napkins, notebook paper, and calligraphic scrolls. That was how I initially learned to speak and write Japanese, a beautiful language whose profound dissimilarity to English opened my mind to new avenues of thought and perception.

Some of the words I heard were not in the dictionary no matter how hard I looked. When I asked the local Japanese about them, they laughed. "That's *Shingu-ben*—the Shingu dialect! Better not to learn those words!" they'd say. There were colorful regional dialects all over Japan, and their casual tone was quite different than the textbook Japanese I studied alone in my room, poring over books I had acquired in Tokyo. *Shingu-ben,* the local version of the Kansai dialect of western Japan, was softer and warmer in tone than the more staccato sounds of standard Tokyo Japanese. For instance, the standard Japanese *Ikanakereba ikenai* (You must go) became *Ikanandara akan* in the local dialect. The standard *So desu ne* (Yes, you're right) was transformed into the down-home, country sound of *So ya no!* I was fascinated to learn that O-Sensei had spoken a similar Kansai dialect. That intensified my resolve to decipher the mysteries of *Shingu-ben.*

By the end of my first year in Japan, I still couldn't understand the newscasters on TV, but I could make myself understood in most conversations, and read and write in a rudimentary way. More important, I enjoyed an increasing comprehension of the inspiring talks on Aikido that the Shingu instructors loved to give. Looking up my teachers' words in the dictionary was a treasure hunt. Each day brought thrilling discoveries, as I learned new words like *zanshin* (continuous awareness), *dai shizen* (great nature), and *tamashii* (spirit). Gradually I became familiar with the specialized spiritual terms O-Sensei had used to describe his art, such as *Ame no uki hashi:* the Floating Bridge of Heaven.

Ame no uki hashi frequently appeared as part of the mysterious vocabulary in the lectures of O-Sensei that Hikitsuchi Sensei would quote to us verbatim. I learned that the Floating Bridge of Heaven referred to a creation story in the *Kojiki*. The *Kojiki*, or *Records of Ancient Matters*, was an oral history of spiritual stories and myths from Japanese prehistory that had first been put into written form in 712 CE.[8] In one sacred story beloved to O-Sensei, the male and female deities *Izanagi* and *Izanami* stood on the Floating Bridge of Heaven, and joining together, gave birth to the first land, the islands of Japan.

But when I sat listening with the other Aikido students and teachers on the mat at the Kumano Juku Dojo, all of us dripping with sweat and focused intently on the practice of Aikido in the here and now, the Floating Bridge of Heaven did not feel like an abstract reference to a story of the past. It was a vivid invitation to venture into the world of the spirit, and to integrate that sacred spirit of creativity into all of our actions. It was a compelling reminder that to O-Sensei, and by extension to all sincere students of his art, Aikido was far more than physical technique.

Motomichi Anno Sensei

In Shingu, Motomichi Anno Sensei was the senior Aikido instructor under chief instructor Hikitsuchi Sensei. There were a number of other high-level *shihan* as well, all of whom had been originally inspired directly by O-Sensei and continued to train and teach at the Kumano Juku Dojo. Each of them modeled for us a clear unity of physical and spiritual practice in Aikido. The teacher who influenced me most deeply, however, with his emphasis on the heart, was Anno Sensei.

My first memory of Anno Sensei is of his smile. It was like a ray of sunlight in the living room of Hikitsuchi Sensei's house, as we kneeled on the *tatami* waiting for him to return. I had only a few words of Japanese, and Anno Sensei knew no English, so we sat in silence, smiling.

Aikido training fosters deep, intuitive connections. Energy circulates between people, hand to hand and heart to heart. Immediately I felt a direct heart connection that endures to this day.

Anno Sensei held a seventh-degree black belt, which was a high and rare honor at that point in Aikido's history. He was the most highly ranked teacher in the area under Hikitsuchi Sensei, who had been verbally awarded the highest level, tenth *dan*, by O-Sensei just before he died four years prior. But you would never have guessed Anno Sensei's elevated status from his friendly and unpretentious manner.

One of the first practices we three Americans had with Anno Sensei was a private class in the afternoon just for us. To our surprise, Anno Sensei wore a beginner's white belt, without his *hakama*, and joined us enthusiastically in training. There was no mistaking who the teacher was, however. Even his simplest movements conveyed an astonishing

Motomichi Anno Sensei on
a visit to the Omoto spiritual
center in Ayabe, Japan, 1980.

28

depth and a soft, relaxed power. When we attacked him, the subtle way he blended with the motion of the attack melted opposition like butter in the sun. I had never felt anything quite like that before. He seemed to be a living model of O-Sensei's declaration, "In Aikido, there is no opponent."[9]

When we first met, Anno Sensei was in his forties, working long shifts around the clock at the paper manufacturing plant across the Kumano River. Like many Japanese men, he was slim and slightly shorter than I was, though his upright posture and sunny presence made him seem larger. He lived with his wife and two sons in neighboring Mie Prefecture, where he had his own dojo, up the coast in Kumano City.

Despite his busy work and family life, Anno Sensei frequently came to the Kumano Juku Dojo in Shingu to train and to teach. With his appearance at the door of the dojo, I would feel a strong current of energy enter the room, as if the lights in the high ceiling of the dojo had suddenly become brighter. He would join us on the mat, moving swiftly and easily, sweeping us up in his big, flowing throws. After class he would toss us around effortlessly, flashing an encouraging smile that kept us coming back for more, long after we began to tire. There was an infectious joy and a sense of freedom in his Aikido.

"Heart"—*kokoro*—was one of the first words I learned from Anno Sensei. I heard him say *kokoro* over and over when he taught class, and again as he sat on the mat with students afterward and talked about Aikido. One day not long after we arrived, I painstakingly prepared a question in Japanese and posed it to him after class.

"*Sensei*, is *kokoro*—heart—the most important thing in Aikido?"

"Yes, I believe so," Anno Sensei answered simply. "People search for many different things in Aikido. I myself am searching for *kokoro*—heart."

In addition to Aikido, he practiced the traditional arts of *Nihon Buyo* (Japanese classical dance) and *Shodo* (Japanese calligraphy).

Anno Sensei sometimes brought freshly brushed pieces of his calligraphy and modestly presented them to us. "I don't have any skill at writing," he would say, "but I'll share my practice with you." His beautiful pieces always conveyed spiritual teachings at the heart of Aikido, such as O-Sensei's motto *Masakatsu Agatsu:* "True victory; victory over oneself." He told us he brushed the words of O-Sensei over and over in order to absorb their meaning. He inspired us by his personal example of Aikido training that extended far off the mat and permeated his life.

From time to time Anno Sensei would invite us along on *shugyo* expeditions as he made pilgrimages to sacred sites or went deep into the mountains to train himself. With excitement and curiosity, Jack, Dick, and I would squeeze into his small Toyota and off we would go for whatever *shugyo* the day would bring. Anno Sensei took us to the ancient capital of Nara, and deep into the Kumano mountains, where we meditated under waterfalls and practiced Aikido swordwork on sacred peaks. We made numerous visits to the Grand Shrines of Kumano that O-Sensei had revered. Following Anno Sensei's lead, in those ancient places of power we undertook purification practices and chanted the *Norito* and Buddhist sutras, as native spiritual practitioners like O-Sensei had done throughout the centuries. Standing in front of the Kumano Hongu Shrine, where O-Sensei had been so many times, my feet grounded in the field of small gray stones, and my gaze rising to the massive shrine roofs with evergreen *sugi* trees towering behind them, I found growing within me a sense of deep connection and natural awe.

Becoming One with Nature

Anno Sensei seemed especially happy and at home in nature. One day he said, "My highest ideal is nature, or the flow of nature. I believe O-Sensei saw the grace of nature—of the universe—and called it *kami*

Linda Holiday at the Kumano Hongu Shrine, 2001.

(sacred or divine spirit). O-Sensei said we human beings must become one with *kami*, and I believe this is what he meant by Aikido. I train with that thought constantly in my mind." Anno Sensei's emphasis on naturalness and heart, and his direct, simple way of conveying the teachings of Aikido, made it easy for him to connect with us and

other Western students. He spoke of O-Sensei with deep respect and affection, and told us stories from the fifteen-year period during which he had learned directly from him.

As a youth growing up in nearby Tanabe, O-Sensei had been inspired by the legends of seventh-century En no Gyoja, the founder of the *yamabushi* (mountain ascetics) of the Kumano area. With Anno Sensei, we hiked the paths of the *yamabushi*, traversing the steep, sacred mountains that had inspired many a Japanese pilgrim. From the high ridges we looked down on the *unkai*, the vast cloud-sea, with mountaintops protruding like rocky

(From left) Jack Wada, Linda Holiday, Anno Sensei, and Dick Revoir on a trip to Japan's ancient capital of Nara, 1973.

islands. Anno Sensei gestured to the wide sky, exclaiming, "This is *Ku*—this is *emptiness!*" Back on the mat in the dojo, I would feel that vast, vibrant, empty sky in Anno Sensei's expansive movements. "Becoming one with nature," a frequent theme in our training, was clearly more than an abstract idea. It was a tangible practice.

Becoming one with nature took on even more meaning as the months passed and the Japanese seasons changed. I had moved to Shingu in the lovely season of cherry blossoms. But this coastal region was known to receive some of the heaviest rainfall in Japan. Even in the springtime, we were frequently drenched by storms as we rode our bikes across town to the dojo. Then, in June, the rainy season formally arrived, bringing weeks of relentless rain as the summer heat and humidity intensified. It seemed impossible to drink enough water after class to make up for the sweat we had lost. The *gis* we wore while training were soaked through and heavy, as if we had been out in the storm. Eventually the searing summer heat was relieved by the cool of early autumn. But in the natural flow of things, it wasn't long before the winter's cold began to make its appearance.

In early December 1973, it was getting seriously cold for a person like me who had grown up in a mild California climate. Mary, Dick, and Jack had just returned to the United States. I rented a small room in a concrete dormitory just across the river from the dojo. Most Japanese buildings were unheated in the winter, so the outside temperature was replicated inside, with little help from tiny charcoal, kerosene, or electric heaters. In the dojo, the windows were thrown open regardless of the weather. In the winter, the canvas-covered mats became slippery as ice, and at times the thermometer on the dojo wall registered temperatures below freezing. But due to the vigorous physical exercise, even my bare feet would eventually become warm during Aikido practice. My nightly soak in the hot Japanese bath, just before bedtime, felt like a godsend.

Daily training at the dojo continued in a steady rhythm of *shugyo* throughout the seasons. The idea was to simply show up and train, regardless of external circumstances, and thereby strengthen oneself. I often heard the people in Shingu say, "Don't let yourself be defeated by ..." ... the heat, or the cold, or any hardship. I was impressed by this philosophy, but as we neared the year's end, I wondered if I could meet the upcoming challenge Anno Sensei had recently told me about.

New Year's Purification Practice

After class one morning, Anno Sensei mentioned the New Year's Purification Practice. He explained to me that every year, the members of
the Kumano Juku Dojo plunged into the cold waters of the Kumano
River to undertake traditional *misogi* purification at the beginning of
the new year. Anno Sensei must have seen the look of apprehension
on my face.

"I'm worried about it, too," he said to me then, kindly, as if confid-
ing a secret. "I think we'd better prepare. Let's not be defeated by the
cold!" He suggested a program of preparation that involved pouring
ten buckets of icy water over my head each night, after the evening
bath. "If you do it, I'll do it, too!" Anno Sensei enthused.

How could I refuse? Late that night, alone in the concrete bathroom at the end of the hall, after I was finally warm from head to toe,
I tipped the wooden bucket over my head, and screamed. Ten times.

The next morning after practice, with steam rising off my sweat-
soaked head, I proudly reported the result of the previous evening's
misogi practice. I figured my screams measured the cold, therefore my
courage. But Anno Sensei was unimpressed.

"Last night I chanted the Heart Sutra three times under a cold
shower," he told me. "Next time *keep* your center, don't lose it!"

Silently I vowed to keep up with him. Every night, for four long
weeks, icy water slapped my steaming skin in the gray bathroom
down the hall. No further sound escaped my lips. I slipped under
the quilts and slept cold but undefeated on the straw *tatami* mats in
my room. When daylight came, I watched clouds of snowflakes, like
airborne schools of tiny fish, drift down and disappear into the wide,
ocean-going currents of the Kumano River. It was hard to imagine
myself in that river.

The long-awaited day was frosty and clear. All the members of the
dojo stood barefoot on the rocky shore, facing the surging expanse

34

of the Kumano River. Following Hikitsuchi Sensei's stern lead, we swung our wooden swords in unison, so fast and hard my arms ached and I began to sweat. Finally it was time to wade together into the river for *misogi* purification.

As the shock of the cold water hit, I heard gasps among the group. Even some of the black belts I'd known in the dojo seemed off-balance, hopping from foot to foot as if running from the river's grasp. But the previous month of struggling with nightly *misogi* had given me the strength I needed. After those weeks of icy water ablutions in the concrete bathroom, the day's fresh air, sunshine, and natural beauty made this long-dreaded step seem easy, inviting. I sank deep into the river's cold, familiar embrace.

I felt a sudden surge of gratitude to Anno Sensei for challenging me to face my fears. Searching for him, I saw him in the river, farther from shore. Anno Sensei was looking toward me with a radiant smile, relaxed and completely at home in the flow of nature. *This is living Aikido,* I thought. This was the example I wanted to follow.

The Power of Harmony

Anno Sensei worked together in harmony with a number of other high-level teachers in Shingu. These teachers had all begun their Aikido training in the mid-1950s, inspired by O-Sensei, and continued to train and teach under chief instructor Hikitsuchi Sensei at the Kumano Juku Dojo. In particular, Anno Sensei, Yanase Sensei, and Tojima Sensei modeled a relationship of mutual respect and affection that influenced me deeply.

In all the teachers, you could feel the result of their years of Aikido *shugyo* humming like an electric current running through them. At the same time they were all relaxed, solid people with an easy authenticity. Each teacher had his own distinct flavor, resulting in a variety of equally delicious cuisines. What a feast it was! It was not uncommon, in Shingu in the 1970s, to be in a class taught by Hikitsuchi Sensei, with Anno Sensei, Yanase Sensei, and Tojima Sensei alongside us as our training partners. Each of them had developed his own way of expressing Aikido, but it was clear that their differences did not put them at odds with one another. Rather, they were complementary, and enriched the community of practitioners at the dojo. Through their mutual respect, these teachers manifested the power of harmony: the central principle of Aikido, and a necessary foundation for peace in a diverse world.

For instance, in contrast to Hikitsuchi Sensei's sword-like intensity and Anno Sensei's emphasis on naturalness and heart, Yanase Sensei's firm strength felt like iron. He was a short, compact man whose precision and upright posture never varied, despite the speed and power of his throws. In fierce silence he would often drill us with rapid techniques for long periods after evening classes, occasionally rewarding us with a single word in English: "Nice." Yanase Sensei undertook as his personal *shugyo* a daily pilgrimage to the ancient Kamikura Shrine, perched on a cliff overlooking the town of Shingu. He would literally run up and down the 538 steps to the shrine—steep, irregular stone steps that were a challenge to climb even at a walking pace. At times Yanase Sensei allowed me to accompany him to the top. There, I got a glimpse of his daily personal practice as we chanted, made offerings, did lengthy purification exercises, and meditated in a small rock cave to the side of the shrine. A devout and serious person, Yanase Sensei could nonetheless be persuaded to sing popular Japanese songs as he drove us around in his sports car to visit his favorite sacred sites in the Kumano area.

And with his round, humorous face and relaxed, cat-like presence, Tojima Sensei presented us with yet another distinct flavor of Aikido. There was a wildness to him that could manifest in lightning-fast *atemi* strikes, sudden boulder-like solidity, or hilarious clowning that would keep us all in stitches. The first night we met Tojima Sensei, at

Left: Linda Holiday trains with Motoichi Yanase Sensei after class at the Kumano Juku Dojo in Shingu, Japan, 1979.

Right: Yasushi Tojima Sensei and Linda Holiday after class in Shingu, 1975. Tojima Sensei passed away in 1995.

the dojo in Shingu, we were astonished to see him fold his legs into full lotus position and walk around the mat on his knees, laughing uproariously. Then he stood up and asked Jack, who had previously studied Karate, to punch him full strength in the stomach. When the punch landed, Tojima Sensei just stood there grinning. Next, he bounced Jack around the dojo with a subtle, close-range "one-inch punch" that gently lifted Jack off his feet and propelled him backward time after time. When you trained with Tojima Sensei, you were always surprised. He felt like an inexorable force of nature one minute, and a kindly uncle the next. Jack, Dick, and I had so many mysterious experiences with Tojima Sensei, on and off the mat, that we privately nicknamed him "Don Genaro," after the mystifying shaman in the Carlos Castaneda books that were popular at the time.

As we trained under Hikitsuchi Sensei, Anno Sensei, and all the other teachers who had studied directly with O-Sensei, our sense

Group photo with O-Sensei in Taiji (in Kumano), c. 1960. Front row, left to right: Ishigaki Sensei (from Shingu), Hikitsuchi Sensei, Fukiko Sunadomari (head of the Women's Aikido Division in Tokyo), O-Sensei, unknown student, and Yoshihiro Kubo Sensei, O-Sensei's first recorded student in Shingu. Standing behind O-Sensei: Yanase Sensei, Tojima Sensei, and Anno Sensei.

of lineage grew strong. We young American students were following in the footsteps of people who directly carried the teachings of the founder of Aikido. Differences of personality, race, nationality, age, gender, or language seemed ultimately irrelevant. All that was required was our sincere desire to train ourselves in the spiritual and physical practice of O-Sensei's Aikido: The Way of Harmony.

There were other notable teachers, too numerous to mention here, and over time many other foreign students as well, flowing in and out of the Kumano Juku Dojo. My own stay in Shingu was interrupted when I ran out of money after the first year and had to return to the United States for a time. I worked as a waitress while continuing to practice Aikido in the dojos that had just begun to multiply in northern California. Living frugally, I saved my pennies and counted the days until I became able to return to my Aikido *shugyo* in Japan.

Taking the Next Step

As my months of practice continued, I found to my surprise that I had become part of the "clan" of the Kumano Juku Dojo. The rhythms of the Japanese language were second nature to me now, and the places of pilgrimage in the Kumano mountains spoke to my soul. I had grown from a young woman who followed an impulse to Japan, into a serious student of *budo* with a sense of spiritual purpose in her life.

There was, inevitably, hardship in this process. I wrestled with the challenges of being an American in a foreign country, and a woman in Japanese society, where the economic, social, and physical dominance of men was unquestioned. Still, Japan had come to feel like a second home to me. I felt an immense debt of gratitude to my Aikido teachers and wanted to learn all I could from them. I struggled with the question of when to return to the United States, where I ultimately completed my university education and took on the intimidating responsibility of teaching Aikido in Santa Cruz. When it became clear it was time to go, it was Anno Sensei who helped me to step forward with courage on the unknown path ahead of me.

One night in 1976, as I was preparing to leave the Shingu dojo and the familiar rhythms of my life in Japan, I expressed my apprehension about the upcoming change to Anno Sensei. "I'm reluctant to go back to America," I lamented.

"Why?" Anno Sensei inquired.

"Training is better here."

"Why do you think so?"

Surprised, I replied, "Because you are here, and the other high-level teachers." Anno Sensei ignored the compliment.

"Don't make the mistake of depending on the presence of certain people for your training," he advised me. "Teachers come and go. My own teacher, O-Sensei, died not long ago. I could have given up when O-Sensei passed away. Instead, I've continued my practice, even though I've found it difficult at times. Don't rely on other people. Do your best Aikido practice wherever you are."

The founder of Aikido had on one occasion, in 1961, left his native Japan to teach in Hawaii and support the development of Aikido there. At the beginning of his journey, he affirmed his vision of Aikido as a path of peace for the entire world.

"I have come to Hawaii in order to build a 'silver bridge,'" O-Sensei said. "Until now, I have remained in Japan, building a 'golden bridge' to unite Japan, but henceforward, I wish to build a bridge to bring the different countries of the world together through the harmony and love contained in Aikido. I think that *aiki*, offspring of the martial arts, can unite the people of the world in harmony, in the true spirit of *budo*, enveloping the world in unchanging love."[10]

It was time for me to return to my own country, to explore whatever personal contribution I could make to the spread of Aikido, as O-Sensei had envisioned it, in the West.

Twenty Years Later
(Santa Cruz, California, 1996)

Fresh white paint gleams brightly on the high, wide walls of the newly remodeled training hall, where an amazing expanse of sea-green mats has recently been hammered into place over a wooden floor by teams of dedicated students. For twenty years now I have been back in America, training and teaching nearly every day, building a strong dojo community focused on O-Sensei's Way of Harmony.

Linda Holiday Sensei and students sit together after a class in the training hall at Aikido of Santa Cruz, California.

"*Aiki* is not a technique to fight with or defeat an enemy," O-Sensei's words continually remind me. "It is the way to harmonize the world and make humanity one family." I've taught class after Aikido class as a "Lecturer in Physical Education" to crowds of young students in the newly built Field House at the University of California in Santa Cruz. Together with local Aikidoists, I have taught people of all ages in the community center downtown, then at our first rented dojo building, then four years later at the second one, aiming to bring people together and to share the gift of Aikido that Anno Sensei and all my teachers have shared with me. I've taken every possible opportunity to study with Aikido teachers in America, including the visiting Japanese *shihan* who were direct students of O-Sensei.

My roots in the community of Santa Cruz have grown deep. I've married a local man who also practices Aikido. Our energetic five-year-old son has brought an immeasurable increase of love and creative chaos into our lives. Now I see the innate innocence of my child in the face of every person I meet. My Aikido students tell me I have become more patient as a teacher since becoming a mother.

Now, in 1996, after a full decade of grassroots fund-raising and more than a touch of grace, our nonprofit educational organization has been able to purchase and completely remodel the spacious, free-standing building in which I am standing today. Working together, our Aikido community has transformed a large community hall into the dojo I have long envisioned: a truly permanent home for Aikido on the central coast of California.

I walk slowly from room to room in a state of gratitude so deep it feels like a dream. In the big training hall, the dressing rooms, library, children's playroom, kitchen, even the hallways—everything I see has been built or brought here by loving hands and dedicated to the practice of Aikido. There are multiple classes every day, from five-year-olds wearing their first *gis* to men and women who have earned their black belts and continue to polish body and spirit on the mat. It is enough to give me faith for a lifetime. And after my lifetime, I feel certain this dojo will still be here, a permanent contribution to the local and international community.

How right and natural it feels, then, to place on these new, shining walls the finishing touch: the beautiful pieces of Japanese calligraphy that Anno Sensei, Hikitsuchi Sensei, and my other teachers have given me. These representatives of the living lineage of Aikido take up residence in the training hall and watch over the classes like benevolent guardians. After class one day, alone in the dojo, I stand and gaze at a piece of Anno Sensei's calligraphy. The smooth, flowing brushstrokes say simply *"Shizen no Sugata:* The Form of Nature."

Unexpectedly, my heart speaks: *Anno Sensei should be here.*

I want Anno Sensei to see what has become of the American Aikido seedling he tended so long ago. To see that the heart of Aikido he

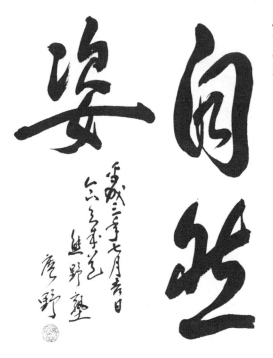

Shizen no Sugata
"The Form of Nature"
calligraphy brushed by
Motomichi Anno Sensei

cherished is blooming in the West. But he is nearly seventy years old now. Would he make the journey?

Flower of the Heart

It takes three more years for this vision to materialize, but the day finally comes when hundreds of students pack the mat for Anno Sensei's classes in Santa Cruz. It is an extraordinary phenomenon of transmission and synergy. Anno Sensei brings the teachings of O-Sensei alive in his classes, and he is clearly inspired in turn by the open-hearted students he meets here in America. This eighth-degree black belt instructor—a direct disciple of Aikido's founder—jokes and laughs with my students. With disarming vulnerability, he tells them of his personal training process and challenges.

Motomichi Anno Sensei teaches a class in Santa Cruz, with Linda Holiday's assistance and interpretation.

"Let's share the Aikido journey!" he exclaims. "Never forget O-Sensei's primary message: Aikido is love."

On that initial visit, Anno Sensei puts brush and ink to paper again. The first piece of calligraphy he gives to me, in celebration of my new dojo and the community that has worked together to make it possible, is "*Kokoro no Hana:* Flower of the Heart."

In subsequent visits, he brings hundreds of pieces of calligraphy with him, bundled into thick rolls in his suitcase, bearing the familiar words of Aikido's founder, including "True Victory Is Victory Over Oneself," "Great Love," and "The Floating Bridge of Heaven." Anno Sensei delights in giving a piece of calligraphy to every single person who attends his classes. He advises them, "Don't judge the skill, or lack of skill, of the calligraphy. Instead, focus on the message it contains. Read O-Sensei's words, absorb their meaning, and put them into action."

Surrounded by eager Western students, Anno Sensei looks at me, shakes his head, and laughs, "Whoever would have thought that a boy from Onodani would find himself here, teaching Aikido in America?"

Sekai Dai Kazoku, "The World Family"; calligraphy brushed by Motomichi Anno Sensei.

~2~

From KUMANO to the WORLD FAMILY

"Aiki is not a technique to fight with or defeat an enemy.
It is the way to harmonize the world and make humanity
one family."

—MORIHEI UESHIBA O-SENSEI

A Boy from Onodani

A rice-farming community situated among gentle mountains and generously flowing rivers, the village of Onodani exudes a rural peacefulness that is soothing to the soul. During the 1970s, when I lived as a foreign Aikido student in the city of Shingu, it was a special treat for me to ride my bicycle across the Kumano River toward nearby Onodani and spend a few hours absorbing the quiet beauty of the Japanese countryside. I pedaled along the interlocking maze of rice paddies, which Japanese villagers had collectively farmed ever since wet rice agriculture was introduced from the Asian mainland more than two thousand years before. Each summer the flooded fields reflected the sky, and the rice shoots grew tall and waved gracefully in unison with the wind. Each fall, after the harvest, the cut sheaves of rice stalks were laid to dry over bamboo structures in an elegant braided precision, resembling row upon row of miniature thatched roofs all across the brown stubbled fields.

It was restful to ride my bicycle slowly along the winding, narrow roads, past the tall groves of bamboo with their feathery plumes. Clusters of small, tile-roofed houses sat atop retaining walls of weathered boulders. Next to each house was a small vegetable garden. Japanese cedars forested the slopes of the surrounding mountains. It was easy to imagine that Onodani and the other rural villages of Kumano had been exactly the same for centuries. Until after World War II, these smooth roads had all been unpaved, and cars had been rare. Compared to Onodani, the small city of Shingu seemed like an urban center. It was in this lushly green, remote, hard-working village that Anno Sensei grew up, endured the hardships of World War II, and matured into his elder years as an international teacher of peace.

The Anno family home is still there today, tucked between a bamboo grove and a hill, with their four small rice paddies stretching back toward the narrow access road. Anno Sensei lives there with his wife, in a modest house next to their extensive vegetable garden. Their two grown sons reside nearby with their families. When the grandchildren were small, they came to play and catch frogs at the edge of the rice fields, just as Anno Sensei—the boy "Motomichi"—had done during his childhood in Onodani.

Anno Sensei's ancestors lived in this village for generations. The Anno family once had plentiful land and funds, until one of his grandfather's brothers, a newspaperman, exhausted the family fortune attempting to buy favor with the increasingly powerful military. "These debts lingered through my father's time," reflects Anno Sensei. "My father's generation did not incur debt, but they had lost nearly everything. That's why my parents worked so hard, and had little money. They often said to us, 'Gaman shinasai—be patient and endure.' They naturally developed a stoic approach to life."

His parents farmed the land and grew rice. His father, a roofer who specialized in traditional tiled roofs, had two children with his first wife, and when she died, married a second time. Motomichi Anno was

Top: A view of the Kumano mountains from Anno Sensei's ancestral home in Onodani, Mie Prefecture, Japan. Motomichi Anno was born there in 1931, and still lives there with his wife.

Left: Anno Sensei with his wife, Chihiro Anno, at their home in Onodani, 2006.

born in 1931, the second-to-last child in a wide span of six siblings. His half-sister Masako and half-brother Susumu had already left home by the time Motomichi was born. His older brother Hiromasa was ten years ahead of Motomichi, and the next child, his sister Yasuyo, was seven years older. The youngest daughter, Kunio, came along a full ten years after Motomichi. There were no siblings close enough in age for young Motomichi to play with, and for many years he was the youngest child, lovingly cared for by his mother and older sister.

But when he was in second grade, his mother gave him a terrible scolding that he never forgot. Motomichi had started to become a willful child, with intense likes and dislikes, demanding to have things his own way and making a fuss when he was not indulged. Finally, his patient mother had had enough. "One day she shouted furiously at me and told me in no uncertain terms that my selfish behavior was completely unacceptable. Up until then, I had rarely ever been reprimanded, so I was truly shocked by my mother's anger. I ran off and cried by myself for a long time. After that one ferocious scolding, I turned over a new leaf and became a well-behaved child." Anno Sensei laughs, "Maybe it was my mother's scolding that inspired in me a lifelong desire to be kind to others."

Around the corner from his house was a small Buddhist temple. The old man who served as the part-time temple priest was kind to young Motomichi and the other children. People in the neighborhood brought offerings to the temple, traditional *manju* sweets made of rice and beans. The temple priest distributed the offerings to the children

Young Motomichi Anno grew up in a rural area of Japan near the Pacific coast.

who visited the temple, dividing the sweets up equally among all of them. "I learned from his example," reflects Anno Sensei. "I developed a natural appreciation for Buddhist teachings. The priest did not 'teach' me to have a feeling of gratitude. My body liked it! That temple priest had a big influence on me as a child."

Motomichi grew up with the rigor and rewards of living close to nature. Winters were cold for Japanese children who lived in virtually unheated houses and wore traditional straw sandals outside. But the beauty of nature surrounded and sustained him. He played happily in the rivers, swimming slowly up to the trout-like fish called *ayu* and catching them gently in his hands. He set traps for river eels, and sold the ones he caught for a little extra money, which he used to buy materials to make model airplanes.

The village families produced most of their own food and supplies. Traders came to Onodani on foot from other villages every day, bringing fresh fish from the coast, *udon* noodles, and other specialties. With baskets hanging from poles on their shoulders, they went door-to-door selling their wares. Motomichi would wait eagerly for the arrival of the honey-peddlers, and savor the sweet samples they would offer him. In the early years of his childhood in Onodani, though living in the midst of the gathering clouds of war, he went to school and played games outdoors, like children do.

Hardships of War

In 1931, the year Anno Sensei was born, the Japanese army invaded Manchuria. For the next fourteen years, Japan was involved in continuous military activities, leading to all-out war with China in 1937 and with the Allied Powers four years later. "I was born into war," Anno Sensei says simply. War with the United States was declared in 1941, when he was ten years old. Increasingly, the daily life of his home, family, and community became focused on war.

"My father was a loyal Japanese subject and an ardent militarist. He strongly believed that everything must be in service to the state. He often said to us, 'Serve the people—serve your country—go and make us proud of you!' I was raised to think it was normal and necessary for young men to join the military, and that to die for one's country was the greatest service one could give," Anno Sensei recollects. "But it was tough on the young people. It was painful for young men to part from their families and girlfriends and go off to be soldiers. As a young child, I didn't fully understand this. But I saw my older brother crying as he went off to war. That left me with an awful feeling."

In the early war years, a military examination was required of all Japanese men at the age of twenty. Passing that exam meant one could be called to mandatory service at any time. Both of Motomichi's older brothers went into the military and were sent off to war. His old-est brother, Susumu, came home one time during the Pacific War, on leave from the Navy. He secretly told Motomichi and the other family members, "Japan is going to lose this war." In the repressive political climate of the time, Susumu risked arrest even to make those remarks to his family.

Food and supplies became scarce. There were no imports. Farmers were ordered by the national government to produce a quota of rice each year and turn it over to the military. Although young Motomichi lived in a rice-farming village, there was little rice to eat. Of necessity, they grew potatoes and squash and ate them instead. Farming families grew barley in the rice fields during the winters, and mixed it with what little rice they had left.

"I enjoyed school until second grade," recalls Anno Sensei. "I liked studying math, Japanese language, and other subjects, and I was often praised by my teachers." But by third and fourth grade, the war effort predominated, and he began to hate going to school. The educational system came to a halt when he reached fourth grade. "There had been some schooling until then, but after that, we didn't even have books. I had a school satchel, but no schoolbooks to put in it. No pencils. I just took a little food with me for lunch."

As the war effort intensified, the age of enlistment dropped to fifteen, and there was strong pressure for every boy of that age to become a soldier. Motomichi watched his older classmates go off one by one. So many men had gone into military service that the remaining families and farms were severely shorthanded and unable to keep up with the work. Motomichi and all the other children went to "school" but were taken out into the community every day, to support the villagers as they attempted to cope with life in the final war years. The children would be ordered to work on the farms, and to go into the forested mountains to carry out heavy loads of firewood that the military had requisitioned for fuel.

Anno Sensei describes himself as a small child, lacking the strength and competitive drive of some of the other children. "Everyone in my class, maybe ten kids, would be lined up to work the fields, to cultivate a long stretch of land. I worked as fast as I could, but the kids with a lot of physical strength would surge ahead and finish the whole length of the field before I was able to complete even half of my row. Then they would all shout at me, 'Work harder! Go faster!'

"I began to hate school. I didn't study at all. And I hated the war. But as I look back on that time now, I think it was good for me. I always wanted to be strong, but I understand how it feels to be weak. Consequently I developed a strong desire for people to live in harmony with each other and to be treated equally. That same feeling is present in my practice of Aikido. The childhood memories of the war preparation period are still alive in my body and mind. In Aikido training, I don't want just to throw someone down. I want people to join together as equals. People of all levels of skill practicing together in joyful harmony—that's what I want."

A Search for Something Meaningful

Black-and-white photos of two clear-eyed young men in uniform—Motomichi's brothers—still hang on the wall of the front room of the Anno family home in Onodani, lending a solemn presence. Susumu and Hiromasa Anno were presumed dead at the end of the war, having served on ships that sank during the fierce battles of the final years. All Motomichi's parents received after the war was a bureaucratic notice from the government to that effect. It was time, once again, for the family to call upon their stoic powers of endurance.

In August 1945, when the war finally ended, Motomichi Anno was fourteen years old. He studied English for three months, from January to March of 1946. Then he stopped going to school. "They told me to go, but I refused. Even if I had gone to school, nothing was happening there. Kids were just playing around. Teachers had no idea what to teach at that point." He lived with his grieving parents in Onodani and worked some part-time jobs, though employment was scarce, and conditions chaotic.

At the end of the war, in spite of Japan's defeat, Anno Sensei recalls a common feeling of relief that it was finally over. However, he and his family found their daily lives had become more difficult. "We

had nothing left," he relates. "Food and supplies were hard to find. People stole food and committed other crimes. It was a chaotic environment in which aggressive people prevailed. That kind of chaos lasted for about three years. After that, things settled down."

When he was twenty, in 1951, Anno Sensei took employment at Kisshu Seishi, the paper manufacturing plant nearby on the mouth of the Kumano River. This was a pivotal decision in his life. He worked there full-time, pro-ducing high-quality paper, for the next forty years, until his retirement at age

Motomichi Anno in his early twenties.

sixty. The work conditions he first encountered were harsh. He was assigned daily twelve-hour shifts, working the day shift one week and the night shift the next. He thought about quitting all the time. But his father had recommended him for the job, and his cousin had intro-duced him, so quitting was not an option. "*Gaman shinasai*—be patient and endure," his parents had taught him. When I first met Anno Sen-sei in 1973 he was in his early forties, and his work schedule at the paper plant had eased to eight hours a day, five or six days a week. He continued to rotate through day, evening, and late-night shifts, which allowed him to be present at the dojo at various times during the day.

As a youth, Motomichi had always been attracted to the martial arts. He would cut a rough approximation of a wooden sword from a tree in the forest and practice sword cuts, imitating moves he had seen. He and his childhood friends played around together, trying to practice Judo. But during the war there were no classes to enroll in. After he began to work at the paper plant, commuting on his bicycle nearly an hour each way, he pumped the pedals even further and studied Judo for a short time in the coastal town of Atawa. Although he enjoyed this formal introduction to *budo*—martial arts—the schedule was not sustainable.

"I had the dreams of a young person," remembers Anno Sensei. "I was always thinking I wanted to study something meaningful, and find something to which I could dedicate myself."

At the age of twenty-three, three years into his full-time employment at the paper plant, Motomichi Anno encountered Aikido and its founder, Morihei Ueshiba O-Sensei. With that fateful meeting, he had found the teacher who would lead his life away from the wounds of war and onto a lifetime path of peace—the teacher whose message was love, and whose method was martial arts.

Becoming a Student of Aikido

In 1954, one year after the Kumano Juku Dojo opened in Shingu, Anno Sensei joined as a student. At that time, Aikido was undergoing a transformation from a private, elite martial art taught only to the upper echelon of Japanese society, to an art of peace accessible and available to all. When Anno Sensei commenced his practice of Aikido, it had just begun to spread rapidly through postwar Japan. However, it was still not widely known. There were no published books on Aikido yet; the only information was word-of-mouth.[11] When Anno Sensei first heard of Aikido, he thought of it simply as a martial art. Having just survived a number of very difficult years in

The founder of Aikido, Morihei Ueshiba O-Sensei, at the Kumano Hayatama Shrine in Shingu, 1953. He founded the Kumano Juku Dojo, one block away from the shrine, that same year.

the chaos of postwar Japan, he hoped that Aikido would help him to become strong.

"It was at the barbershop in my home village of Onodani that I first heard about Aikido. I went in for a haircut, and the barber and I got to talking. When I said I was studying Judo, he informed me there were Aikido classes in Shingu. I didn't know anything about Aikido, but the barber told me there was an incredibly strong martial arts instructor in Shingu who was teaching something like Judo." The barber's younger sister, Minako, had married a man named Michio Hikitsuchi, who was one of the senior students of this amazing teacher.

Anno Sensei rode to Shingu by himself on his bicycle. The dojo was in the same location it is in today, in a quiet neighborhood near the Kumano Hayatama Shrine. At that time, the dojo was a newly built, modest wooden building. When Anno Sensei paid his first visit, the world of Japanese *budo* was still a small, closed society. There were sliding, wooden-slat windows at the level of the floor and high on the wall, designed to prevent people outside from seeing what was going on inside the building.

"When I first saw the Aikido dojo in Shingu, I thought it looked terribly old-fashioned," recalls Anno Sensei. "The first person who appeared in the entranceway was wearing a black *hakama* [traditional long divided skirt], which added to the impression of antiquity. Nobody in Judo or Karate wore a *hakama* to practice. Another person, covered in sweat, joined the first person at the door of the dojo, and the two of them looked to me like people from an age past. I wondered if Aikido was a kind of *kobudo* [a classical martial art]."

Anno Sensei silently wondered if he was meeting the founder of Aikido himself. But the man didn't let him see the inside of the dojo. He questioned Anno Sensei in a stern tone of voice: "Where did you come from? How old are you?"

When Anno Sensei replied that he was twenty-three years old, he was firmly informed that no one under the age of twenty-five was allowed to enroll. The man in the *hakama* also told him that a certain number of personal guarantors were required.

Disappointed, Anno Sensei paid another visit to the barbershop.

"Help me out!" he pleaded with the barber. "I went to the dojo, but they wouldn't let me in."

This time Anno Sensei composed a letter with his personal history. He described himself, and stated that he wanted to join the dojo and become a student of Aikido. The barber agreed to ask for the help of his sister, Michio Hikitsuchi's wife. Anno Sensei then gave his personal history letter to Mrs. Hikitsuchi, and after a short while, he was overjoyed to receive special permission to join the Kumano Juku Dojo.

"I no longer remember the details of my very first class, what techniques we practiced, or who first introduced me to Aikido," Anno

The founder of Aikido in the original Kumano Juku Dojo in Shingu, in the mid-1950s. From left: Motomichi Anno, O-Sensei (the founder), and Michio Hikitsuchi.

Sensei notes. "I simply joined in. I entered the dojo shyly, changed into my *gi*, sat down, and bowed in with the other students."

As soon as Anno Sensei joined the Kumano Juku Dojo, he heard people talking about the founder, O-Sensei, who came periodically to Shingu to teach. Anno Sensei heard that O-Sensei would be coming sometime in the next few weeks.

"My first impression upon meeting O-Sensei was the same as the impression I've had every time since then," smiles Anno Sensei. "I just loved him."

The Founder's Awakening

When Anno Sensei first met him, Morihei Ueshiba O-Sensei was seventy years old. He had been a living legend in the world of Japanese martial arts for more than thirty years.

Born in the coastal town of Tanabe in the Kumano region in 1883, young Morihei had grown up close to nature, among the many traditional Buddhist temples and Shinto shrines of his hometown. His parents had made an arduous pilgrimage through steep mountains to the Kumano Hongu Shrine to pray for his birth, and they considered Morihei to be a child of the *kami* (sacred spirit) of Kumano. Morihei was a dreamy child, immersed in spiritual studies from the age of five. His father took him down to the beach to engage in Sumo wrestling with other village boys, to strengthen him physically. That was the very beginning of O-Sensei's lifelong dedication to the practice of martial arts and spiritual disciplines, which he eventually blended together to create the transformative new art of Aikido.[12]

As a young man, O-Sensei was powerful, restless, and inspired. He practiced various martial arts as he explored the world of commerce in Tokyo and returned home to Tanabe to marry. He continued to pursue his martial arts training during his four years in military service, in Japan and also on active duty in Manchuria during the

Russo-Japanese War (1904–05). After his discharge from the army, with his abundant energy and courage, O-Sensei decided to become a pioneer in the northernmost Japanese island of Hokkaido. The government was providing incentives for groups of pioneers to settle there, as a way to ease the transition of members of the former samurai class after the formal abolition of feudalism just a few decades before. In addition, there were many veterans who had returned at the end of the Russo-Japanese War and were desperately in need of work. In *A Life in Aikido*, Kisshomaru Ueshiba describes his father as being "on fire with this 'frontier spirit,'"[13] determined to provide an alternative for the people he saw in economic distress.

In 1912, O-Sensei led a group of Tanabe families, eighty people in all, to establish a brand-new village of Shirataki in the Hokkaido wilderness. There they encountered severe blizzards, repeated crop failures, and other challenges, which O-Sensei met with impressive resilience and leadership. His son relates, "I'm awed by his stubborn determination. . . . I always remember something he used to say: 'I like to create something where there wasn't anything before.'"[14] The village of Shirataki still exists to this day.

It was also in Hokkaido that O-Sensei began to study with the legendary martial arts teacher Sokaku Takeda, whose art of Daito-ryu Jujutsu was a revelation to him and exerted a strong technical influence in the subsequent development of Aikido. When asked about his teacher in an interview decades later, O-Sensei said, "Takeda Sensei opened my eyes to *budo* [martial arts]."[15]

In 1920, after the death of his father, O-Sensei made another bold move, taking his family—his wife, their three children, and his mother—to live in a religious community in Ayabe, not far from Kyoto. There he dedicated himself to spiritual studies with Onisaburo Deguchi, the charismatic cofounder of a new Japanese religion called Omoto: "The Great Origin." Omoto promoted a big vision of the world as one family, united beyond barriers of nation, culture, language, or religious affiliation. This philosophy inspired O-Sensei as he integrated his extraordinary natural aptitude for martial arts with a deepening spiritual practice.

Onisaburo Deguchi recognized O-Sensei's outstanding abilities and strongly encouraged him to teach his martial art at the Omoto center. After O-Sensei opened his first dojo in Ayabe, teaching "Daito-ryu Aiki Jujutsu," as he called it at the time, his reputation as a phenomenal martial artist spread quickly through Japan. People came from all over to observe, to study, and occasionally to challenge him. One of these challenges, in the spring of 1925, catalyzed a most profound experience, which led to the birth of modern Aikido as a path of love and spiritual awakening.

The challenger was a naval officer who was a master instructor of Kendo, the art of the sword. He was confident and armed with a *bokken*, a heavy wooden sword, which, although it lacked a sharp blade, was a deadly weapon in its own right. O-Sensei faced him empty-handed. The naval officer struck at O-Sensei with the sword again and again, with increasing power and speed. But to his amazement, O-Sensei simply and easily evaded his blows, moving out of reach without striking back. As the man continued his fierce attacks, he was unable even to touch O-Sensei. It was as if O-Sensei moved and existed in a different world, which violence could not reach. Finally, exhausted, the challenger laid down his sword and admitted defeat.

Afterward, O-Sensei recalled walking through the garden, where he became rooted to the ground in astonishment. "I felt that the universe suddenly quaked, and that a golden spirit sprang up from the ground, veiled my body, and changed my body into one of gold. At the same time my mind and my body became light. I was able to understand the whispering of the birds, and was clearly aware of the mind of God, the Creator of this universe. At that moment I was enlightened: The source of *budo* is God's love—the spirit of loving protection for all beings. Tears of joy streamed down my cheeks. Since that time I have grown to feel that the whole earth is my house and the sun, the moon, and the stars are all my own things. I had become free from all desire not only for position, fame, and property, but also to be strong. I understood, '*Budo* is not felling the opponent by our force; nor is it a tool to lead the world into destruction with arms. True *budo* is to accept the spirit of the universe, keep the peace of the world, correctly produce, protect, and cultivate all beings in Nature.'"[16]

At the time of this pivotal experience, O-Sensei was forty-one years old. He spent the rest of his life actualizing his vision of love and peace through the practice of his new *budo*.

In 1926, O-Sensei was invited by a Navy admiral, an exceedingly powerful and influential man, to the capital of Tokyo. There, O-Sensei was met with a very enthusiastic reception as he demonstrated his art and taught it to the military and notable members of society. In 1927, he moved with his family from the countryside in Ayabe to the halls of power in Tokyo, where he was celebrated as an extraordinary teacher of Japanese *budo*. Members of the nobility and military leaders flocked to his classes and trained intensively, inspired by O-Sensei's phenomenal power and presence.

First Classes in Shingu

It was in 1928, just three years after O-Sensei's awakening to the "spirit of love and protection for all beings" at the heart of *budo*, that he first came to Shingu to teach. There was no formal dojo (training hall) in Shingu at that time. O-Sensei gathered about fifty students, who studied with him in a variety of temporary facilities—in a sake-brewing company's warehouse, in people's houses, outdoors—wherever they could find room to train.

O-Sensei's first recorded student in Shingu was a man by the name of Yoshihiro Kubo, a professional photographer and prominent citizen. He was instrumental in the later founding of the Kumano

Juku Dojo in Shingu, after the postwar American occupation had ended. It was Kubo Sensei who appeared at the door of the Shingu dojo the day Anno Sensei first came to inquire about becoming a student of Aikido.

Michio Hikitsuchi, who would become the chief instructor of the Kumano Juku Dojo for half a century, was introduced to O-Sensei as a child, when O-Sensei first began to teach in Shingu. Both of Michio's parents had died, and he was raised by his grandmother, a strict woman who had studied the Japanese martial art of Naginata. She urged him to study Kendo, the Way of the Sword. Young Michio showed tremendous talent in the martial arts. He studied Kendo, Judo, Iaido (sword-drawing), Yari (spear), horsemanship, and other arts. He was awarded a high-level black belt in Kendo when he was only fifteen years old.

O-Sensei and his wife, Hatsu, (seated) with Yoshihiro Kubo, O-Sensei's first recorded student in Shingu (standing, left), and Michio Hikitsuchi (standing, right), 1955.

In those days, the world of Japanese *budo* was a closed-door, rather secretive society. To study O-Sensei's art, one needed to be at least twenty-five years old and be vouched for by multiple sponsors. O-Sensei must have recognized Michio Hikitsuchi's unusual potential, for he accepted him as a student in 1937, at the age of fourteen. A strong connection was forged, and Hikitsuchi Sensei remained devoted to O-Sensei as his teacher and spiritual mentor for the rest of his life.

In his elder years, Hikitsuchi Sensei would reminisce about O-Sensei's dedication to Aikido as a path of love and harmony. "O-Sensei was strict with himself and kind to others. All the time

O-Sensei would say that the purpose of Aikido was to become one with nature, make one's own heart the heart of nature. O-Sensei talked about the need to rid oneself of the desire to fight with the opponent, about the need to create harmony. O-Sensei would say, 'Aikido is the *budo* of love. You must give happiness and joy to your partner. . . . Offer happiness. Be compassionate. If you do that mutually, you will make harmony and be like a family.'. . . O-Sensei said, 'I am alive to make the world one family.'"[17]

From the late 1920s until the war intensified in 1941, O-Sensei was very active in spreading his art in Japan. In 1931, he established a large private dojo in Tokyo, where he taught his new art, which he called by various names such as *Aiki Bujutsu* and *Aiki Budo*. He was frequently requested to teach at universities and military academies, where he had connections at the highest levels of Japanese society. Records of the time indicate a constant, dizzying array of classes, intensive seminars, and private demonstrations, in Tokyo, Osaka, and other places. Despite his busy schedule, O-Sensei frequently returned to teach in Kumano, where he said he felt at home.

The Emergence of Aikido

In 1942, O-Sensei abruptly stepped back from his involvement with the military. He resigned all his official teaching positions in Tokyo and moved with his wife 100 miles north to the village of Iwama, where they owned some uncultivated land. There, as they cleared and farmed the land, producing food for their family and others, O-Sensei quietly pursued his practice of martial arts and spiritual purification in the relative peace of the countryside. Privately, he expressed an intense frustration at the direction his country was taking. "There are getting to be more and more people in the military who are reckless and indiscriminate with their power. They have forgotten the importance of helping people, of relieving suffering. . . . Harmony, love, and courtesy are essential to true *budo*, but the people who are in power these days are only interested in playing with weapons. They misrepresent *budo* as a tool for power struggles, violence, and destruction, and they want to use me toward this end. . . . I have no intention of allowing myself to become their tool. I see no other way but to go into retreat."[18]

During this time of spiritual retreat, O-Sensei constructed an "Aiki Shrine" on his land in Iwama, and formally dedicated it to forty-three sacred *kami* that he felt were the guardian spirits of Aikido. It was during this time that he formally established the name of his art as Aikido: "The Way of Harmony."

"Although the name *'aiki'* has existed since ancient times, I decided to call my unique path *'Aikido,'* because the words for 'harmony' and for 'love' are both pronounced *'ai.'* Accordingly, the word *aiki*, which was used by warriors of the past, differs fundamentally from what I mean by *aiki*," O-Sensei was frequently heard to say. "*Aiki* is not a technique to fight with or defeat an enemy. It is the way to harmonize the world and make humanity one family."[19]

Even when the defeat of Japan was imminent, O-Sensei remained resolutely optimistic about the path of reconstruction ahead. "Don't worry—hereafter, the true Aikido will emerge,"[20] he declared. He was confident that Aikido would have an important role to play in the establishment of a peaceful society, and his vision did not waver. "The ultimate goal of *aiki* is the creation of heaven on earth," O-Sensei later explained. "In any case, the entire world must be in harmony. Then we do not have a need for atomic and hydrogen bombs."[21]

Despite the years of chaos and suffering that followed the war's end, O-Sensei and his close students in Tokyo proceeded to set up the Aikikai Foundation, receiving in 1948 the prized authorization from the Ministry of Education to spread Aikido in postwar Japan. In the application submitted by O-Sensei's son and supporters, the spiritual ideals of Aikido were clearly articulated, and the words about the future expansion of Aikido throughout society were prophetic:

"Aikido is an art of profound significance. Once it is made available to all, it will spread far and wide, connecting with all levels of society rather than only with an elite. Its potential for expansion is boundless. In order to understand it, however, one must become involved and actually practice. . . . Even though Aikido techniques may be applied in life-or-death situations, Aikido itself is connected to the love of the heart."[22]

"Kumano Is My Spiritual Home"

The Kumano Juku Dojo in Shingu was one of the first branch dojos of the Aikikai Foundation to be constructed in the postwar expansion of Aikido. Kisshomaru Ueshiba, O-Sensei's son and successor, described it this way:

"Shingu would become one of the two centers for Aikido in the Nanki [southern Kansai] region, as important as Tanabe, O-Sensei's birthplace. O-Sensei had paid a visit to the shrine at Kumano Sanzan in January of 1949, and earnestly encouraged Michio Hikitsuchi to open a dojo. . . . 'Michio-san, Kumano is my spiritual home. I would be very happy if you built a great dojo in Shingu. The spirit of Japanese love, rooted in Takemusu Aiki, will certainly provide the foundation for building a new Japan. I will do whatever I can, so please do your part also.' Michio Hikitsuchi was moved by this encouragement to open Kumanojuku in 1952, and pledged himself to the expansion of Aikido."[23]

Building a dojo was a major undertaking in postwar Shingu. Financing was secured through a group investment cooperative and the leadership of Kubo Sensei, O-Sensei's first student in Shingu, who served as the first chief instructor of the dojo. The Hikitsuchi family

The founder of Aikido supervises the construction of the original Kumano Juku Dojo in Shingu, 1952. The current, enlarged dojo is on the same site.

provided a plot of land just one block from the Kumano Hayatama Shrine. This beautiful Shinto shrine, founded in the pre-history of Japan, is one of the most sacred pilgrimage sites in Kumano, and one which O-Sensei had revered since he was a child. O-Sensei came down from Tokyo to personally supervise the construction of the Kumano Juku Dojo, which formally opened in 1953.

O-Sensei's son Kisshomaru Ueshiba later reflected, "O-Sensei used to refer to the Kumano-juku Dojo in Shingu as 'My dojo,' and made frequent visits there from about 1955 on. He had his own name-plate displayed at the entrance of the dojo, and to this day, Michio Hikitsuchi has kept it there, as if it were indeed O-Sensei's dojo."[24]

One year after O-Sensei's dojo opened in Shingu, Anno Sensei became a member. The dojo that he entered in 1954 was the first of three successive dojo buildings on the same spot, each one an enlargement of the one before. The original Kumano Juku Dojo, constructed under O-Sensei's supervision, was a wooden building with a small training area of twenty-one tatami mats—less than 400 square feet in size. Its simple walls, canvas-covered tatami mats, slatted wooden windows along the floor, and large wooden structure containing the dojo's Shinto shrine have all been preserved in the subsequent dojo buildings of 1959 and 1973, creating a strong sense of continuity with the past.

In 1959, the original dojo building was significantly expanded. The matted training area was preserved as the central portion of the new building, while additional space was added, along with glass windows that let in more light. This resulted in a larger training area of sixty tatami mats (about 1,000 square feet), which supported the practice of many people who came to learn O-Sensei's art of Aikido there.

In the second Kumano Juku Dojo building, Hikitsuchi Sensei demonstrates Aikido swordwork with the assistance of Anno Sensei, 1960s.

A Lifelong Practice

When Anno Sensei began his Aikido training, he was working full-time at the paper manufacturing plant, and his commute by bicycle was close to an hour each way. Later, after he married a young woman from a nearby village, they moved into employee housing at the plant. This was closer to Shingu and the Aikido dojo, but his family responsibilities increased, especially after the birth of one son, and then another. Anno Sensei attended as many Aikido classes as he could. After a shift at work, his coworkers would go out drinking together, but he would go off to the dojo to train. "My friends at work didn't understand my choice at the time," recalls Anno Sensei. "But now, some of them tell me they wish they had made a commitment, in their youth, to a lifelong practice like Aikido."

About five years into his practice, Anno Sensei's commitment was severely tested. While riding a motor scooter, he collided with a truck and suffered a serious neck injury. It was months before he could move his arms again, but his love of Aikido led him back onto the mat. Moving his feet and his body as a whole, he practiced Aikido without the use of his arms. His perseverance through that very difficult period led him to develop the relaxed, natural posture and complete lack of force in the arms for which he is widely admired.

People often ask Anno Sensei what has enabled him to persevere in Aikido training for more than fifty years, in spite of injury and while balancing his work and family responsibilities. He points to the support he received over the years from both O-Sensei and Hikitsuchi Sensei. O-Sensei was often very kind to him and encouraged him to keep going in his commitment to Aikido.

"In those days I was young, one of the youngest people in the dojo. One day, O-Sensei said to me, 'You are a fine young man because you are *sunao* [sincere; open-hearted].' It felt wonderful to be called *sunao* by O-Sensei," remembers Anno Sensei. "Although I didn't think

I merited the compliment, I resolved then and there to become *sunao*, and to be *sunao* forever, and to treasure those words of O-Sensei to the end of my days.

"O-Sensei gave me important words to live by, and I have never forgotten them. When I've gotten discouraged in Aikido, I've called upon those words, and resolved to continue to train myself, and to become

the sincere and open-hearted person that O-Sensei said I was. Great teachers leave their students with positive and inspiring words, and those words teach us for as long as we live. That's the kind of teacher O-Sensei was."

"In addition, Hikitsuchi Sensei has helped me to persevere in my practice by his constant exhortation to train," Anno Sensei continues. "If I got lazy and stopped training for a while, Hikitsuchi Sensei would telephone me and tell me to get back to class. O-Sensei's words to me were extremely kind, and

The founder of Aikido stands with Michio Hikitsuchi Sensei at the entrance of the newly constructed Kumano Juku Dojo in Shingu, 1954.

I am also thankful for the stern phone calls of Hikitsuchi Sensei, which led me to return to practice again and again. Through continuing my prac-

tice, I have come to love Aikido so much that I feel I will be able to keep training regardless of leg or back pain, or any other obstacle. Three factors have brought me here to this day: O-Sensei's kind words about sincerity, which I have kept in my heart, Hikitsuchi Sensei's phone calls bringing me back to the dojo . . . and, through my continued practice, beginning to understand the heart of Aikido, which has led to great joy."[25]

Postwar Aikido Community

Postwar Aikido of the 1950s and '60s was a small, intimate community on the verge of a rapid expansion. Close students of O-Sensei tended to know one another, or to have heard about the students in other areas. There was a sense of an extended family centered around O-Sensei, even though there was considerable distance between the various dojos O-Sensei visited and supported. "Many branch dojos were just starting to open—in Osaka, Kobe, Wakayama City, one after another," reminisces Anno Sensei. "O-Sensei must have wanted to go to all the new dojos to help them. He needed to develop instructors who could carry on the teaching when he was not there."

Anno Sensei was the youngest student at the Kumano Juku Dojo when he began, but as he continued to practice, his role quickly evolved. Inspired by O-Sensei and Hikitsuchi Sensei and sincerely dedicated to his practice, Anno Sensei was promoted rapidly through the black belt ranks. He became one of O-Sensei's senior students in Shingu, and a senior instructor at the Kumano Juku Dojo. Each of Anno Sensei's ranking certificates, through his sixth-degree black belt in 1969, was signed by O-Sensei himself. Anno Sensei has held an eighth-degree black belt for the past thirty-five years. The fact that each of his early certificates bears a number of about thirty—meaning that he was only the thirtieth person to receive that rank—offers a glimpse into the small size and closeness of the Aikido world at that time.

When O-Sensei came to teach in Shingu, he would often bring one or more of his close personal students with him from Hombu Dojo in Tokyo. On occasion, he would leave one of them at the Kumano Juku Dojo to undertake a period of intensive *shugyo* training. Anno Sensei recalls that some of O-Sensei's senior students in Tokyo would bring groups of students to Shingu for multiple-day training sessions. Fukiko Sunadomari, head of the Women's Aikido Division at

Motomichi Anno demonstrates Aikido techniques with a wooden staff, at a demonstration attended by O-Sensei at Tankaku Elementary School in Shingu; 1950s.

An Aikido presentation at Tankaku Elementary School in Shingu, 1950s. Seated to O-Sensei's right is Koichi Tohei, one of O-Sensei's senior students in Tokyo (later, the founder of the Ki Society).

the Aikikai Hombu Dojo in Tokyo, frequently accompanied O-Sensei to Shingu and can be seen in the photos of the time.

Soon after the Kumano Juku Dojo opened, O-Sensei brought with him from Osaka a man by the name of Seiseki Abe. He was a devoted student of O-Sensei's, as well as a teacher of *shodo*, Japanese brush calligraphy. O-Sensei and Abe Sensei stayed in Shingu for about a month, during which time Abe Sensei offered *shodo* lessons to a group of people in the dojo, at O-Sensei's suggestion. It was there in Shingu that O-Sensei began his study of calligraphy with Abe Sensei. "Morihei Sensei [O-Sensei] would watch me teaching like that, and gradually began to take an interest himself. Before I knew it he

Hiroshi Tada Sensei, one of O-Sensei's personal students in Tokyo, leads a group of Aikido students from Waseda University to the Kumano Juku Dojo, 1961. Front row, left to right: Shizuo Imaizumi, Hiroshi Tada, Michio Hikitsuchi, and Tadaharu Wakabayashi.

O-Sensei stands at the entrance of the recently opened Kumano Juku Dojo in Shingu, c. 1954. From left, standing: Seiseki Abe, O-Sensei's personal student and teacher of calligraphy from Osaka, Japan; Michio Hikitsuchi; O-Sensei's grandnephew Yoshitaka Hirota, and unknown student in cap.

was saying, 'Well, perhaps I'll do a few myself. . . .' The first thing he brushed was the word *'aiki,'*" recalled Abe Sensei in an interview in 1981. "Morihei Sensei had a certain tension in him whenever he took up the brush, I think because he always expressed his entire being through the tip of the brush. Using the ink as a medium, he transferred his ki into the characters as he brushed them. Look at his works today and you can immediately sense the amazingly strong ki imbued in them." Abe Sensei remarked, "It is writing that will forever be vibrant and alive."[26]

Heart-to-Heart Connection

In the close circle of senior students in Shingu, Anno Sensei was deeply inspired by the devotion Hikitsuchi Sensei showed to O-Sensei, and the quality of wordless communication that was evident between them. "I was drawn to that connection," says Anno Sensei. "It is the heart-to-heart connection that I have loved most in Aikido. Naturally, I wanted to develop good technique. But as I continued my training, it was the feeling of deep connection that attracted me and has stayed with me."

Hikitsuchi Sensei, who had lost both of his parents by the time he was seven, thought of O-Sensei as more than just an instructor. "Although I was his student, I always viewed O-Sensei as my father," he explained in an interview. "O-Sensei moved like a *kami*. . . . I therefore endeavored to absorb everything as it was—to do exactly as O-Sensei did. . . . My mind was always on O-Sensei. He knew that but didn't say anything. It just happened naturally. This is true, sincere action—devotion. One mustn't think, 'Oh, he will like this: I will please him.' That is not devotion. Sincere service is service with the whole heart."[27]

In this kind of close relationship between teacher and student, much of the personal transmission takes place outside of normal class times. A *deshi* or personal student serves the teacher in the course of everyday activities and is ready for special training opportunities at any time of day or night.

Hikitsuchi Sensei always enjoyed telling the story of one such private training session, which took place in August 1957. O-Sensei summoned him to the dojo at 2 A.M., and "transmitted to me the innermost teachings of *Sho chiku bai no ken* [The Sword of Pine, Bamboo, and Plum]. O-Sensei had a *bokken* [wooden sword] made of brown *biwa* [loquat] wood and another black *bokken*. . . . He used the black *bokken*, and we practiced together. It was very intense practice with nothing but the sounds of our *bokken* ringing out into the night. At a certain point, I received O-Sensei's strike on my *bokken* and—bang!—the tip of his *bokken* broke off. 'Enough! *[Sore made!]*' he said, and we stopped.

"As I looked around for the missing two inches from the tip of O-Sensei's *bokken*, he cried out, 'Is this what you are looking for?' And he then pulled the missing *bokken* tip out from inside his *keiko gi*

The Kumano Hongu Shrine, established in the mountains of Kumano in prehistoric times (see page 76). A major pilgrimage destination, it was designated a World Heritage Site by UNESCO in 2004.

[training uniform]. That was mysterious! How did the tip of the *bokken* get into his *gi*? Had he somehow reached out and caught it? What had happened? After all, the tip had broken off when our *bokken* had struck one another at full speed. I was truly stunned when he pulled the missing piece out from his *gi*."[28]

Pilgrimage to Kumano

The magnetic power of the three Grand Shrines of Kumano—Hongu, Nachi, and Hayatama (in Shingu)—drew O-Sensei to Kumano over and over through his life, and led to the establishment of the dojo in Shingu. In the shrines of Hongu, Nachi, and Shingu, there is a quiet vibrancy, an ancient sacredness in the midst of the natural beauty of the mountainous Kumano area, that recalls the origins of Shinto—

The founder of Aikido on one of his many pilgrimages to the Kumano Hongu Shrine. Bowing in the *haiden* prayer hall, he has made the traditional offering of a green leafy sprig of *sakaki*. The round object in the middle of the altar is a symbolic mirror.

"The Way of *Kami*"—in Japan's earliest history. Even today, in modern Japan, Kumano represents a primordial, mystical unity with the beauty and blessings of nature.

The Japanese of ancient times worshipped the mysterious forces of nature as indigenous people everywhere tended to do, with awe, gratitude, ceremony, and offerings. In the earliest days, there were no shrine buildings as there are now; sacred space for ceremonies was designated by the use of straw ropes *(shimenawa)*. You can still see the spiraling *shimenawa* indicating the transition to sacred space, hanging above the shrine gateways and encircling natural objects of special beauty and power, such as trees and large boulders. Kumano's Nachi Falls, the highest waterfall in Japan, is itself revered as a sacred *kami*. As you gaze up from the base of the falls, you can see the *shimenawa* stretched between the trees at the top, where the water cascades off

At the Kumano Hongu Shrine (from left): Anno Sensei, Hikitsuchi Sensei, O-Sensei with a child, head priest Munetaka Kuki, another priest, and Fukiko Sunadomari, accompanying O-Sensei from Tokyo.

The founder of Aikido pays his respects to the Kumano Hongu Shrine with a short ceremony of bowing and clapping, and possibly chanting; accompanied by Hikitsuchi Sensei.

the cliff. White folded paper streamers, called *shide*, hang down from the sacred rope, fluttering in the wind.

The Kumano Hongu Shrine is primarily dedicated to four *kami*, which are ceremonially enshrined in the large *honden* shrine halls situated on a forested hill above the town of Hongu and the Kumano River. On one level, *kami* can be thought of as Shinto deities who play dramatic roles in the native myths of Japan, similar in function to the Greek or Norse gods and goddesses. On another level of interpretation, the *kami*, although native to Japan, are clearly representative of certain universal energies.

The four main *kami* of the Hongu Shrine are primal ones. The largest hall enshrines *Izanagi no mikoto* and *Izanami no mikoto*, the mythological male and female *kami* of creation who stood upon the Floating Bridge of Heaven. According to the oldest stories in Japan, *Izanagi* and *Izanami* brought into being the islands of Japan—symbolizing the whole material universe—through their creative union on the Floating Bridge. The two other shrine halls at Hongu house two very significant *kami* in Shinto, who were born through an act of *misogi* (purification) performed by Izanagi: *Amaterasu omikami*, the sun goddess, who is the primary "heavenly" *kami*, and *Susano-o no mikoto*, younger brother of the sun goddess, representing the "earthly" *kami*. In one well-known myth, *Susano-o* slew a fierce eight-headed serpent and pulled from its tail the sword called *Ame no murakumo no tsurugi*, which came to be known as one of the three sacred Imperial Regalia of Japan. *Susano-o*, also known as *Take haya susano-o no mikoto*, is considered to be the central *kami* of the Hongu Shrine. O-Sensei was often heard to identify this powerful *kami* with the essence of Aikido.

Hikitsuchi Sensei has said that he accompanied O-Sensei to the Kumano Hongu Shrine more than one hundred times. Anno Sensei frequently went with them. They would drive up into the Kumano mountains for a day's journey, or stay overnight in one of the hot spring *(onsen)* inns near the Hongu Shrine. This was the shrine to which

79

Hikitsuchi Sensei (right) supports O-Sensei as he steps out of the *honden* area of the Kumano Hongu Shrine. To O-Sensei's right, in dark *hakama*, is the former head priest, Munetaka Kuki.

O-Sensei's parents had made the strenuous pilgrimage from their hometown of Tanabe to offer prayers for his birth, more than seven decades before. "O-Sensei's face would light up at the very mention of Hongu," remembers Anno Sensei. "Whenever I heard O-Sensei was going to Hongu, I wanted to go with him. I loved to see O-Sensei there."

On April 15 of each year, the Kumano Hongu Shrine holds its ceremonial festival or *matsuri*. As a young American Aikido student in 1973, I vividly recall the first time I went to Hongu, accompanying Hikitsuchi

The founder of Aikido signs the guest book at the Kumano Hongu Shrine. To his right is Hikitsuchi Sensei; in back, former head priest Munetaka Kuki.

Sensei to this annual spring festival. The evening before, in a turbulent rainstorm, we drove up the narrow, winding road from Shingu, between forested mountains jutting up on either side of the Kumano River. In the village of Hongu, we found lodging at the traditional inn for pilgrims, at the base of the steep slope leading up to the sacred

The founder of Aikido walks up the long stairway to the Kumano Hongu Shrine, with Fukiko Sunadomari (left) and Michio Hikitsuchi (right).

shrine grounds. The morning dawned clear. "Purified by the storm," declared Hikitsuchi Sensei. With a sense of wonder, I followed him up the long stone stairway he had climbed so many times with O-Sensei.

Reaching the top, we were greeted by clouds of pale pink cherry blossoms and crowds of Japanese people who had gathered in solemn celebration. Below the majestic cypress bark roofs of the shrine buildings, there were several Shinto priests wearing colorful *hakama* and ceremonial garb from a thousand years ago. They moved slowly and gracefully, making ritual offerings of rice, fruit, and vegetables that had been elegantly arranged on delicate wooden trays. As the doors to the innermost shrine were opened, the priests uttered a mysterious, sustained, rising sound that resonated powerfully.

After the ceremony, I was introduced to the head priest *(guji)*, Munetaka Kuki, who had known O-Sensei very well. Despite his prestigious position, Kuki Guji was a relaxed, humorous man. He seemed unfazed by my surprise appearance as the only foreigner attending the festivities, and he welcomed me with genuine warmth. It was only four years since O-Sensei had last visited the shrine.

Kuki Guji's son, Ietaka Kuki, who has now succeeded his father as head priest of this venerable shrine, recalls O-Sensei's many pilgrimages to Hongu. "As a younger man, O-Sensei would run up the steps to the shrine; but as he aged, he wouldn't run. As a young boy, I sometimes watched from the top of the stairs as O-Sensei ascended them. Sometimes it was frightening, because he would go in his *geta* [wooden sandals] faster and faster, and as he neared the top, his eyes seemed to glow as if he were coming home."[29]

O-Sensei's Offering

For the April 15 *matsuri* festival, a simple wooden stage is sometimes erected in front of the shrine buildings, to be used for special performances and demonstrations considered to be sacred offerings to

O-Sensei offers a demonstration of Aikido at the Kumano Hongu Shrine.
The ropes and white paper streamers indicate a sacred area.

the *kami.* O-Sensei offered his art of Aikido on that platform. There is one film of O-Sensei's "offering demonstration" *(hono embu)* at the Kumano Hongu Shrine. In it, O-Sensei looks tiny and frail with age, but he gleams like a light in his white kimono. Hikitsuchi Sensei helps him onto the stage with a tender, protective touch. O-Sensei walks purposefully to the center, holding a long wooden staff. He kneels to bow reverently, and claps his hands twice to greet the Kumano *kami.* A breeze begins to stir the white *shide* (paper streamers) hanging from the sacred ropes surrounding the platform.

O-Sensei stands up and begins to move the staff as he often did, first holding it vertically in front of his heart, then raising it twice with slow intensity, lifting his face to the sky. Shifting the staff to his right side, he rises up on his toes as he begins a sustained, rising chant. The white paper *shide* are now flying horizontally in a strong breeze, as if O-Sensei has called the wind. He begins to swing the long staff in expanding spirals, first one direction, then the other, punctuating the flowing movements with clear upward thrusts that look like O-Sensei has plugged into the power supply of the universe. His body sways slightly, as if he is holding on with both hands to a rope suspended from heaven.

The wind whips through O-Sensei's white beard and the long sleeves of his kimono as he suddenly sweeps the long wooden staff around him, followed by a series of strikes and blocks that are almost too fast for the eye to follow. He performs the dynamic movements of the warriors of old, transforming them into a purifying, sacred dance of love and reverence. Finally his staff comes to rest. O-Sensei bows and stands still again, upright and surrounded by the energy of the shrine he loves. The wind has quieted, and the white *shide* streamers hang peacefully again. Then O-Sensei calls to Hikitsuchi Sensei, who attacks him repeatedly, first barehanded and then with a wooden sword. O-Sensei walks through all the attacks, unarmed and unharmed, with a smile on his face. He is, after all, at home.

A New Dojo in Kumano

"Aikido wa Kumano no ki ya!—Aikido is the ki of Kumano!"

When O-Sensei made this declaration, surely he was referring to the sacredness revered in the nature of the Kumano region since ancient times. But Anno Sensei heard O-Sensei say this so frequently that in the mid-1960s, the idea came to him that it would be fitting to establish an Aikido dojo literally in the city of Kumano, a small town less than an hour up the coast from Shingu. It was not far from Anno Sensei's childhood home in Onodani.

Anno Sensei began to visit the Hana no Iwaya Shrine on the outskirts of Kumano City. This shrine is mentioned in one of Japan's first historical books, *Nihon Shoki*, compiled in 720 CE. In the most ancient Shinto manner, there are no actual shrine buildings housing the *kami* (deities) at Hana no Iwaya; the object of veneration is a massive white cliff, across the highway from the pounding Pacific. In February and October of every year, the local citizens work together to make and install a huge straw rope from the top of the cliff to the beach, symbolizing an enduring connection with the *kami*. Hana no Iwaya Shrine is also revered as the mythological grave of *Izanami,* the female *kami* of the male and female pair who united on the Floating Bridge of Heaven and gave birth to the land. A small shrine, unassuming in appearance but powerful in spirit, Hana no Iwaya played a part in the founding of Anno Sensei's dojo in Kumano City in 1969.

O-Sensei had originally been invited to teach his martial art in Kumano City in 1932. These prewar classes were organized by a local man named Okamuro. Intrigued by the idea of bringing an Aikido dojo once again to Kumano City, Anno Sensei contacted Mr. Okamuro and secured his blessing on the new dojo project. Then, while visiting Hana no Iwaya Shrine one day, Anno Sensei happened to meet a couple of local women who were so impressed with the sincerity of his words about Aikido that they spontaneously offered him land nearby, on which he could build a dojo. Anno Sensei used all of his personal resources to finance the construction of a small dojo building on that land, anticipating the day that O-Sensei would come to the new dojo in Kumano.

A Person of Greatness

When Anno Sensei saw O-Sensei in Shingu in early February 1969, he had no idea it would be the last time O-Sensei would travel to the Kumano area. But after O-Sensei went back to Tokyo, Anno Sensei had a strange dream. He dreamed that O-Sensei was behind a wall—that he could hear him, but couldn't see him. Then the word came from Tokyo that O-Sensei was seriously ill. In April 1969, at the end of a long and rich life, O-Sensei succumbed to liver cancer at the age of eighty-five. Anno Sensei accompanied Hikitsuchi Sensei to Tokyo twice during O-Sensei's final days.

"When I went with Hikitsuchi Sensei to see O-Sensei at his home in Tokyo during his final illness, his condition was still stable and he was resting in bed. Hikitsuchi Sensei spoke to O-Sensei, and O-Sensei said to him, 'Michio-san, the *kami*....' Then Hikitsuchi Sensei chanted the *Norito*," recalls Anno Sensei. "O-Sensei did not have the strength to get up. He lay there quite still, listening. At that time I thought, he is truly a *kamisama* [divine spirit] now.

"Hikitsuchi Sensei and I were there with O-Sensei all day. I noticed there was an oxygen mask for O-Sensei, the kind that someone would have to hold up to his face for him. With a pair of chopsticks and some string, I rigged up a support for the oxygen mask and placed it right next to him. Noticing that, O-Sensei brought his hands together in a gesture of gratitude."

Anno Sensei speaks of this moment with deep emotion. "That is my most vivid memory of O-Sensei. He looked just like a Buddha, like *O-Jizo-san* [Buddhist protector of children] . . . so beautiful and dear that I wanted to drink him up with my eyes and absorb him completely. He seemed to manifest a true oneness with nature—a true thankfulness for everything. That sight, of O-Sensei expressing gratitude, is burned into my memory.

Morihei Ueshiba O-Sensei, founder of Aikido (December 14, 1883–April 26, 1969).

"Looking at O-Sensei that day, I reflected on what a difficult time it was for him. If I had looked at him with my intellect, I would have concluded that he was seriously ill and wouldn't live long. But in my heart, I felt his presence to be eternal. I had no feeling that O-Sensei would die . . . and I still feel that way.

"In all the time I knew him, and to this day, I have felt O-Sensei's existence as something absolute. O-Sensei was, and is, a person of greatness. I don't have the feeling that he has died, or that I have parted from him. I think O-Sensei will live forever."

Carrying on the Mission

Two months after O-Sensei passed away, hundreds of people gathered in the Kumano Juku Dojo in Shingu for a formal commemoration of the passing of Aikido's much-beloved founder. There was a special aspect to this *mitama sai* or "spirit ceremony." O-Sensei's white hair and beard had been preserved in a traditional manner and divided into three parts; each part was then given, as a symbol of spiritual connection, to a place that had been special to O-Sensei. That great honor came to the Kumano Juku Dojo during the *mitama sai* on June 26, 1969. On that day, O-Sensei's spirit was formally enshrined in the dojo by priests from the Kumano Hongu Shrine. (The Ueshiba family tomb in the Omoto center in Ayabe and the Aikido dojo O-Sensei had built in Iwama were also honored by receiving portions of O-Sensei's hair after his passing.[30]) From that time on, Hikitsuchi Sensei conducted a *mitama sai* ceremony in memory of O-Sensei, in the dojo in Shingu, on the twenty-sixth of every month. He would offer *Norito* chants, speak eloquently of O-Sensei's spiritual message, and urge everyone to carry on the mission O-Sensei had envisioned for his art of Aikido in the world.

In the fall of 1969, six months after O-Sensei's passing, Anno Sensei's new dojo up the coast in Kumano City opened its doors. Students poured in to commence their study of Aikido. A priest of the Kumano Hongu Shrine came to the dedication of Anno Sensei's dojo, bearing the *mitama* (spirit) of the Kumano Hongu *kami*, which was formally

Motomichi Anno Sensei at the ceremonial opening of his dojo in Kumano City in September 1969. Sitting behind him is Yoshihiro Kubo, O-Sensei's first student in Shingu. By the wall, in white, are Michio Hikitsuchi Sensei and a Shinto priest (in hat) from the Kumano Hongu Shrine.

enshrined in the dojo that day. After that, Anno Sensei taught regularly in his own dojo in Kumano City as well as carrying increasing responsibility as a senior instructor at the Kumano Juku Dojo in Shingu.

The World Family

Less than four years later, the Aikido community in the Kumano region welcomed the startling appearance of the first foreign full-time Aikido students, from far-away America. We took up residence in Shingu and dedicated our days and nights to Aikido training there, under the direction of Hikitsuchi Sensei, Anno Sensei, and the other instructors who had learned directly from O-Sensei. At times we also attended classes in Kumano City, in Anno Sensei's personal dojo, a simple wooden building close to the Pacific Ocean and Hana no Iwaya Shrine.

The Kumano Juku Dojo
in Shingu, Japan, 2012.

In the spring of 1973, when we first arrived, the historic Kumano Juku Dojo in Shingu was about to be remodeled and enlarged one more time. I often saw Japanese carpenters in split-toed boots working high up on bamboo scaffolding around the building. Hikitsuchi Sensei had just concluded a fund-raising drive, which enabled him to increase the dojo to its present size of 100 *tatami* mats (1,800 square feet) on the ground floor, as well as extra training and living areas on the second story. Once again the heart of O-Sensei's first dojo in Shingu was preserved right in the center of the building. Even today, to practice in the center of the Shingu dojo is to train in one of O-Sensei's original dojos built after the war.

The grand reopening of the Kumano Juku Dojo, in October of 1973, was a poignant celebration of Aikido's growth and vitality four years after the loss of its beloved founder. Attended by O-Sensei's son and successor, Kisshomaru Ueshiba, as well as numerous Aikido dignitaries from other areas, the event was a day of solemn remembrance of the founder. There were inspiring Aikido demonstrations by Hikitsuchi Sensei and Kisshomaru Ueshiba Doshu, speeches and toasts, a classical Japanese dance performance, and hours of feasting, as we all sat together on tatami mats in the newly enlarged training hall. This symbolic event in Shingu coincided with the acceleration of Aikido's international expansion and the increase of foreigners coming to Japan to study Aikido. In the Aikikai Hombu Dojo in Tokyo—headed at that time by the second Doshu, Kisshomaru Ueshiba—as well as in Shingu, Iwama, and other Aikido centers, the enthusiastic influx of students from other countries clearly showed Aikido's evolution to an art of global scale.

Hikitsuchi Sensei, Anno Sensei, and all our teachers in Shingu spent an extraordinary amount of time with us young Westerners, communicating to us the meaning of Aikido—its origins and its relevance to the challenges faced by the modern world. O-Sensei's words echoed in the voices of our teachers. We came to feel that all of us were natural members of the living lineage of Aikido, connected to

O-Sensei's son and successor, Kisshomaru Ueshiba, offers an Aikido demonstration on the occasion of the grand reopening of the Kumano Juku Dojo, 1973.

Michio Hikitsuchi Sensei bows to begin his Aikido demonstration on the occasion of the reopening and expansion of the Kumano Juku Dojo, 1973. His demonstration partners, left to right: Dick Revoir, Peter Shapiro, Mary Heiny, and Tomio Ishimoto.

the founder, O-Sensei, and the "World Family" he had envisioned. This was more than an intellectual concept. O-Sensei had conveyed this vision through Aikido training, a profound, pragmatic practice of embodying the peace that we need in our world. Each time any of us stepped on the mat and attempted to express the principles of harmony through our own bodies, the seeds of the world family grew.

Conveying the Heart of Aikido

For over half a century, Anno Sensei has devoted himself to the continuation of O-Sensei's martial art and spiritual message, teaching steadily and inspiring thousands of students. An eighth-degree black belt since 1978, Anno Sensei is among the most highly ranked Aikido teachers in the world today. He is one of the last remaining master-teachers *(shihan)* of Aikido who received direct instruction and inspiration from O-Sensei. When he was sixty years old, Anno Sensei retired from his employment at the paper plant, and dedicated his time to Aikido, as he began to travel outside of Japan to teach. In 1999, the Aikido community in California was honored to receive the first of Anno Sensei's frequent visits to teach in Santa Cruz, which drew together students and teachers from a wide spectrum of dojos. Soon he was teaching in European countries as well, conveying in each seminar O-Sensei's message of love and purification, along with a rigorous practice of technique.

In February 2004, fifty years after he first stepped onto the mat to begin his training, Anno Sensei stepped forward to succeed the late Hikitsuchi Sensei as the chief instructor of the Kumano Juku Dojo in Shingu. A humble man by nature, Anno Sensei leads by example. In his eighties, he still gets on the mat nearly every day. When his slim, upright body begins to flow through the circular movements of Aikido, they seem as smooth and natural as breathing. Teaching beginning students and advanced black belts with equal respect and care, he invites them to take part in O-Sensei's vision of a harmonious world. In 2009, Anno Sensei was given the prestigious Distinguished Service Award from the Japan Martial Arts Association, for his lifetime dedication to teaching Aikido.

While honoring the origins of Aikido and the founder's spiritual roots in Japan, Anno Sensei gently insists that Aikido is not ultimately Japanese: It is an art of universal truth and international significance. Foreign students traveling to Shingu to study Aikido often describe Anno Sensei's generosity in teaching them and personally escorting them on pilgrimages to sacred sites in the Kumano region. He conveys the heart of Aikido in a simple, natural way that bridges differences of language and culture.

In October 2009, a group of American students and I attended the fortieth anniversary celebration of Anno Sensei's original dojo in Kumano City. It was a joyous, festive event. Elementary school students and teenagers gave spirited, flowing Aikido demonstrations alongside Aikidoists from numerous countries, and local adults, some of whom had studied with Anno Sensei for forty years. We sat crowded together in the small wooden dojo building, under big windows looking out on the forested mountains of Kumano, and listened to Anno Sensei's resonant voice.

Anno Sensei with visiting Aikido teachers from the United States, Danielle Smith and Linda Holiday, after morning class in Shingu, 2008.

"Train hard in the infinite techniques of Aikido, but don't study technique alone," Anno Sensei encouraged everyone. "You must take your study further, into new and wonderful areas. Don't lose your way. Do the kind of technique that will allow you to become one with your partner, one with all people, one with the universe, and one with *kami*. To accomplish this, you need a heart of gratitude. Please practice Aikido with that feeling. What matters most is the heart."

Motomichi Anno Sensei receives the Distinguished Service Award for Aikido from the Japan Martial Arts Association, in Tokyo, 2009.

Aikido is a relatively young art, although it has spread throughout the world with amazing speed. The founder, O-Sensei, lived until 1969. At the present time it is still possible to receive Aikido instruction from a small number of teachers who studied directly with him. But it is the nature of time to flow on, and of generations to pass, and to pass on their wisdom to those who will receive it. Anno Sensei has devoted his life to studying the heart of O-Sensei's teaching. He often reminds us that *all* people who learn Aikido are the inheritors of O-Sensei's legacy, and bear the joyful responsibility to convey it to the next generation.

The heart of Aikido is in your hands.

The HEART of AIKIDO: TEACHINGS of MOTOMICHI ANNO SENSEI

Motomichi Anno Sensei speaks from the heart to a group of students in California, 2004.

INTRODUCTION TO PART II

In Part II, Anno Sensei speaks directly to you. With the simple transparency of water, and the honest humility of a lifelong spiritual seeker and teacher, Anno Sensei invites you to join him in exploring the heart of Aikido.

These deep reflections on the teachings of Aikido have been selected from extensive taped interactions between Anno Sensei and Western students and teachers. They are drawn from formal classes in Aikido dojos, and conversations in more intimate settings with Anno Sensei's closest students as well as beginners, artists, musicians, teachers, and professionals in many fields. I have translated Anno Sensei's remarks from Japanese to English, and I've edited this wide-ranging collection of talks to convey the depth and immediacy of his communication.

Imagine you are sitting in a circle of Aikido students, on the mat after a vigorous training session. During the class, Anno Sensei has exhorted everyone to express personal integrity, love, and a spirit of deep harmony in all interactions, even when under attack. As one student after another leaps up to attack Anno Sensei, he embodies that teaching. Blending naturally with their movements, he draws them close, then releases them to a fall or roll that seems to imbue his partners with a mysterious joy. Now, Anno Sensei says he is only beginning to understand the depth of Aikido. Although it is a startling statement from a teacher of his level, his sincerity is palpable. He warmly encourages everyone to join him in a profound and mutual study, to grow in understanding together. You begin to feel he is speaking right to you. Then Anno Sensei sits down, looks invitingly at the circle of students, and asks for questions.

There is a particular quality of radiance that occurs when sincere students bring their full attention and open hearts to an interaction with an elder teacher. This energizes the teacher to express what is most profound in his or her experience. These poignant moments happen again and again as Anno Sensei teaches, as he responds to questions from Western students, with whom he invariably has a relaxed and intimate connection. Whenever I sit with Anno Sensei and interpret his teaching—whether it is in Santa Cruz, San Francisco, Seattle, or Japan—there is a clear sensation of a heart transmission taking place.

As you read the following chapters, you have the rare opportunity to sit with Anno Sensei and study with him. Take your time as you read and reflect on each of the teachings. Listen to Anno Sensei's voice as he speaks of his teacher, O-Sensei, the founder of Aikido. Consider how you can apply his training insights and methods to your own life. Let Anno Sensei's eloquent, simple words lead you to the heart of Aikido.

—LINDA HOLIDAY

∼3∼
LEARNING from the FOUNDER of AIKIDO

Ever since Anno Sensei started coming to California to teach in 1999, people have responded with excitement to the vivid way he brings O-Sensei right into the room. Anno Sensei speaks of the founder of Aikido with the authenticity of one who knew him as a teacher and as a person. He freely shares the inspiration he felt as he studied with O-Sensei in Kumano, during the last fifteen years of the founder's life.

People always ask Anno Sensei, "What was O-Sensei like as a person? What did it feel like to be in a class with him—to be thrown by the founder of Aikido?"

Anno Sensei's face lights up when he speaks of his personal experiences with O-Sensei, and of the deeply spiritual teachings O-Sensei integrated into his practice of *budo* (martial arts). It has been an honor to translate for Anno Sensei over the years as he remembers O-Sensei, and to feel the light and love still vibrant in him as he speaks.

—Linda Holiday

Ki, "Life Energy"; calligraphy brushed by Morihei Ueshiba O-Sensei (signed on left: "Tsunemori," one of several personal names used by the founder).

All Things Are Born of Ki

When I began my study of Aikido, the first words of O-Sensei I heard were *Banbutsu subete ki yori shozu:* "All things are born of ki [energy; spirit]."

I heard this from O-Sensei, but I didn't understand at first what it meant. The concepts in Aikido can be difficult to grasp, and their essence is profound. To reach an understanding of these concepts, O-Sensei taught us over and over, in a concrete and tangible way.

Banbutsu subete ki yori shozu means that all things in the universe have come into being through ki [energy; spirit], through the harmonious relationships of ki. All things are made of ki. We human beings are the same. We are born through the exchange of ki between men and women, the ki connection of our fathers and mothers. We do not work by ourselves, but depend on the power of many things—many relationships of ki.

Consider rain. It starts out as water, and through the power of the sun it turns to vapor and is drawn upward. Then it cools and descends again, in a cycle. All things come into being through the exchange, the interplay, of ki with ki. O-Sensei perceived this—the way ki works with ki—and he called it Aikido ["The Way of Harmony with Ki"].

Aikido is not just the training we do on the mat. Through the practice of technique, we experience the power of ki and come to know the inter-relationships of ki. Far more important than throwing someone is fully understanding the power of ki.

Stand on the Floating Bridge of Heaven

"Here, push on my head," O-Sensei would say, as he would invite two or three people to push on him. O-Sensei would sit there on the tatami mat with his legs outstretched, and there was absolutely no reason why we couldn't expect to push him over. But to my amazement, when I pushed hard, my own feet would slip out from under me. Then one of the people pushing on O-Sensei would start to fall, and we'd all come crashing down. It was impossible to resist.

Trying to take hold of O-Sensei was like trying to grasp water. Even if you manage to get it in your hands, the next thing you know, it's gone. You can't hold on to it. Like a cloud—you can't grab a cloud no matter how hard you try. I would try to grab O-Sensei's arm with all my strength, but it was an entirely different feeling than grabbing someone else's arm. Try as I might, I was unable to use my force. O-Sensei may have been moving before I was able to get a good grip on him, but I couldn't tell when he began to move. His ki was in motion. His mind was not fixed in one place.

We must train until we have a natural state of mind: a mind like water, like a cloud. We must continue our practice until we have no consciousness of having an opponent at all. We must go completely beyond winning and losing. If the other person comes to grab you here, you have moved there. If they try to push you here, you have gone over there. There's nothing to hold on to. After a while they get tired and can't continue to attack. That's the way I felt, when I had the opportunity to train with O-Sensei.

People enjoyed it when O-Sensei did demonstrations of amazing feats. Then, he would speak about the purpose of Aikido and use the names of the *kami* [sacred spirits; Shinto deities]. O-Sensei didn't talk about things like footwork, or how to use your strength, or how to relax. When O-Sensei taught about technique, he would talk about

The founder of Aikido, O-Sensei, demonstrates immovability in the original Kumano Juku Dojo in Shingu, Japan. Anno Sensei (wearing black belt) tries unsuccessfully to move O-Sensei's arm, along with Hikitsuchi Sensei (on left) and another student (pulling with a belt); 1955.

kami. He conveyed the most important points of the techniques in that way.

Before O-Sensei led us in the purification practice of *shin kokyu* at the beginning of class, he would say, "First, you must stand on the Floating Bridge of Heaven [*Ame no uki hashi*]." I wasn't sure what he meant, and like the others around me I was impatient to train. Looking back on it, I feel that O-Sensei was telling us how to stand in a fundamental, natural posture. I understand what O-Sensei said about standing on *Ame no uki hashi* to mean that we must begin in a natural state of mind, a fluid state of mind that is not fixed in one place. Stand naturally, with your mind on the Floating Bridge of Heaven: a clear, egoless state of mind.

O-Sensei demonstrates immovability from a seated position. Anno Sensei, Hikitsuchi Sensei, and another student attempt to push O-Sensei over, while a fourth student pulls.

As it is a *floating* bridge, using a lot of strength is unnecessary. You can't use force or resistance, and neither can you simply go limp. O-Sensei's words "Stand on the Floating Bridge of Heaven" point to a natural way of standing that is not a matter of what you do, but rather an indication of the existence of an incredible power.

It is important to let people know what O-Sensei said. Then, in the future, those who are interested in what he taught will think about his words, and explore what O-Sensei meant when he told us, "First, you must stand on the Floating Bridge of Heaven."

Pushing on O-Sensei

O-Sensei's ki was powerful and expansive. He seemed to completely absorb the ki of others. When O-Sensei would extend his arm, holding a wooden sword, two or three of us pushing from the side could not make it move. This was truly a mysterious experience. People have asked me, "Did you really push hard? Maybe you could have pulled him." When O-Sensei would call me up again and say, "Push on my head!" I would think, *this* time I'll push with all my might. Each time, I would approach O-Sensei with the resolve to give a good solid attack, but something would change even before I reached him. It was an indescribable feeling . . . as if I were pushing on emptiness. I was defeated from the beginning.

O-Sensei would take a vigorous stance, and while one person was pushing on him, he'd call for another. Everyone would get swept up into the same feeling. We'd push and push, still expecting that we could move him—it was incredible! What I felt was that somehow, inexplicably, O-Sensei absorbed everything I did. I felt no resistance to my push. Try as I might, I was simply unable to exert all of my strength.

If you push on a small tree branch, you feel you can push strongly. But if you touch the trunk of the tree, you feel somehow that you can't push. Pushing on a wall or on a big boulder is the same. You don't have a way to use your strength. You feel your physical power is useless.

Anybody who attacked O-Sensei for real was thrown. People would try and try to push O-Sensei over, and just when they seemed to be pushing with every ounce of their strength, they would be thrown. I would hear stories about tremendously strong people, even Sumo wrestlers, who thought they could best O-Sensei. They, too, were thrown and admitted defeat.

The power O-Sensei had was truly awe-inspiring. Yet I was not afraid of him, because I perceived in O-Sensei no intention to hurt or harm. I believe that O-Sensei absorbed the fighting spirit of his opponent. He took it away. Right from the beginning, my ability to push was taken from me. O-Sensei had already absorbed it.

People ask me about the significance of the amazing feats O-Sensei performed. What was he trying to show us? I think O-Sensei may have been trying to convey the fact that there is a mysterious power we can experience on the path of Aikido. Perhaps O-Sensei could not fully express that in words, but he could demonstrate it so that people would know it existed. My feeling is that O-Sensei may have left those remarkable feats behind like a message: *There are mysteries here. Keep training!*

Ai, "Love"; calligraphy brushed by the founder of Aikido.

No Opponent

O-Sensei said, "There is neither time nor space, only the universe as it is. All I need is to stand here. If you think of winning, you defeat yourself."

O-Sensei may have been standing on the same mat as his students, but his state of being was vastly different. O-Sensei was not standing in the relative world. He was standing in a world in which the great sky was constantly clear. His world could not be reached by the power of people who burned with the desire to fight.

For O-Sensei, there was no opponent, no "other." He told us, "To make enemies, to defeat opponents, and to think that this is Aikido, is a serious error. Aikido is love."

When we practice Aikido, we learn specific physical techniques, such as *shiho nage* [four-directions throw]. We attempt to do each technique skillfully. But that's not what O-Sensei was doing. His heart was already in a state of unity with the other person. He was absorbing and drawing the whole person to him, and wrapping that person up in love, and that process would result in a technique like *shiho nage*.

O-Sensei was believable. Because of his masterful technique, he was able to teach about the heart. People listened to him.

He said, "I completely envelop my opponent's heart with the heart of love."

The Heart of O-Sensei's Practice

To want the heart of O-Sensei's practice is to search for the heart of *Dai Ai:* Great Love. To go beyond an ordinary understanding of love, in search of a greater love. I felt this in O-Sensei.

O-Sensei was amazingly powerful, but it was power without pain. Sometimes he threw us very hard, but his power had an entirely different feeling than the strength of other people. Although his techniques were extremely effective, you could say that he threw us with love. O-Sensei threw strong people strongly, and he threw newer students in a way that was appropriate to their level. I had the vivid feeling that the heart of love was present in each technique. If I were to describe O-Sensei's techniques in terms of food, I'd say they were delicious!

If you saw O-Sensei, you would understand. He had a mysterious power. You could say that O-Sensei expressed everything with the power of Great Love, which gave you the most wonderful feeling. Clearly, within O-Sensei there was *something* invisible and unfathomable that welled up from the inside and was expressed in his technique and in his words . . . you could feel it.

I cannot duplicate what O-Sensei manifested, but when I feel I am getting closer to the heart of his practice, the closer I get, the more joy I experience. I think, *Ah! Could this be what O-Sensei felt?* I continue to practice Aikido because I want to understand O-Sensei's spirit. How did he feel, inside, when he did an Aikido technique like *kokyu nage* [breath throw]? My greatest desire is to draw closer to the feeling of O-Sensei's practice—to the spirit that made his technique possible.

O-Sensei studied many forms of Japanese *budo.* He dedicated himself to the practice of all sorts of martial arts. He attained the summit, and understood their essence. But he did not feel satisfied with what he had learned.

In Kendo, the Way of the Sword, there have been many wise teachings about the difference between "the sword that takes life" and "the sword that gives life." But O-Sensei was not satisfied with that level of insight. He pursued his spiritual practice further. He realized that the essence of *budo*—the martial way—is love. I believe that in the long history of martial arts in Japan, O-Sensei was the first person to teach that love is the essence of *budo*. Aikido was born from that realization.

As we practice Aikido, it is necessary that we, too, realize that the essence is love. The heart of love, born from *budo,* is Aikido. We practice Aikido in order to realize this.

"True *budo* [the martial way] is a work of love. It is a work of giving life to all beings, and not killing or struggling with each other. Love is the guardian deity of everything. Nothing can exist without it. Aikido is the realization of love."[31]

～ Morihei Ueshiba O-Sensei

The founder of Aikido at the train station in Shingu, accompanied (left to right) by Fukiko Sunadomari from Tokyo, and Motoichi Yanase and Michio Hikitsuchi from Shingu.

Greatness in Small Things

In the early years of the Kumano Juku Dojo, O-Sensei came down from Tokyo to Shingu every month or so. He often stayed for a week at a time. O-Sensei didn't have a fixed schedule of when he would come down to this area. From time to time he would think of Kumano, and decide to make the long pilgrimage to the Kumano shrines.

O-Sensei would travel down from Tokyo by way of Osaka, or by way of Ise. In those days, it was eight hours by train from Osaka to Shingu. There were no express trains in the earliest years. From Ise, the train stopped at every single station, and the train went only as far as Owase. Then O-Sensei had to ride a bus through the mountains from Owase to Kumano City, which took about four hours, and then catch another train from Kumano City to Shingu. Whether he came by way of Osaka or Ise, it was a very long journey.

O-Sensei's practice inspired people to a high degree of commitment. When the news arrived that O-Sensei would be coming down to Shingu from Tokyo, the dojo would fill with increasing numbers of people training with excited anticipation. I would get the word from Hikitsuchi Sensei that O-Sensei was coming soon to Shingu, and I would look forward to O-Sensei's arrival. It was inspiring to receive his teaching, and everyone would be really focused while training. Students would train hard even after O-Sensei went back to Tokyo. Gradually, though, laziness would overcome them again and the number of people on the mat would decrease.

I will never be able to forget how completely dedicated O-Sensei was in his practice and in his teaching. When O-Sensei journeyed to Shingu on the overnight train, he would arrive very early in the morning. Then he would immediately begin the morning practice. If you or I were to arrive in the early morning like that, we would probably be exhausted, excuse ourselves from morning class, and start with the afternoon practice. But O-Sensei absolutely never did that sort of thing. Once he was in

Shingu, O-Sensei would teach every day. He would teach class as soon as he arrived, whether it was morning or evening. He was very disciplined about that. He led a much more orderly life than the rest of us.

If practice was scheduled to begin at 7:00, O-Sensei would start practice exactly at 7:00. He would begin to practice even if there was only one other person there and that person was someone like me, far below O-Sensei's level. If it was time for class to start, he simply started. I think most of us find this degree of discipline to be difficult. We might say, "It's cold today, so let's wait a little longer," or "Let's start practice after another two or three people show up." Even in these simplest ways O-Sensei was wonderful. I think the fact that his greatness showed itself even in small things indicates that he was great through and through.

O-Sensei in the Kumano Juku Dojo

In the old days the *genkan* [entrance] to the Kumano Juku Dojo was small, like the front door of an ordinary house. We students would enter the dojo through the *genkan* and walk down a hall to a tiny dressing room. On the way, we would pass a room with a traditional Japanese bath for O-Sensei's use, and a kitchen that was used for preparing his meals. O-Sensei's own room was six tatami mats [about nine-by-twelve-feet] in size, with a smaller adjoining room. In the early years, O-Sensei would sleep in his room in the dojo, and Hikitsuchi Sensei's wife and his grandmother would cook food for him. Hikitsuchi Sensei's grandmother often cooked O-Sensei *okaiyu-san*, a simple dish of rice cooked in green tea, which was favored by people from O-Sensei's hometown of Tanabe. O-Sensei used to joke affectionately that she cooked him so much *okaiyu-san*, he was starting to get tired of his favorite foods!

Students changed into their *gi*s in the dressing room and proceeded into the training area before class. There we did warm-up exercises and practiced *ukemi* [techniques of falling safely], waiting for O-Sensei to appear. As soon as O-Sensei entered the room, we would all kneel formally on the mat. Hikitsuchi Sensei or Kubo Sensei would follow O-Sensei into the room and sit down. Then O-Sensei would face the dojo shrine and chant the *Norito* [Shinto prayers], and our legs would begin to ache in anticipation of an extended period of kneeling in *seiza.*

O-Sensei always chanted the *Norito* at the beginning of the first class of his stay in Shingu. After that first class, he would start the classes in a variety of ways. Sometimes he didn't chant, but went right into *shin kokyu* [a purification practice]. Then he would speak to us about Aikido. We lined up for class along the sides of the training area, in a *U* shape. We sat there listening to O-Sensei speak.

When O-Sensei taught Aikido, he spoke at length, but we found it difficult to understand him. He frequently referred to spiritual terms in the *Kojiki* [*Records of Ancient Matters,* a collection of sacred stories and myths about the *kami* from ancient Japan]. Reflecting back, it seems to me that O-Sensei was using terms from the *Kojiki* and the *Norito* to explain technique and to teach Aikido. When O-Sensei led us in *shin kokyu* at the beginning of class, he would speak of the Floating Bridge of Heaven, and he frequently referred to *Izanagi* and *Izanami* [the two deities of creation, male and female, who stood on the Floating Bridge of Heaven]. He would say their names while he demonstrated Aikido techniques.

O-Sensei told all of us to study. He said that everything came from the *Kojiki.* "If you don't study the *Kojiki,* you won't understand Aikido!" he would declare. But most of us had the feeling that it was enough just to study technique. If we had done what O-Sensei recommended, perhaps we would have come to understand Aikido more quickly.

"In Aikido, you manifest the *Kojiki* with your body," he told us. I believe that means to study what is written about *kami,* understand it, and ultimately integrate that understanding into your own body. As

O-Sensei would say, "Make it your own flesh and blood," and express it in your actions every day.

At the beginning of class, O-Sensei would often lecture on these matters for thirty minutes or so. When he was feeling particularly inspired, he might speak for a whole hour. He would "stand on the Floating Bridge of Heaven" and the sound *u-u-u-u* would float out of him in a rising chant. After doing things like that for some time, he would give a brief demonstration of a technique and instruct us to practice it. Then we would try to figure out what he had done. That was how we learned from O-Sensei.

O-Sensei generated a feeling, an energy, around him. Being in a class with O-Sensei was like being drawn into a mysterious atmosphere, like dissolving into the universe. When O-Sensei would chant *u-u-u-u*, you would ride the wave of his sound. You know what it's like on a rainy day, when you look out into the mist, and all you can see is clouds and rain, and the indistinct shapes of mountains? That's the kind of world you entered, with O-Sensei. You would feel drawn to the mountain in the mist.

Beyond Strength

When I began Aikido training, in 1954, my intention was to become strong by studying a martial art. But I soon heard from O-Sensei that Aikido was not a matter of becoming strong and defeating others. It was a practice of *agatsu:* victory over oneself. O-Sensei used to tell us *"Tsuyoku naru na!*—Don't become strong!" That puzzled me. People who were training in the early days didn't yet understand the spiritual side of Aikido, or what Aikido was. Most of them thought of Aikido only as a martial art.

When I first saw O-Sensei's practice, I sensed it was different from that of other people, but I couldn't tell exactly how. By the time I had my first class with O-Sensei, I had already received some instruction in technique from Kubo Sensei, who was the head of the Kumano Juku Dojo at that time. Even though the techniques Kubo Sensei taught us were effective, and one could say they were the same techniques that O-Sensei did, receiving them from O-Sensei was an entirely different experience.

If you practice Aikido, I think you can understand this from your own experience. Let's say you receive the same technique, *nikyo* [a joint lock], from two different people. The first person's *nikyo* is extremely painful, but when you receive the same technique from the second person, it feels good and is effective at the same time. A new student's *irimi nage* or *shiho nage* feels quite different than the same technique done by someone with years of experience, doesn't it?

O-Sensei's technique was simply amazing. It was not always pain-free, but there was a powerful energy to it. He had no openings [no *suki*], but I did not find him fearsome. When you are thrown by someone who is filled with physical power, it can be frightening. At lower levels of training, it is possible to make a mistake and cause an injury. The spirit of love is not yet consistently present in our practice. Sometimes it is there; sometimes it is not. But there was something in O-Sensei that transcended speed and power. He seemed to be filled with the spirit of love. With O-Sensei, I felt safe taking *ukemi* [falls].

Anno Sensei takes a fall from O-Sensei in the original Kumano Juku Dojo in Shingu, mid-1950s.

Training with O-Sensei

When O-Sensei demonstrated techniques in class, he would first call up the most experienced students to be thrown as his *uke* [training partner]. He would instruct Hikitsuchi Sensei to attack him, saying, *"Michio-san, dete koi!—Michio,* come out here!" When I was a beginner at the dojo, I watched the students who O-Sensei threw first. People like Okizaki-san and Sugawa Yoko-san had previously practiced Judo and took beautiful *ukemi.* I longed to be like them. I would anticipate their arrival at the dojo and ask them to train with me. It was after I was promoted to *sandan,* third-degree black belt, that O-Sensei began to call me up to take the first falls.

Sometimes O-Sensei would throw the most experienced student, followed by the others. At other times he would only use one person as his *uke.* The first *uke* had absolutely no idea what to expect and needed to have extremely skillful *ukemi.* O-Sensei didn't announce, "Now I am going to perform *kotegaeshi,* so come up here and take the fall for it." These days, people often announce the technique in advance, saying "Next, we will do *shiho nage."* But that seems unnatural to me. O-Sensei would simply say, *"Chotto, dete koi*—You, come out here." We had no idea what he was going to do. It was a real challenge to take *ukemi* well under those circumstances!

When O-Sensei began to call me up to take *ukemi,* I was ecstatic. Being thrown by O-Sensei was an incomprehensible experience. I wasn't told what to do. I simply tried my best to keep up. Just to stay connected with O-Sensei took all I had. When O-Sensei threw me, I couldn't tell how I had been thrown. When other people threw me, they would use techniques that would follow a certain sequence leading up to the fall. But with O-Sensei it was a different feeling. I would be thrown smoothly before I knew it.

Regardless of how many people O-Sensei would call up before me, when I went to attack him I would be thrown with such a lightness that

115

I would have no idea what was going on. Afterward, I would realize it had been a certain technique like *kotegaeshi*. Or I would be thrown— *pow!*—and it would turn out to be the form of a *shiho nage* or *kokyu nage* throw. I would be thrown without understanding how it happened.

It was a wonderful feeling when O-Sensei would allow me to be his *uke* for certain techniques, like *kotegaeshi*. He would throw me crisply and I would take a clean fall. I was so happy when things went well. When O-Sensei threw me with a technique that required a fall at which I was unskilled, then I felt small, and I didn't enjoy it as much. But when it was time for *kotegaeshi* . . . When O-Sensei picked me up and threw me, I'd fly through the air. I enjoyed that!

People often ask me what it was like practicing with O-Sensei in those days. It was wonderful. Training was fast-paced, and it was pretty rough on us, much more than now. The feeling of the practice was incredibly intense. O-Sensei was so sincere with each person that the students were equally sincere. Because of this, no matter what sort of technique we practiced, there was an intensity—a total, whole-hearted involvement.

After O-Sensei demonstrated a technique, he watched us train. But it was more than just watching. He was not merely looking at what we did. The feeling we got from O-Sensei was, "Practice with your whole heart what I just showed you. Give it your all!"

The founder of Aikido observes students training as he teaches a class in the original Kumano Juku Dojo, mid-1950s. Hikitsuchi Sensei takes *ukemi* on the left.

A Sincere Attack

O-Sensei seemed pleased when his students gave a sincere attack, without preconceptions. If the attack was *munetori*, a lapel grab, he wanted us to grab for the lapel with full commitment. Not to attack while thinking, "I wonder what technique will be applied to my arm?" Not to anticipate, "Next time I think he will turn to the inside for *shiho nage*. Or maybe it will be *kotegaeshi*."

My feeling was that if we attacked while thinking or anticipating, it was not an enjoyable practice for O-Sensei. He wanted our complete, honest commitment. He wanted us to strike sincerely and fully, without speculating about what the other person would do. But we often strike with the anticipation that we will be thrown and take the fall as *uke* [receiver], don't we? When I look back on training with O-Sensei, I remember that he was happy when we gave him a sincere, wholehearted attack.

But O-Sensei used to hate it when his *uke* grabbed his beard! People were supposed to take hold of the cloth material of his *gi* [training uniform], but they would grab his long beard by accident. It would get caught in the grab. He would tell us, "Don't you grab my beard!" That was his biggest weakness.

Ukemi [the practice of receiving] is not simply "taking the fall." It is not about hitting the mat with a big bang. The art of *ukemi* starts at the very beginning. You must perceive and understand what the other person wants. That's *ukemi*.

I don't remember O-Sensei calling out the names of the attacks he wanted from us. But he would give a small indication. He expected us to see that small *suki* [opening] and attack accordingly. You can observe that sort of interaction in the video footage of O-Sensei. If his *uke* did not respond right away to his subtle signs, O-Sensei would seem dissatisfied, as if saying to his students, "Why didn't you pick up on that?" That's what taking *ukemi* from O-Sensei was like.

118

But it is difficult to perceive those subtle signs, isn't it? The wordless communication of an opening [suki] is a subtle invitation, akin to saying "Come here!" It is incredibly enjoyable when the uke perceives the opening and comes in with the appropriate attack. It is not so much fun when "the sign" goes awry, and you go in with a yokomen uchi [diagonal strike] when a shomen uchi [straight strike] was called for in that situation! That lack of perception means our practice is not yet complete and we need to continue to train ourselves.

New students don't always perceive the beginning of the technique, so we verbalize, "Please grab me here," and then allow the uke to grab. By repeating this practice, intention is conveyed. At first you say, "Come and strike me with shomen uchi!" You say it in words. Then you might make a sign with your hand. Then, you make that sign in a natural way, inside your heart.

Morihei Ueshiba O-Sensei, at the age of seventy, sitting in his room at the
Kumano Juku Dojo, 1953. The scroll behind him was written by the co-founder
of Omoto, Onisaburo Deguchi.

No Openings

O-Sensei had no *suki*—no openings. He had a consistent focus, even when he was talking or drinking tea. It was not a harsh strictness, but a natural intensity. He didn't act one way during class and another way afterward. The rest of us tend to lose our concentration after class is over. We say, "Hey, that was a great class!" But I never saw O-Sensei conduct himself that way.

At times I would accompany O-Sensei on the train from Shingu to Osaka. His posture was always impeccable. It took many hours for the train to reach Osaka, and O-Sensei would sit up straight the entire time. It was a natural state for him. I would try with all my might to match O-Sensei, to maintain my posture like his. But by the time we passed Katsuura, twenty minutes out of town, I would start to slump in my seat. I would be defeated! O-Sensei had that kind of personal discipline. Both his body and his mind were upright and correct. He was very highly respected.

To say that O-Sensei had no *suki* [no openings] means that he was fully present in form and spirit. Whenever O-Sensei was speaking, or eating a meal, or sitting on the *tatami* mats in his room, he sat upright, with full awareness. That meant we couldn't listen to O-Sensei with less than our full attention. We couldn't lean on the table and make casual remarks. O-Sensei's focus was that intense. When a teacher has that kind of intensity, it affects the people around him or her. They become more focused, too.

I would like to develop more of the kind of clarity and strictness O-Sensei had. In Aikido terms, you can express this quality as *shinken shobu*. A dictionary will tell you that *shinken shobu* means to fight with a live blade—a *shinken*, a real sword. This refers to competition, a real fight. But I think it is essential to look at the larger meaning of *shinken shobu*: the importance of living our day-today lives without *suki* [openings; gaps in awareness]—with whole-hearted concentration.

What is needed is integrity. If you don't put into practice what you say, others will notice this fact and lose their respect for you. If you integrate your practice in your daily life, this will earn you the respect of others.

No matter what wonderful, wise-sounding words I say to you now, if I get lazy and lose my focus afterward, it is clear that I need more practice. We need to apply our practice to every moment. Don't give up.

Consistent awareness means always . . . even now . . . this very moment.

The founder offers a demonstration of Aikido sword work with Michio Hikitsuchi Sensei in front of the Aiki Shrine in Iwama, Japan, 1950s. Morihiro Saito Sensei, close student of the founder and longtime chief instructor of the Iwama Dojo, can be seen sitting on the mat, on the far right.

Live-Blade Practice and Love

O-Sensei said, "*Bu wa ai nari: Bu* [the martial essence] is love." I believe this love is intimately connected to the intensity of our training focus.

To reach an understanding of Aikido as love, you have to be *shinken* [completely focused; as if wielding a real sword]. You need to commit yourself, body and soul. Without a wholehearted focus, you won't be able to effectively love yourself or someone else. You can't half-heartedly achieve a true love. It has to be *shinken*. It must be real.

If we want to be able to teach Aikido truly as love, then we need to train with a *shinken* [live-blade] concentration. We need the kind of love that can attack and be attacked with full commitment. That's what it's going to take to reach a true understanding of Aikido as love.

Ask yourself: Am I training wholeheartedly? Or am I taking a half-hearted approach, out of fear that I might hit someone accidentally? When others are watching, am I holding back or diminishing my own practice in attempt to make things go smoothly? To reach the higher levels of Aikido, we must not let these kinds of concerns get in the way of our practice.

Hikitsuchi Sensei often pointed out the importance of having a *shinken* focus. He trained with O-Sensei when no one else was around. I imagine this allowed him to be truly *shinken*—real. Hikitsuchi Sensei didn't have to worry about others watching, or wonder if he might look like he was being disrespectful to his teacher.

Many times I heard Hikitsuchi Sensei tell the story of the time he and O-Sensei engaged in an intense practice with wooden swords in the middle of the night. Apparently Hikitsuchi Sensei reached such a state of focus that he actually cut off the tip of the *bokken* [wooden sword] that O-Sensei was wielding! It seems that they were both incredibly happy about what had occurred. You can't do that sort of thing halfway. I feel that is how to grasp the essence of Aikido, which

123

is connected to a real love. When teacher and disciple train whole-heartedly together, that is a true state of love.

Love is not just about personal relationships, or the love between teacher and student, or between friends. Of course there are some people with whom we connect easily, heart to heart. It is much more difficult to love each and every person, isn't it? We can't simply make the claim that we understand Aikido as love. I often feel that I fall short in my attempt to truly practice Aikido. I want to become able to give love to absolutely anyone. But I fail at this, and find my inspiration again, on a daily basis.

Aikido must be practiced every day. That is how Aikido will continue to live.

"Hanashi Ni Naran!"

Occasionally O-Sensei would refuse to teach or to demonstrate his Aikido.

O-Sensei could instantly tell who was sincerely paying attention and who was not. He was not fooled by superficial appearances. A highly ranked group of black belts from another martial art might appear to be watching intently, but if they had no serious intent to learn, O-Sensei would perceive that. At times O-Sensei would declare, "There are *bureimono* [rude people] here," and refuse to proceed.

It was because of the high stature he had reached that O-Sensei was able to take that action. People snapped to attention simply because O-Sensei declared there were rude people present. They became more sincere and watched with a greater intent to learn.

Occasionally, at the dojo in Shingu, when O-Sensei felt that we students were not showing enough intent to learn, he would exclaim *"Hanashi ni naran!"* and leave the room. *Hanashi ni naran* [worthless; not worth talking about] means that O-Sensei didn't feel motivated to teach us. Even though we wanted to learn Aikido, we had not pre-pared ourselves sufficiently.

After O-Sensei left the room, we would redouble our efforts to train in such a way that he would want to teach. Then O-Sensei would come back and instruct us again. It would have been terrible if he had left and not returned! But when O-Sensei would exclaim, *"Hanashi ni naran!"* all the students would suddenly wake up. We would practice with increased concentration and a better spirit.

Some people receive a scolding from their teacher as a sign of love, and vow to make positive changes in themselves. Other people resent the scolding as unwarranted criticism, and think, "I'm out of here!" How you receive your teacher's words is of utmost importance.

The founder of Aikido demonstrates *atemi* (striking techniques) with Motomichi Anno in the original Kumano Juku Dojo in Shingu; mid-1950s.

A Lesson at Osaka Stadium

One time I accompanied O-Sensei to Osaka as his *otomo* [personal attendant]. We traveled to Osaka Stadium, where O-Sensei taught an Aikido class. The man in charge of the Osaka Stadium dojo was an important, influential person in his thirties or forties, much older than I was. O-Sensei directed me to train with him during the class. There I was, training with the head of that dojo, and I must have put a technique on him that was too rough. I had a black belt, and I was anxious to make a good showing, so I was trying to do strong technique. O-Sensei was watching us.

Suddenly he shouted, *"Dame ya!"* ["No good! Stop that!"] Immediately, O-Sensei called me over and let me know in no uncertain terms that I had done something wrong. He said to me, "It is unacceptable for you to be rough and out of control like that!"

Later, O-Sensei kindly told me not to worry about it. As we ate a meal together after class, he clarified that it was good to have strong technique, and he encouraged me to train hard. But during the class, he had vividly communicated to me that it was not appropriate to treat my partner the way I did. It was rude for a young person like me to be insensitive to an older person in charge—the very person who had invited O-Sensei to teach there.

I don't remember O-Sensei ever correcting our techniques in class. But at Osaka Stadium, he scolded me because I had been too rough. O-Sensei taught me that it is essential to take a good look at who your training partner is, and act appropriately.

When you come from countries far away to train with us in Kumano, for example, it would be wrong for us to train too hard with you. You've traveled a long distance; your body is tired, and you've come with the intention to train sincerely with everyone. Speed and power are not the highest goals. We need to understand that, and to train as fully as possible, based on that kind of discerning awareness.

126

O-Sensei's Example

O-Sensei didn't teach through explicit instruction. He taught by example. When O-Sensei led us in the *misogi* purification practices of *torifune* and *furutama,* for instance, he didn't instruct us in specific procedures. We would just follow along. It was the same when he demonstrated technique. O-Sensei didn't tell us, "This is what I'm doing—this technique begins with *shizentai* [natural stance], and here is the footwork." I never heard him teach that way. We just observed the amazing things he did, and then tried to practice what we had seen and experienced. That's why the Aikido teachers who studied directly with O-Sensei all have different technique.

O-Sensei didn't explain technique. He didn't even use names for the techniques. He frequently used the term *kokyu* [breath], but he didn't say, "This is *kotegaeshi* [a wrist twist]. This is *irimi nage* [an entering throw]." I believe the technical terms in use today were developed by senior teachers to assist in the instruction and popularization of Aikido. But I never once heard from O-Sensei's lips, "This is *shiho nage* [four-directions throw]." The direct learning from O-Sensei was unlabeled.

O-Sensei was always changing the way he did things. During one stay in Shingu, O-Sensei would train in a certain way, and the next time he was here, he would do things differently. He was constantly researching and making rapid progress. The *torifune* practice O-Sensei did in earlier years evolved and changed. During his last years, he would often practice with a *yari* [spear], a short staff with a sharpened point, which he brought with him from Tokyo. Toward the end of his life, O-Sensei didn't do specific techniques like *irimi nage*. He would walk, and people would fall. His technique had become simply walking. He would just utter "Ahh!" and it would be over.

It is natural that each person perceived O-Sensei's demonstrations in a different way. Aikido teachers who learned from O-Sensei are teaching what they remember of what O-Sensei did, so the footwork and method of each teacher is different. This has led to the development of numerous "styles" of Aikido. O-Sensei didn't explicitly say to his students, "You have to do it this way, and this is exactly what it is." There are numerous diverse interpretations of Aikido, due to the manner of teaching O-Sensei employed.

Even now, when you watch videotapes of O-Sensei, don't you each see something different? It's natural.

"There is no form and no style in Aikido. The movement of Aikido is the movement of Nature, whose secret is profound and infinite."[32]

~ MORIHEI UESHIBA O-SENSEI

A formal portrait of Morihei Ueshiba O-Sensei, in Shingu, Japan, 1960.

Take a Step Closer to O-Sensei

You ask if it is possible to come to be like O-Sensei, the founder of Aikido. I do think it is possible. But how far you go in O-Sensei's direction depends on how much you apply yourself.

If you want to take a step closer to O-Sensei, pay attention to what he said. "*Aiki* was born of the form and heart of *kami*," O-Sensei said. Make this your central focus as you practice. Think of all the powers of nature as the heart of *kami*. Imagine waves, clouds, and all the forms in nature as the form of *kami*. Make a deep study of what has brought these forms into being. Then you can express that perception in your practice of technique.

If you learn from *kami* [spirit, nature], you will draw closer to O-Sensei. If you live long and train in the same spirit as O-Sensei, if you apply yourself continuously to the practice of becoming one with nature—with *kami*—then depending on the ability you were born with, you may even go beyond O-Sensei.

People say that O-Sensei was the kind of teacher who comes only once in a thousand years. I agree. But I think a person could reach O-Sensei's level, if they had natural ability and put in the same amount of effort. Even if you didn't have O-Sensei's natural aptitude for *budo* [martial arts], if you were to put in twice the effort, you might still reach O-Sensei's level.

If we want to take a step closer to O-Sensei, we have to apply ourselves. If we want to get closer than that, we must apply ourselves more. There is no other way.

But the nature of our effort is crucial. It's not a matter of just trying to become strong, or striving to become like O-Sensei so that we can act superior to others. What is essential is the heart. We need to hold the sincere desire for *everyone* to progress along the Path. That's the kind of spirit that O-Sensei had.

When O-Sensei was a child, he had already memorized the Buddhist sutras and the Shinto *Norito* chants and had an active spiritual practice. So in a sense he was ahead from the start. But this should not be a source of discouragement for us. At any time, we can engage in the kind of practice that O-Sensei did, and make progress. It is important to ask ourselves if we are going to stay at our current level for the rest of our lives. Or will we take another step?

You could think of yourself as a candle. Your body is the wax, and your heart is the wick. When your wick is lit with the fire of Aikido, you begin to shine. As your light increases, the people around you are brightened as well. And because your light has been lit by Aikido, you devote yourself to your practice.

I would like to give light like a candle. The wick of the candle is important, and the wax is also essential. Body and heart must work together. If the body—the wax—goes first, you can't burn for long. And a broken wick won't do either. I need to secure my candle, make sure it doesn't crack or fall over. I want to protect this light against wind and rain, and keep my fire burning until all the wax is gone. Give my full effort until the end.

I pray that the candle burns with the flame of Aikido. I would like to take one step closer to O-Sensei. I would like to communicate Aikido—the real thing—to others. My hope is for everyone to increase in radiance, together. When I feel the desire to be of service to everyone, my heart becomes warm.

You ask if it is possible to come to be like O-Sensei. Make your heart into the wick of Aikido, study the words of O-Sensei, and grasp the purpose of O-Sensei's Aikido. Light your wick with O-Sensei's light: the desire to unify all people into one family. If you keep that flame burning, I believe you will come to experience a mysterious power: a great light, heat, brightness, and joy.

Shi Jin Shi Ai, "Greatest Benevolence, Greatest Love";
calligraphy brushed by the founder of Aikido.

~4~

The HEART of AIKIDO

With wisdom distilled from a lifetime of practice, Anno Sensei invites each person to focus on the heart. He communicates as a companion on a shared spiritual journey. He says, "Aikido training is a way of taking off the layers that cover up what is inside. If each of us could shed those layers, we would all shine with the same light."

In this chapter, Anno Sensei speaks of the fundamental spiritual principles at the heart of Aikido, and articulates a practice of gratitude based in the interdependence of all life. He describes essential practices expounded by O-Sensei, such as self-reflection and "victory over oneself." Speaking simply and encouragingly, Anno Sensei responds to questions from Western students about heart and spirit in Aikido. He gives us a window into his own training, and shares his approach to the challenges and opportunities that a deep practice of Aikido presents.

—Linda Holiday

What Is Aikido?

What is Aikido? Ultimately, Aikido is love. This is the founder's teaching and must not be changed. Aikido training is a method that allows us to reach a state of love.

I want to have a loving heart. I want to live in harmony with everyone. I believe we all do. Despite that intention, we think, "I don't like this person, or that person." "That's no good, that's wrong." We get into conflict with other people. We want to be in harmony with everyone, but we are not. We need to keep training in order to purify the heart.

O-Sensei described Aikido as a process of uniting with the ki of emptiness *[ku no ki]* and the ki of true emptiness *[shin ku no ki]*. I feel it is the process of emptying ourselves, and purifying our hearts, that leads us to a state of love. In Buddhism there is an expression, "Emptiness beyond emptiness." *Mu* [emptiness; void] beyond *Mu*. I believe this may be what O-Sensei referred to as true emptiness. Beyond emptiness lies "true emptiness."

Love beyond love . . . Love becomes Great Love. Harmony becomes Great Harmony. Great Love is not a matter of thinking. It is a continuous state of being. In order to develop that state, it is essential to polish and purify ourselves continuously.

Aikido training is a method by which to reach Great Love and Great Harmony. Aikido is a path, and that is the objective of the path. It is possible to go along this path but lose sight of the true goal. We could end up trying to make our technique clean and beautiful, instead of making our hearts clean and beautiful. When O-Sensei spoke, he pointed out the goal, and he gave us advice on how to progress in that direction. He referred to a continuous process of self-reflection. He told us it was necessary to develop ourselves spiritually, intellectually, morally, and physically. He spoke frequently of cultivating the heart.

134

What are you focused on, as your goal? In order to reach your destination, your heart must be in alignment with the direction of the journey. It is not enough simply to become strong. The heart is essential.

Imagine a beautiful flower. If its blossom represents Great Love, you could say we are at ground level. We don't yet know what color of flower we will produce. We don't understand our own weak points, and we may not clearly perceive our own strengths. For that, we need to find a good teacher. We put forth our full effort to send out strong roots and to draw water up from the ground, so that the plant can blossom. We train ourselves, study hard, and absorb many things, so that we can bloom beautifully. So that we can embody the heart of Great Love.

Anno Sensei teaches in California, 2012.

The Fundamentals

The most important objectives to keep in mind are Great Harmony, Great Love, and Gratitude. These are the fundamentals of Aikido.

Aikido practice is a method of incorporating the fundamentals of Great Harmony, Great Love, and Gratitude into one's own heart. To integrate these fundamentals into Aikido technique, I have to eliminate the sense of winning and losing. The feeling of competition must be completely transmuted into the heart of gratitude and harmony. If I am able to do that, I will transcend issues of relative strength or skill. When thoughts of strength versus weakness, or comparisons of technical skill, start to creep into my mind again, I need to let go of them through more training, and return to the heart of Great Harmony.

What you think about, what you hold as your objective, is incredibly important. As we practice Aikido technique, we need to focus consistently on the fundamentals of harmony, love, and gratitude. If we forget about the fundamentals, we will begin to think again in relative terms of "strong" and "weak." And that is the path that leads to war.

Beyond Ordinary Gratitude

When I was a child, I was taught the phrase *Okagesama*: "It is thanks to you." There is a big meaning in that brief expression, which parents teach to their children early in life. To say *Okagesama*, "It is thanks to you," over and over, cultivates a big spirit.

There is a subtle difference between the usual word for gratitude *[kansha]* and *okagesama*. If you just say "Thank you," and that's the end of it, that is not what is meant by *okagesama*. *Okagesama* goes beyond the level of ordinary gratitude. It is the understanding that our lives are sustained by nature, by other people—by everything around us. With that understanding, the meaning of "gratitude" undergoes a profound shift.

The heart of gratitude is essential. What is the foundation of our lives? What allows us to live? It's not enough to consider only human beings, or to think only of visible, material things. We must remember the source. The essentials of life are things like water, air, and sunlight. *Kami*—Great Nature—is the center of everything. *Okagesama* implies gratitude toward *kami*.

O-Sensei told us, "First, you must stand upon the Floating Bridge of Heaven." I believe that the Floating Bridge of Heaven is a state of being. But this state of being is dependent upon each person's level. No doubt O-Sensei was standing on a marvelous bridge, floating in the universe. We, however, find ourselves "standing" firmly right here on the floor! I believe that when our sense of gratitude increases, we are moving toward the state of being that is the Floating Bridge of Heaven.

Concepts and words of gratitude are not enough. You could say all the right words, "My life is sustained by *kami*, and I am grateful to this person, and that person," and still find yourself standing separately, alone, on the level of the floor. O-Sensei went beyond that level. He felt he was standing in connection with the entire universe. I believe

137

that if we devote ourselves to our daily practice, we, too, over time, will approach that state of being.

In the very first book on Aikido, O-Sensei wrote that the purpose of Aikido is to develop people of sincerity. Sincerity requires gratitude. It works the other way as well: If you are sincere, you will develop a sense of gratitude. The techniques of Aikido must not devolve into winning and losing. How wonderful if our techniques were to become acts of gratitude!

Anno Sensei teaches an Aikido seminar in San Francisco, 2004.

A True, Sincere Human Being

When I started Aikido training, my greatest desire was to become strong. I didn't think about spiritual matters at the beginning. But I thought O-Sensei was wonderful. He was small yet strong.

O-Sensei was strong, but his strength was of a different nature. It was not the kind of strength that caused pain or injury in others. You could say that inside his power was the heart of love, but I didn't think in those terms yet. I just wanted to be strong. O-Sensei often spoke of "Truth, Goodness, and Beauty." I was mysteriously drawn to the beauty and goodness in O-Sensei's power.

As I kept training, I studied O-Sensei's words. I wasn't sure I understood what they meant, but I read them over and over. For instance, "The purpose is to make true, sincere human beings." I read those words of O-Sensei and I loved them.

I would like to become a true, sincere human being. But let's say I lose my temper and have an argument with someone. I still want to develop the heart of Truth, Goodness, and Beauty. So I remember that arguing with others is not the way of *Aiki*. When I reflect on my argumentative behavior, I feel embarrassed. I think about the reasons I lost my temper. Maybe I was thinking only of myself in a prideful way. Perhaps I got so upset because I was in pain. If I open my heart in self-reflection, I will remember that everyone suffers. Then I may be able to let go of my anger. If I have even a small capacity to reflect on my behavior, resolution is possible. Without self-reflection, the argument might be the end of the relationship.

Aikido is a path that builds the ability to reflect and to conduct ourselves well. It would be an embarrassment to walk the path of Aikido yet be unable to reflect on our own behavior. This needs to be an area of constant, lifelong practice. O-Sensei frequently spoke to us about the process of self-reflection.

When O-Sensei occasionally exclaimed *"Hanashi ni naran!"* ["Worthless!"] to us students, we felt strongly moved to reflect on our behavior. Ordinarily, if someone calls you "worthless," you respond defensively. If your behavior is criticized by one of your peers, you might reply, "Well, if that's the way you feel, do it your own way!" But the power of O-Sensei's presence was different than that. If he said *"Hanashi ni naran, na,"* even in a soft voice, you would immediately reflect on yourself. O-Sensei's words would put you in that frame of mind.

O-Sensei spent eighty years developing Aikido. He didn't make it all by himself. Before he formalized the path of "Aikido," he studied with many teachers and knowledgeable people. What O-Sensei developed, over the course of his whole life, is already here for us. We need to put forth more effort to understand what O-Sensei taught, and to share it with others without delay. This, too, is the heart of self-reflection.

Kaerimiru, Hajiru, Kuiru, Osoru, Satoru, "Self-reflection, Shame, Remorse, Fear, Enlightenment [The Process of Self-Reflection]"; calligraphy brushed by Motomichi Anno Sensei.

省恥悔怯悟

素岐書

The Process of Self-Reflection

O-Sensei taught us to engage in a step-by-step process of self-reflection: *Kaerimiru, hajiru, kuiru, osoru, satoru.* I believe this five-step process is a very important teaching for the continuation of Aikido in the future. The significance of self-reflection is universal.

The first step, *kaerimiru* [self-reflection], means to look inside and reflect on your own behavior. To question yourself and to evaluate what you have done.

The second and third steps are *hajiru* [to be ashamed] and *kuiru* [to regret, to have remorse]. If you become aware that you did something wrong and you regret what you did, that is self-reflection. To experience remorse [*kuiru*] is also self-reflection. Looking back at the past, at what has brought you to this point, perhaps what you see is a series of mistakes. You might wonder if you have focused too much on making money. You think, "Too bad! How I wish I had realized this earlier, tried harder, done better. . . ."

The next step is *osoru* [fear]. *Osoru* is also essentially self-reflection. When I reflect on the fact that I don't have much time left in which to change my ways . . . that's when the fear comes in. "Why didn't I realize this before?"

Let's say I notice that a student's attendance at class has become irregular. When I see the student next, I speak to him about the importance of training frequently, and ask him to come to each class without fail. What if the student then disappears altogether from the dojo? I need to reflect on the effect my words may have had. How frightening to realize that I may have actually discouraged the student from continuing with Aikido, the exact opposite of what I had intended to do. *Osoru* [fear] brings us to a new level of understanding: *satoru.*

This is the process of self-reflection. As you repeat this process over and over, and increase your understanding, you begin to experience *satori* [understanding, enlightenment]. When you reach this new realization, you must actually put it into action, so you don't simply repeat your past mistakes. Putting realizations into actual practice is the biggest challenge, but it is also the best part, isn't it? O-Sensei frequently spoke of "bringing the spirit out." What I believe he meant by that is to put our spiritual realizations into practice—to take actions that are visible to others.

O-Sensei emphasized the importance of this process. With your mission in life constantly in your mind, it is good to engage over and over in the process of self-reflection: *kaerimiru, hajiru, kuiru, osoru, satoru.*

Living Spirit

Traditional teachings of Japan are typically not presented in a rational, logical way. This is different than the teaching methods in modern society. At a university, for example, you are taught knowledge in a clear, explicit way, in order to avoid misunderstandings. If there are several interpretations, they will still be laid out clearly. But the teachings of O-Sensei are different from that.

O-Sensei always used terms with multiple meanings. For instance, it would be difficult to settle on a single definition of what he meant by the word *tamashii* [spirit, soul]. Your understanding of the concept *tamashii* will depend on your own spirit. So you could say that it is a difficult task to understand what O-Sensei taught—or you could say that it is an enjoyable one!

Another word that O-Sensei frequently used was *ikutama. Ikutama* is a compound of two characters: *ikiru* [to live], and *tamashii* [spirit]. Thus the simplest interpretation of *ikutama* could be "living spirit." But a truly living spirit—what it means to be truly alive as a human being—is deeper than the mind. It is deeper than intellectual knowledge, deeper than your thoughts and feelings.

I feel that that intellect, heart, and spirit are three layers of the self. Intellectual knowledge resides on the surface. Heart adds a sense of what's good and bad, of values, to intellectual knowledge. You can understand with your heart, and be known as a person with a good heart. But hearts and minds are changeable. They can be influenced in one direction or another. Even when you're doing something important, someone can come along and invite you to idle away your time at a karaoke bar, and in spite of yourself, off you go. . . . A state of mind can change at any time. It's not that going off to a karaoke bar is a particularly bad thing to do. But when you enter the realm of the spirit, you stay true to yourself, consistently.

The founder of Aikido, O-Sensei, was consistent. No matter how searchingly I looked at him, regardless of the angle from which I viewed him over all the years, O-Sensei absolutely did not vary—so I found him absolutely believable. I feel we all need to develop that kind of spirit. Not the mind that says, *I did well today, so I'll slack off tomorrow.* That kind of inconsistency means we have not yet fully developed the spirit.

When you first learn an Aikido technique, you acquire knowledge about it. After training more, you are able to perform the technique somewhat freely. At that point you are able put your heart into it. After even more training, you may be able to do that technique without thinking at all. That's when the technique emerges from your spirit. When your training partner strikes with sincere intent and the movement of a technique emerges spontaneously, without thought or consciousness, that is the power of the spirit.

If you try to learn with your intellect, it is more difficult to absorb the teachings on a deep level. The mind looks at something and says, *I don't want that; I want this instead.* But as you simply continue to train, something changes. What changes is deeper than your intellectual knowledge, deeper than mind or heart.

In the beginning, we perceive form. We admire the beautiful execution of an Aikido technique. After a while, we can perceive the feeling with which it is done—the heart of the person doing the technique.

The founder of Aikido, with Michio Hikitsuchi and two others, 1960s.

Later, we can become able to perceive a person's deepest intentions. The very same technique, however skillfully performed, can be done with a focus on winning and losing, or it can be done with the feeling of joining with your partner. Each different intention will show itself within the form of the technique. When you can perceive what is in the deepest center, a person's deepest intentions, then you have entered the world of *tamashii:* the spirit.

The greatest challenge is to absorb O-Sensei's teachings into your own *tamashii*—to make them resonate within your own spirit. I believe that Aikido training is the process of moving more and more in the direction of the spirit.

"Willingly begin the cultivation of your spirit."[33]

~ MORIHEI UESHIBA O-SENSEI

144

A Path for Us to Follow

To cultivate a heart that sees clearly, the heart of *okagesama,* we continue our practice of Aikido. It is a gradual process, not something we can accomplish all at once. As we take small steps, our capacity increases. It is important to develop our sincerity and to engage in self-reflection.

In the development of sincerity or truth, there are different levels. At first you might be sincere in your words. After training and polishing yourself more, there will be another level of truth. Even if you feel that you have already purified yourself, it is always possible to polish yourself further.

A person who has polished himself or herself emits light. O-Sensei was truly wonderful in this regard. There was a consistent radiance in the way he conducted himself each day and in his words. I felt mysteriously drawn to the words I heard him say. And when I sat next to O-Sensei, I felt completely safe with him, despite his tremendous power. A wonderful light shone from him. It was an expansive radiance of harmony, of love, and of gratitude.

O-Sensei often spoke of *shin zen bi:* the light of "Truth, Goodness, and Beauty." We need to polish and purify ourselves in order to turn into light that will give joy to everyone. If you become light, all people and everything on the earth will rejoice. We practice Aikido in order to unify ourselves with Truth, Goodness, and Beauty: the heart of *kami.*

Even the smallest plant is doing this. A plant humbly receives power from the world around it. Receiving the ki of heaven, the ki of the sun, and the power of water, the plant puts forth its full effort for a lifetime, blooming and giving joy to others. What a wonderful example for us to follow! Over the course of a year, the plant grows and develops into beauty that causes us to exclaim in delight. Bearing fruit, it provides the seeds for the next generation. It is unified with the heart of *kami.*

You could focus on the desire to become the kind of human being who brings joy to the entire world. To become radiant with light and, as O-Sensei said, "one with the universe." Of course this is incredibly difficult to do. But if you take one step at a time, or even half a step, as people do in walking meditation, you will draw nearer to your goal. O-Sensei left a path for us to follow, which leads to real truth, real goodness, and real beauty—to unity with the heart of *kami*. He called this path "Aikido."

IN DIALOGUE WITH ANNO SENSEI: THE HEART OF AIKIDO

In the following section, Anno Sensei responds to questions from students about cultivating the heart of Aikido.

Anno Sensei with an American student visiting the Kumano Juku Dojo, 2006.

Focus on the Heart

Sensei, as we continue to practice Aikido, how can we keep our inspiration fresh, as you have done for so many years?

There was a nearly blind person who trained with us in Kumano. He taught me a great deal about matters of the heart. I feel I learned more from him than he learned from me. The advice I would give to any student of Aikido is this: Focus on the heart. Don't get caught up in technique; study the heart of the art.

If you want to do Aikido, it is important to train hard. But you also need to bring into your practice the spiritual message of Aikido's founder. No matter how long and hard you train in technique, you will at times reach a wall, a place from which you feel you cannot go any farther. At times like that, when you feel confused and discouraged, read O-Sensei's words. Study them deeply. Absorb them. Ask yourself, What is it that O-Sensei was trying to get across? Make your own personal commitment to practice in the spirit of O-Sensei's teachings. This will allow you to progress to another level of your training.

The forms of Aikido techniques are likely to change over time. The question is, will they change in a positive direction? Will we concentrate on becoming stronger than other people? Or we will develop technique that is clean and natural? O-Sensei used to say, "Technique changes each and every day." As we train, something changes in our hearts, and our technique reflects that.

It is important not to get stuck in judging someone's technique as good or bad. Don't be limited by a judgmental way of thinking. The main errors we need to avoid are in matters of the heart. I try to avoid evaluating whether a certain instructor's technique is "correct." Don't get stuck focusing only on technique. More important than the form of the technique is the intention behind it. Study carefully the intention of Aikido, its purpose and spirit. Strengthen your heart while you

147

strengthen your technique. Then, you can pursue whatever technique you like—whatever "style" of Aikido appeals to you.

You can devote yourself to developing beautiful technique and a peaceful mind. Or you can concentrate on winning and losing, and that competitive attitude will manifest in your technique. When you look at a painting, don't you have a natural response to what the painter has tried to convey in form? When you view a piece of calligraphy, you can feel the spirit with which it is written. And if you look, you can see a person's training spirit precisely expressed in their Aikido technique.

We need to remember that the primary goal of Aikido is harmony and good relations between people. If we don't cultivate a harmonious heart along with technical skill, there will be a lack of integration in our practice, which will show up in behavior off the mat. So we must train ourselves rigorously, not only in technique, but also in the spirit of Aikido that O-Sensei taught.

As O-Sensei frequently said, "More than technique, study the heart."

"Aikido is *ai* [love]. You make this great love of the Universe your heart, and then you must make your own mission the protection and love of all things. To accomplish this mission must be the true *budo* [martial way]."[34]

~ Morihei Ueshiba O-Sensei

The Secret of Aikido

I hear people refer to "the secret of Aikido." Is there actually a secret of Aikido? If so, how can I find it?

The secret of Aikido can be found in the calligraphy that you see on the wall right over there—O-Sensei's *Masakatsu Agatsu:* "True victory; victory over oneself."

True victory means doing the right thing—conducting yourself with ever-increasing integrity. Victory over oneself means defeating the laziness in your own heart. Winning over yourself, then, is what makes it possible to do the right thing, to achieve true victory. I think this is the essence of Aikido. We engage in Aikido training in order to become enlightened to this "secret."

Yet it is not a secret. And it is not something that is limited to any particular dojo. The spirit of Aikido is found in our family lives and every-where in the world. Aikido exists throughout the entire universe. The question is, how will we awaken to this reality?

You won't realize the essence of Aikido by amusing yourself with idle pursuits. It is neces-sary to undergo hardship and to purify yourself. You have to train with other people in ways that are challenging, even painful, in order to tran-scend those challenges and realize the true nature of Aikido. Gradually you come to know the joy of moving in unison with others. We unify with other people and with nature, and live joyfully in the world. My understanding is that Aikido training is a way of developing in ourselves the ability to be a source of joy to others.

The easiest of all of O-Sensei's teachings to keep in mind may be *Masakatsu Agatsu:* "True victory; victory over oneself." It is possible, and helpful, to return to that thought over and over again while you are training.

Masakatsu Agatsu, "True victory; victory over oneself"; calligraphy brushed by Morihei Ueshiba O-Sensei. Signed (at bottom): "Morihei."

Agatsu: Victory Over Oneself

If "True victory is victory over oneself," how do you avoid seeing yourself as an adversary? Seeing yourself as bad, or as the enemy?

As much as possible, I think well of myself. I think of my own heart as being wonderful. I need to continue to train and develop myself in such a way that I can always think well of myself. This is the meaning of *Agatsu:* victory over oneself.

Although I think well of myself, there is another side to my heart, which wants to defeat other people. These two parts of the human heart struggle with each other. When the positive side shows itself, it is important to appreciate and nurture it. When the negative side comes out, we need as much as possible to let it go, to eliminate it. I believe this is the purpose of Aikido training.

I am motivated to continue my training because I want to improve myself. I have not yet polished all of myself. I experience collisions and conflicts with other people, and I have not yet developed the strength to love everyone. So I feel I must continue to train myself, to develop a wonderful spirit.

You could say that there are good desires and bad desires. There is the desire to polish oneself, to develop into a person who can bring joy to others. And there is the desire to defeat others, and to possess more than others. Everyone has both good and bad desires. Certainly in Aikido, we all want to become skillful in technique, to get "good" at Aikido. But we must transform our desire to be stronger than others into the desire to train hard so that our practice will benefit others.

"A mind to serve for the peace of all human beings in the world is needed in Aikido, and not the mind of one who wishes to be strong or who practices only to fell an opponent."[35]

∼ MORIHEI UESHIBA O-SENSEI

In the Spirit of Joy

How can we cultivate a heart of harmony and compassion through the practice of Aikido?

It is important to study the words of the founder of Aikido and attempt to understand them. And in order to attempt to understand O-Sensei's words, you need to do the physical training. You won't fully understand what O-Sensei meant if you simply read the words over and over. You train—you read—you train—you read . . . and through this process you come to understand the teachings of Aikido.

Recently I taught the first class for a group of beginning students. I gave each of them a copy of O-Sensei's "Guidelines for Aikido Training." When beginning students read those guidelines now, I imagine they have quite a different feeling than I do, reading them again after many years of training.

For instance, the third guideline is "Practice always in the spirit of joy." This seems to be a simple point that anyone would understand. But after you continue to practice for a long time, you come to understand that its significance is profound. Over the years, as you experi-

Anno Sensei teaches in California, 2010.

151

ence conflict with other people—differences of opinion about training, or major disagreements leading to repeated problems—you develop a deeper understanding of what it takes to get along with people. What it means to practice always in the spirit of joy. You realize that you need to develop a big heart.

Then you start to think about the importance of harmony between people all over the world. North and south need to be able to get along together. People in organizations, those with more experience or position and those with less, need to have friendly relations with one another. You reflect on the significance of "four directions" [shiho] and "eight directions" [happo]. Then you come to appreciate what a large meaning is contained in the simple directive, "Practice always in the spirit of joy."

Think about the earth, how it exists in harmonious relationship to the sun, the moon, the stars—the whole universe. That universal harmony must be in your own heart as well. Even if we can't completely embody the harmony of the universe, it is essential that we move in that direction.

The Capacity to Reflect

What can I do when I find myself in conflict with my partner during an Aikido class?

When you start to get into conflict, recall the words of the founder of Aikido, O-Sensei, "Practice always in the spirit of joy." Reflect on your own thoughts and feelings. You have an unpleasant feeling at that moment, don't you? You think, "How can I practice in the spirit of joy?"

Joyful practice depends upon your capacity to reflect. If you are engaged in a battle with your partner, it is quite difficult to think clearly. You need to dissolve the attachments in your mind, and let go of the intention to defeat the other person. O-Sensei spoke of the importance of self-reflection [kaerimiru]. When you encounter a

Anno Sensei demonstrates an Aikido technique with Linda Holiday at Aikido of Santa Cruz, 2000.

problem, engage in self-reflection. Reflect on why the problem has occurred. However, as you begin to reflect, you will often conclude that you are fine, but there is something wrong with the other person. If that is your assessment of the situation, it is unlikely that there will be a good result!

O-Sensei spoke of "winning correctly" [*tadashiki ni katsu*]. When we hear the word "winning," the first thing we think about is defeating someone else. So we need to reflect on the teaching of "winning correctly" and develop a correct understanding of it. O-Sensei frequently referred to "Winning correctly; winning over oneself" [*Tadashiki ni katsu; jibun ni katsu*]. I love these words of O-Sensei. But they are challenging to put into practice.

Winning over oneself, or "self-victory," is a difficult concept. You could misinterpret it to mean you must be utterly determined to win, to not be defeated by anyone. Upon deeper reflection, though, you see that "winning over oneself" expresses the importance of making correct choices. It is necessary to train yourself, to become the kind of person who will move in the right direction.

The most challenging thing is to see yourself clearly. How do you judge yourself? It is natural to think, "I am correct!" When you think you are doing the right thing, it is important to look at yourself with eyes wide open. If you look with your ego, you will look good and the other person will look bad. Even if your actions are completely off-base, you'll think you are right! You need a heart that is *sunao*—open, clear, and unbiased—in order to see yourself clearly.

Recognizing that the thought of winning and losing has appeared in your mind is what allows you to let go of it. When the feeling of competition arises, the real challenge is to return to a natural state of mind. If I can find within myself the intention to proceed in a relaxed and natural way, then I am more easily able to let things go. It may still take an effort, but it is easier when I have a natural feeling. Other people will feel that relaxation in me and will be influenced by it. Gradually, a feeling of harmony increases.

It is important to continue your practice forever. As you practice, you continue to become aware of your weak points, and you feel the desire to train in order to correct yourself. O-Sensei, the founder, trained himself intensively for many decades. After all that practice, near the end of his life he remarked, "I feel like I'm just beginning to understand Aikido."

A Heart That Is Sunao

You say it is essential to develop a heart that is "*sunao.*" What is the most important aspect of the meaning of *sunao*?

Sunao means a beautiful heart . . . the kind of beauty that is pure, innocent, and completely clear. Transparent. If your heart is transparent, you can connect easily to other people, can't you? You don't worry. You only worry if your heart is cloudy.

In Aikido training, being *sunao* enables you to learn easily. If you introduce a color into clear water, the water turns that color. But if you put the same color into murky water, you can't see it. When you practice using a sword, if you exert more power on one side than the other, you won't be able to cut straight despite your best intentions. When your heart becomes *sunao*, completely clear, that's when you will be able to do a straight strike.

When I teach a new technique in class, it seems to me that the new students pick it up faster than the more experienced students. They don't have entrenched habits that get in the way of learning. Once the advanced students have learned the form, they

Mary Heiny Sensei teaches an Aikido seminar in Maryland, 2009.

develop skill quickly, but beginning students are quicker to take in something new. It is important to become *sunao* and be able to learn new things, even when you have been training for a long time.

Sunao doesn't mean simply agreeing to everything. It doesn't mean agreeing to something that is wrong. O-Sensei's teaching of "True victory" [*Masakatsu*] is very important in this regard. The spirit of "True victory" is to say yes to what is right, and no to what is wrong.

"Winning correctly" also means not being defeated by what is wrong or bad.

The clear, open heart of an infant is very different from the clear, open heart of a middle school or high school student. It is different again in an adult, or in a person who has trained himself or herself diligently for many years. Regardless of your stage in life, it is important to become *sunao*. And to carefully assess whether something is right or wrong. If you believe something is bad, but you agree to it anyway, that is not *sunao*. If something is wrong, you need courage in order to speak your mind. To say, "You are making a mistake." That is difficult. So we train ourselves, in order to develop a heart that is *sunao*. To find one's own true heart, which is completely clear.

If my mind is packed full of thoughts, it is not *sunao*. If I think, "He probably won't like it if I say no to him, so I won't," or "It won't go well if I say that to her, so I'll agree with her temporarily and things will go more smoothly," these are ego-based thoughts. I end up like this if I don't actually know right from wrong, and I am just trying to make things go smoothly.

This is quite challenging. If you are in an ongoing relationship, in order to be able to proceed, you may need to be patient, to find a path of harmony, and not abruptly say something that would cause a parting of ways. Sometimes you will need to compromise. How clear and open can you be? You can't get by with only the simplest *sunao* of an infant.

It all comes back to "True Victory," doesn't it? True victory is overcoming one's own weaknesses. As you continue to practice, you go in the direction of what is true and right, and you develop the capacity to let other people know when you feel something is wrong. We practice Aikido in order to develop a strong heart. A true heart. A heart that is *sunao*.

Confidence

How can you envelop someone else in the spirit of love when you doubt the spirit of love in yourself?

I feel the same way. I don't feel completely confident of my ability to love. But I believe that Aikido training gradually develops that confidence. As you continue to train, you develop more skill, and as a result, you have more confidence. Then you have more ability to give to others.

O-Sensei told us that although technique is important, even more important is the spiritual aspect of Aikido training. It is essential to develop the heart of harmony—a heart that is kind to everyone. We must integrate that heart into the practice of the physical techniques of Aikido.

A student recently apologized to me. She said, "I'm sorry that my ukemi is not good." But the essence of *ukemi* [the art of "receiving"] is not a matter of physical skill. What is more important is that you have enthusiasm and a sincere desire to train yourself.

When I think about my own practice, I could judge myself as lacking in technique, knowledge, or spirit. But I don't give up. I want to follow O-Sensei on the path of Aikido. I want to go in the direction of the spirit that O-Sensei manifested. You could say that I have confidence. I think what I have is faith.

Show Your Real Self

You emphasize the importance of opening the heart, yet it is so common to become fearful, critical, or competitive. How can we develop a heart that is open and expansive?

As I train, I would like to develop a bigger heart. But what I focus on is not whether my heart is big or small, or the expansiveness of what I am showing to other people. I think mostly about simply being myself, and not worrying about how that looks to other people. Not trying to make things different than they are. Being my natural self.

There could be a better answer to your question, but I am giving you my real thoughts. When I'm talking with you, I'd like whatever is inside me to emerge naturally. My words may come out smoothly or I may trip over them. But even if I trip, it's the real me, stumbling out.

Don't we all experience the desire to show ourselves to others as better, more polished, than we really are? It's best to let that go. Show your real self. This is important in the practice of Aikido technique as well. We all want to improve, and to show others how skillful we have become. But the techniques of your true self must emerge naturally.

We All Shine with the Same Light

Sensei, I appreciate the ways you shine a light on my training and reflect back to me, like a mirror, the areas in which I could train harder, improve, or explore. How can I develop this quality of illuminating light?

Through Aikido training, each of us polishes our own heart, and as we become reflective, we are made radiant by the light shining from other people. When another person's light reaches me, I, too, shine. By polishing ourselves mutually, we shine mutually.

If you train and polish yourself, if you come to be clear like water, you will be able to perceive other people clearly. If you polish your own heart, you will be able to see other people's hearts. But if you look at others through "dirt" in your heart, they will appear dirty. You won't be able to see them clearly. We must first polish and purify ourselves; then we can perceive the true light of others.

It's the same in nature. By receiving the light of the sun, the moon shines. The earth becomes radiant as well, and everything on earth receives the gift of life.

158

When your heart becomes clear, it is beautiful. Then you can perceive the hearts of other people. It is a source of strength to talk with others who are also trying to go in this direction, people who are engaged in a process of self-reflection and purification. No matter how long a person has trained, or how wonderful a person he or she is, if their ego stands in the way, it can be difficult to see them. But if a person can let go of competitiveness, his or her wonderful qualities become visible to others.

Don't all babies inspire love? Babies are sweet and lovable because they haven't studied anything. They are innocent, clear. When we are just born, we have no sense of self. We are *Mu* [emptiness, void].

I believe that every person's heart naturally shines. And that the heart, or spirit, which each of us receives from the spirit of the universe, is the same in all of us. But as we grow up, this clear and beautiful spirit is covered up by the acquisition of intellectual knowledge, and by family matters, and we may become stuck in a feeling of competition with others. The "self" we receive, and the knowledge that we acquire, are fine. But I believe that it is our practice to completely let go of them.

Two students train together in an "All Ages Aikido" class in Santa Cruz, California, 2008.

Aikido training is a way of taking off the layers that cover up what is inside. If each of us could shed those layers, we would all shine with the same light. It is the same in learning technique: starting fresh, learning, letting go; learning and letting go . . . *Mu* [emptiness], *Yu* [existence], *Mu, Yu, Mu* . . . a continuous process.

If you keep training, you will shine.

Study the Leaf

Sensei, you often say that what you received of O-Sensei's teaching is only a fraction of what he taught. Now that we are studying with you, we have the same feeling, that we are able to receive only a fraction of what you are teaching. And if in turn, our students receive only a fraction of what we can teach, what will happen to Aikido in the future? Will Aikido students learn a fraction of a fraction of a fraction?

That is a possibility.

If Aikido is a tree, then what you learn from your teacher is one leaf. But if you apply yourself to studying that leaf and its purpose, for instance its role in producing food and its relationship to the trunk of the tree, it is possible that you can come to understand the whole tree. If I am taught one part, then I must study it very deeply in order to understand the whole.

Why do human beings have two ears, two eyes, and two nostrils? I was taught that the reason we have two of each is so that we can perceive—hear, see, and smell—all aspects of something. When you hear O-Sensei's teachings, listen well with both ears so you can receive the meaning deeply. When you look at something, don't just look at the surface of it, or what is on the front. Look keenly at what is inside as well. That's why you have two eyes, to see the *omote* and the *ura*, the front and the back. That's the way you need to pursue your learning.

Why do we only have one mouth? This is important to consider. Having only one mouth teaches us the importance of words. Once you say something, it is out in the world and you can't take it back. So you have to be very careful about what you say.

Ears, eyes, and nostrils are all for absorbing. We need to be aware of what we are drawing into ourselves, and absorb only the good. When we put things out into the world through our mouths, we need to think carefully about what we are saying, and put out only the

160

good. But people say many things that should be left unsaid, and neglect to say many things that need saying.

In the Japanese tea ceremony, when you receive the tea bowl, you turn it around so you can view all sides of it before you drink the tea. Until you look at the other side of the tea bowl, you can't see what is different on the other side.

I have a teacup in my hands right now. You could say simply, this is *Mihama-yaki,* a piece of pottery made in Mihama. The calligraphy on the cup lets people in other areas know about the *Kumano Kodo,* the ancient Pilgrimage Paths of Kumano. If you look even more deeply at the cup, you may comprehend more of its meaning. You may get a sense of the person who made it, and the person who gave it to you. He didn't give you just any gift. He gave you something that expressed his love for Kumano, and his desire that you keep a connection with Kumano, and learn about the history and culture of this area. That's all contained in this cup.

When you receive that tiny fraction of Aikido, study it from all angles. If you continue to look deeply at it, you will gradually become able to perceive O-Sensei's spirit and be fully connected to O-Sensei's Aikido.

Take Musu Aikido (a phrase referring to Aikido at the highest level of consciousness and creativity); calligraphy brushed by Motomichi Anno Sensei.

~5~

AIKIDO TRAINING: POLISHING the SPIRIT

Anno Sensei always affirms the importance of physical training in Aikido. Now in his eighties, he still gets on the mat nearly every day. He exhorts us, "Train, train, train . . . until you have a natural stance, natural form, and natural joy."

In this chapter, Anno Sensei articulates a multitude of ways in which the spiritual principles of Aikido are cultivated in the process of Aikido training. He shares his personal methods of practice as he discusses on-the-mat dynamics, the meaning of *ukemi,* the importance of a noncompetitive mind, and learning from nature.

One of the remarkable aspects of Anno Sensei's teaching is his willingness to engage in candid conversations with Western students and teachers. It is a startling, disarming experience to hear such a high-level Aikido instructor respond to a student's question with "I don't know," and then follow it up with an insightful discussion of the issues involved. He affirms our common humanity and encourages us to deepen our practice.

—Linda Holiday

"Take-musu ai-ki, the martial art that is love and love that is none other than martial art."[36]

～ Morihei Ueshiba O-Sensei, founder of Aikido

A Paradox

Martial arts have long been employed to achieve victory over an opponent. One could say that the original purpose of *budo* [martial arts] was to protect what is true and right, so that we could live in peace. I believe that people are meant to live together in harmony. However, we still mistakenly fight with one another. *Budo* has come to be used for personal gain, to protect our own sense of being "right."

It's like the United Nations. The United Nations was created to foster harmony between nations. But the self-interest of each country turns it into a competitive arena and makes it difficult for the United Nations to fulfill its original mission.

O-Sensei established Aikido for the purpose of bringing harmony out of conflict. But if there are feelings of territoriality and competition between leaders, it is easy for things to deteriorate. It is important that each of us train in such a way as to resolve this paradox. That is our practice of Aikido.

Aikido is often said to be a martial art *[budo]*. As a martial art, it is not a sport, and there is no competition in it. But I think Aikido is simply Aikido. I believe that Aikido is something that was born from *budo* and transcends it.

O-Sensei explained to us that the heart of *kami* [spirit, nature] is *shin zen bi:* "Truth, Goodness, and Beauty." Aikido is the method of training we undertake in order to express the heart of *shin zen bi* through our own bodies. The way I see it, we do the martial art training in order to realize the spirit of Aikido—the spirit of truth, goodness, and beauty. Through *budo* training, we come to understand what Aikido is.[37]

Spirit in Form

Aikido technique is the expression of spirit in form. Study the spirit, and manifest it in technique. If you don't actually train, if all you think about is spiritual matters, you need technique. If all you do is technique, you need spirit.

Remember that spirit is our source. We are born of *kami* [spirit; nature] and our lives are sustained by *kami*. At the end of our lives, we return to nature. Back to the source.

Spirit comes first. I believe that if you make the spirit primary, if you give it the central place in your mind as you practice technique, then what you are doing will become Aikido.

Yatagarasu, the three-legged crow, is the ancient symbol of the *kami* in Kumano. The three legs of *Yatagarasu*

Yatagarasu, the three-legged crow; ancient symbol of the *kami* (divine spirit, sacred nature) in the Kumano region of Japan.

represent courage, wisdom, and compassionate love. It is essential that we bring all aspects of the spirit together in Aikido. Love alone is not enough. You need strength. You need courage. You also must have effective technique. And you need to have a heart that brings people together in harmony and gives joy to others.

Unity with Nature

When I practice Aikido, new ideas float up in my consciousness. New ways of thinking and behaving are born. My whole self is renewed. Through training, I am polished and purified. Little by little, I become closer to nature.

The word *shizen* [nature] has many different meanings. What I'm thinking about now is naturalness: doing things naturally, without strain. Learning technique without rigid calculation. That's what I mean when I say, "Become more natural."

Shizen also refers to the natural environment. When my own natural feeling is the same as the flow of nature, then you could say that I have become "one with nature." It's hard to describe this in words. I express the feeling of my practice using nature as an example. I say "like the wind" or "like a wave." I know things are going well when I feel that kind of unity with nature.

If you practice Aikido, I believe you will develop that way naturally. But the way you think has an effect.

"Is it natural movement?" I ask myself. Not fighting with an opponent, but becoming one with nature . . . not struggling with my partner, but moving myself. Even with this intention, I still tense up at times. When I do, I tell myself, "That's no good; I must drop that tension and move naturally." This feeling is central to my practice, and I keep it in my heart, so it tends to manifest. Likewise, if a person has the intention to defeat an opponent, that form will naturally manifest in technique.

I feel it is good to be fluid and flexible in training. First, relax and let go of the tension in your body. It is natural to experience tension at the beginning of your practice. Even when you are told to relax, you may naturally tense up. Sometimes the more you think about letting go of your tension, the more it increases. But it is best to let it go. Later, gradually, you can add increasing amounts of power. The process in training is to transform your physical power into the power of ki.

Muri, Muda, Mura

When I was young, I loved to train fast. But O-Sensei told us, *"Tsu-yoku naru na!*—Don't become strong!"* I had no idea what he meant by that, and I'm still pondering his words. Generally speaking, people train because they want to become strong in some way. Why would O-Sensei tell us "Don't become strong"?

Perhaps he wanted us to relax, and to become one with our partners. It is common to try to do things quickly, and to attempt to force your partner to do something. We all wanted to be strong, but O-Sensei told us the complete opposite! And we didn't understand what he meant when he said, *"Bu* [the martial essence] is love." We thought *budo* was for winning over others, and O-Sensei said it was love.

Training slowly is actually more difficult than training quickly. Anyone can go fast, but it takes skill to be able to go slowly. When you practice the basic techniques slowly, you get rid of errors and let

Anno Sensei teaches a seminar in San Francisco, 2004.

go of things that are nonessential. You start to develop a more ideal, perfect form. That's the principle of becoming one with nature.

As an ideal in any technique, I focus on eliminating three things: *muri, muda,* and *mura*—strain, waste, and inconsistency. To eliminate *muri* is to let go of any strain or force. To eliminate *muda* is to get rid of extraneous things or useless movement. To eliminate *mura* is to develop a steady rhythm and to get rid of inconsistencies—for instance, the inconsistency of doing really well one instant and really poorly the next.

For many years I have concentrated on these three practices, as well as developing center and balance. For the purpose of this practice, I want to move in an expansive way. Slowly and expansively, while maintaining my posture and balance.

Everyone likes to go fast. Speed is necessary, but rushing is bad. It is best when speed emerges naturally.

Goals

When new students join my dojo, I ask them why they have chosen Aikido. I give them a new student application form and ask them to write about their goals in training. It seems to me that people who clearly articulate their goals tend to continue their practice. They have their own ideas, and they want to undertake some sort of spiritual study. The people who don't write anything down tend to stop training after a short time.

The practice of Aikido technique is good physical exercise. It develops communication skills, and it is enjoyable to train with other people. But if that is all, you may not continue your practice.

I want to emphasize how important it is to keep your personal goals, and the goals of Aikido, in mind. If you have a clear sense of where you are headed, you are more likely to keep going. The goal of Aikido is to cultivate a heart of love and a spirit of sincerity. If you embrace this goal as your personal objective, then I believe you will be able to sustain your practice. And what you are practicing will become Aikido.

Let's say your goal is to get a gold medal in the Olympics. You get really good at what you practice, and you receive the gold medal. If that were all you wanted, you would stop at that point. People who have trained hard enough to become Olympic gold medal champions inspire others with their achievements. However, stopping at that point can be seen as a kind of failure. In Aikido, it is important to continue past that point. Of course, I have great respect for those who train themselves with tremendous effort and reach such a goal. But I feel it is important to keep going.

Quite a few people in Aikido stop training after receiving their black belts. I wonder if they stop training because they lack the desire to be of service to others. It is so important to want to share your joy with other people.

Don't Wait for an Attack

In the present age, O-Sensei said, we cannot achieve victory simply through the use of force against an attack. This is no longer a world in which we can think in terms of fighting against each other. It is a time and a world in which we must cooperate with others. O-Sensei often told us that Aikido was born in order to serve humanity as we move into the future. And now we find ourselves in the twenty-first century.

In Aikido, we practice a technique called *shomen uchi ikkyo*. There are many different ways to practice this common Aikido technique. Sometimes people receive the *shomen uchi* strike and then deliver the *ikkyo* technique in return. You can also interpret this technique as an exercise in which you take the initiative to move first, in order to draw out the *uke* [attacker]. When I first learned *shomen uchi ikkyo*, we practiced it by intercepting the attack as the *uke* raised his or her arm

169

to strike. But toward the end of O-Sensei's life, he told us that it was too late to wait for the attacker to begin to strike.

O-Sensei frequently taught that we must not wait for an attack and then react to it. One way to practice this principle of not-waiting is to extend your arm quickly and directly towards the *uke,* taking the shortest possible line. Since you travel a shorter distance than the *uke,* who is raising a hand to strike, you may be faster. The important question, though, is not how you can move faster than the attacker, but how can both people progress together? How can we become one?

Bu wa ai nari: "The martial essence is love," said O-Sensei. He told us, "If you want to learn technique, study the heart." How can we stop thinking only of winning over an opponent, and instead unify our hearts with others? We take up this challenge with our practice of the technique of *shomen uchi ikkyo.*

Linda Holiday Sensei demonstrates *shomen uchi ikkyo* with her son at Aikido of Santa Cruz, 2012.

At the beginning of class, we practice *torifune* [the "rowing exercise"] in unison. In *shomen uchi ikkyo,* we are doing a similar practice of moving everything together. Not just one hand and then the other. Sometimes we make the mistake of trying to press forward on one side only. But we need both sides. We need to go forward with everything together, in a natural way.

Right from the beginning, without waiting for the other person to strike at you, take the initiative to go forward, with the feeling of giving a gift to your partner. Take the shortest path. Don't raise your hand above your head to strike at them; don't come around from the left or the right. Go right in on the shortest path to the other person's heart.

In earlier years, O-Sensei may have trained in a different way, with one person striking and the other person quickly blocking and parrying the blow. But O-Sensei's practice changed and evolved. He taught us to change our approach to technique. For some people, striking and blocking may hold more interest, or they enjoy it more because it is what they think of as *budo.* Others have taken a new approach based on O-Sensei's later teachings. O-Sensei told us that technique is born anew each and every day. He said we must not stay in the same place and do the same thing over and over. I believe that O-Sensei came to feel we must take the initiative, and take the shortest route to building a world in which we move in unity with others.

Please hold these thoughts in your mind as you practice the techniques of Aikido.

IN DIALOGUE WITH ANNO SENSEI:
AIKIDO TRAINING

In the following section, Anno Sensei responds to questions about Aikido training, from Western students and teachers.

Anno Sensei speaks and Linda Holiday translates, at an Aikido seminar in California, 2010.

Simple Things

Aikido is called natural movement, but we find it a challenge to do seemingly simple things, for instance to keep our hands in front of our center, take natural steps, or turn our hips. I've heard you quote O-Sensei as saying, "It is difficult even to take a single step." Why is it difficult to do simple things?

I don't know! Simple things are hard for me, too.

We all eat. Eating is an ordinary, common experience. But there is a difference between eating when you really want to, and being made to eat. When you are a child, you may be told, "Eat this, it's good for you." But eating something because you really enjoy it is a different experience. It's natural.

In Aikido training, at first, you are taught how to do the techniques. You are told, "Do it this way." Trying to do what someone has told you to do tends to be less natural. If you decide to do something yourself, you will tend to do it most efficiently, without extraneous things getting in the way. That's a more natural way of doing things.

O-Sensei used to say, "Study the workings of nature, come to understand them, then put them in your center [hara]. Incorporate the workings of nature into your own body—make them your own flesh and blood. Then manifest them." That's the way O-Sensei expressed himself.

In Aikido training, you receive instruction. It's important to absorb that, and to practice until you understand it with your own body. Then it will come out of you naturally. But it is essential to develop a *true* understanding of nature. Correctly perceive the truth of nature, and make that understanding a part of yourself.

In a sense, it becomes more challenging the longer you practice, as you continue to make progress and to grow. When I look back on my previous training, it seems that I was focused entirely on throwing. I felt I was doing my best, but my perspective has shifted. Now I feel I must do everything with my spirit. I need to integrate the practice so thoroughly into my body that it reaches my spirit. For that to happen, I feel it is essential that I concentrate on moving my center firmly and energetically. That will transform my practice of Aikido technique.

If you look at O-Sensei's techniques in the final years of his life, he appears to be doing nothing. It was as if he were simply walking, uttering sounds like "Ahh..." and making simple, natural movements, which threw people. His movements were much simpler and more refined than my practice is now. I aim to go in O-Sensei's direction. But in order to reach that state of simplicity, it is necessary to do many kinds of training.

O-Sensei grew old, yet a young, vigorous Sumo wrestler in great shape was powerless against this elderly man. Why? Sumo wrestlers train very hard to use their hips and attack quickly. O-Sensei understood that, so he was able to throw him freely. He could handle his opponent with ease, because he understood what the Sumo wrestler was doing. O-Sensei had personally experienced that sort of training and more.

When I was young, I lowered my center using physical strength. But as I have grown older, my physical strength has gradually diminished. Now I must use my ki and focus on my center. I have habits of physical movement that I have done for a long time. Even when I intend to lower my hips and turn, I notice that my hips have become high and have stopped turning again. It is difficult to change one's habits and do something new, isn't it? So we need to have a sincere and open attitude toward learning new things.

O-Sensei often spoke of the importance of having a heart that is *sunao:* simple, receptive, and open to learning. For instance, you need to be able to change what you are doing, immediately, in order to follow the instruction of a person who is teaching class. If one teacher says to stand tall, you stand tall. If another teacher tells you to get low, you get low. But it's not so easy, is it? If you normally look in a certain direction during a technique, and then a teacher tells you to turn your head to a different direction, it's hard to change that in the moment. But it is very important to develop this ability. This is the way you develop the ability to change your patterns and use your own body freely.

"Those who train in Aikido must never forget that the teaching has to be forged in one's very body."[38]

~ Morihei Ueshiba O-Sensei

Turning the Body, Turning the Mind

When you teach class, you remind us not to focus on throwing people, but rather to concentrate on correcting ourselves and polishing the spirit. You tell us to focus on elements of practice such as turning the hips, maintaining straight posture, and looking beyond our partners. Is that the way we polish our spirit?

How wonderful it would be to have full mental and physical flexibility! To be able to turn freely, all the way in one direction . . . or the other direction . . . or halfway. . . or not at all. I would like to develop complete freedom of body and mind.

I want to be able to make use of all parts of myself freely. Hips, feet, hands, eyes . . . Through practicing that, I feel I am polished and purified. I'd like to be able to move at will, to have complete freedom. But I am not free. I lose my balance. It's not only the balance of the body that is so difficult, but the balance of the mind as well.

Carefully consider how you can become one with your partner, both physically and mentally. When you collide with someone, think about why that happened. You may realize it was because you did not change your position.

When you pick up a ceramic cup and look at it, at first it seems to be completely flawless. But when you turn the cup around to look at the back, you may see there is a crack. When you are turning and harmonizing with your partner, there are many aspects to focus on. You may start to turn part of your body, and then realize that you haven't turned your gaze—your attention is still fixed on your partner. And after you move your gaze, you realize that your foot hasn't moved at all!

Developing a real integrity of the body is a challenge. You can turn your hips, yet be unable to move the rest of your body. The hips turn, but the hands don't move, or the feet are at a bad angle.

It is good to focus on turning the hips. After developing the ability to turn the hips freely, focus on "turning" the mind. We experience many different emotions in the course of Aikido training. Sometimes we feel, "I did it! I did the technique!" Sometimes we experience a satisfied feeling that isn't about throwing at all. Yet other times we clash with our training partners, and sparks fly. What I really want is to become one with the other person, with a powerful feeling of gladness.

It is most enjoyable when you and your partner are both going in the same direction. When you are sitting in your garden in the evening with a group of friends, and you look at the moon and remark, "Isn't the moon beautiful tonight?" and everyone looks in the direction of the moon, there is a feeling of unity. When you are looking all by yourself in one direction and your partner is looking in another, there is a certain balance that is missing. When an Aikido technique

Anno Sensei demonstrates an Aikido technique at a seminar in California, 2012.

is clean and beautiful, both people—the person who throws and the person who receives the throw—are carried along in a current going the same direction.

Like a Mountain

When I try to move forward to do a technique such as *ikkyo*, I feel like I'm just pushing on the other person's arm. I can't figure out how to join with my partner. How can we become one?

Try to find the most natural, relaxed posture. If you bend over at the waist and thrust your arm at your partner, you won't be able to make the technique work if you encounter any resistance. The technique will be ineffective no matter which direction you try to move. It is important to improve your own posture, and to find a posture without any strain. Then you can become one with your partner.

A natural, efficient posture is like a mountain. A mountain does not lean over or lose its shape. First, you need to develop this kind of posture in yourself so that you will be firmly centered. Your partner may also have that mountain-like steadiness. Then you need to go even further in order to develop your own good posture and to become one with your partner.

If you are grabbed by a person who is like a large mountain, you may feel that you can't move. But somewhere there is a path by which you can climb that mountain. When you look at a huge, magnificent mountain and you want to climb it, you have to reflect, how can I get up there? Where does the path begin that will take me there? How can we reach our goal safely and naturally, without strain? That's what the practice of Aikido technique is: the search for that path.

"This is not mere theory. You practice it. Then you will accept the great power of oneness with Nature."[39]

~ MORIHEI UESHIBA O-SENSEI

Look Up

In practice, you emphasize the importance of looking up. You ask us to free our gaze . . . to be able to freely change the direction we are looking. Why is that?

My intention is to move naturally, to express natural form without any strain or force. In order to develop that ability, I cultivate the feeling of uplifting the spirit. There is a natural tendency for the gaze, and the spirit, to drift downward. To counter that tendency, I encourage movement in the opposite direction. I want the spirit to expand upward, so I say, "Look up, toward heaven!" I want to look beyond myself, to expand my view, to see the whole universe. I feel that is a purifying process for my spirit.

Sometimes we end up looking at other people—our partners and "opponents"—instead of viewing heaven and earth. In order to look up to heaven, I have to set aside the desire to throw my partner. Instead of the feeling of throwing your partner, you can cultivate the feeling that you are uplifting your partner's spirit.

Anno Sensei demonstrates
Aikido at a seminar in
California, 2012.

Everything Teaches Me

You speak of cultivating a sense of connection with heaven and earth, with everything around us. Do you engage in any practices outside the dojo that foster that connection?

Actually, it's the opposite. It is because I practice Aikido that no matter where I go in my daily life, everything teaches me about that connection.

For example, when I look at a flower, I think, "How beautiful!" Flowers face upward in the most beautiful way. I reflect that I could develop a form like that—not drooping, but rising upward, naturally. I wonder what it would be like to *be* that flower. Then I carry this feeling into my practice of technique. I learn from the flowers. I think of Aikido and nature as one.

Young flowers bloom energetically, but as they age, they wilt and weaken. So I feel it is best to face upward like a flower toward the sun, bloom beautifully, and be full of life. I always encourage people to look upward, toward the sun and the heavens, when they are practicing Aikido technique. Doesn't it make everyone happy to see that? They think, "How beautiful!"

This doesn't mean you simply look up all the time. It is natural to bloom, bear fruit, and then go in a downward direction again. We have a saying in Japan, "The more the fruit ripens, the more the plant bows its head."

179

A Beginning Student's Practice

In Aikido, our practice is to become one with our partners, but I find this a challenge, especially with newer students. How can I establish a connection with an *uke* [training partner] who seems to be tense and afraid, and does not come toward me?

When I am practicing Aikido, I have the intention right from the beginning to move toward my *uke*. Try to take the attitude of approaching your partner on your own. Take the initiative to go toward them and greet them. If you have the attitude of going to greet the other person, then he or she will tend to develop that same feeling.

If you find it a particular challenge to connect with newer students, then I suggest that you become a newer student, too. Join them in their newness. Go slowly, step by step, and concentrate on precision.

If you practice with a beginning student in the same way you would practice with someone who has a black belt, they will naturally become afraid. But if you adopt the feeling of someone who doesn't know anything, the beginning student will feel safe. It is good to undertake a beginning student's practice.

With a student who knows nothing—hold the feeling that you don't know anything either! Then focus on feet, and hands, and go step by step. Build up your knowledge together.

Self-Correction

In Aikido training, when I try to concentrate on my center, I become aware of tension in my lower back. I also notice that my feet are tense. Even when a technique is going well, I often find that my feet are in an odd position or my toes are curled. What should I do to dissolve the tension in my body?

Cultivate the feeling of breathing up from your feet and toes, into your back. Try holding that image as you breathe. Think of the roots of trees. Trees absorb nutrients from the earth through their roots. Breathe deeply while drawing the breath up from your "roots." Absorb the breath of earth. Breathe with your whole body, not just the upper half. That would be a good feeling with which to practice.

It's common to believe you have to do things quickly. But when your practice has deteriorated, it is important to take the time to correct yourself. You can adjust your posture, change your position, and relax your toes. Don't rush yourself. If you don't engage in this process of self-correction, your mind will be distracted by your partner and your desire to throw them. It is more important to think about how to straighten up and correct yourself. Your feet, your hands, your face . . . and your heart.

Developing stability in the midst of movement is a challenge. I suggest you practice big movements, and practice them slowly. If you repeat them many times, you will over time become able to do them quickly and easily. But if you always try to do techniques quickly, you end up losing your balance. It's best not to rush. Ask your partner to wait for a moment. You can realign yourself and then begin your movement again.

The same principle holds true in the practice of calligraphy. No matter how many *kanji* characters I write, if they are written hastily, I will not improve. I have to reflect on my practice. Adjust the angle of my brush. Evaluate my posture. Straightening my posture takes effort, but if I want to write something beautiful, it is essential that I correct myself. Later on, after I have developed myself further, I may be able to write a beautiful character even if I'm leaning a little to one side.

True Emptiness

Sensei, how can I develop more stability? When I am your *uke* [training partner], you invite me in and then move in an expansive circle. Even when the circles of movement are huge, you seem stable and balanced. When I try the same movement, by the time I get to the end, I've lost my balance and I start to fall toward my *uke*.

I believe it is a matter of movement and flow. Move expansively to take your partner's balance, and place yourself in the center. If you want to move big, you need strong roots. Your hips have to be stable.

Imagine that you are stirring a glass of water. When you stir the water quickly, the center deepens, and what is around it expands. In Aikido training, when you descend in a spiral, your partner is spun out in a large circle. You could say that you become the empty space in the center [*Mu:* emptiness, void]. That would be the ultimate, to become *Mu*.

O-Sensei frequently spoke of "the ki of emptiness" [*ku no ki*] and "the ki of true emptiness" [*shin ku no ki*]. Perhaps the empty space at

Anno Sensei teaches a class
at Aikido of Santa Cruz, 2012.

182

the center is related to the emptiness to which O-Sensei often referred. He would say, "Connect yourself and your technique to the ki of emptiness and the ki of true emptiness." Maybe he meant that you become this emptiness. You make yourself empty, and draw the other person to you as you turn.

The Spinning Circle

As I went in to receive a technique from you, I was trying to grab onto something solid. But I felt as if I were caught by a rotating energy. Every time I fell in, I would start flying back out again. I'd be reaching in while my feet were going out.

That is the kind of feeling I hope to generate in my practice. If you feel it when you are receiving a throw, that may mean that you are starting to perceive the ki of "emptiness" and "true emptiness." I aspire to that feeling in practice, but it is hard to get my body to move like that, to turn the whole body at once. You can't make this kind of phenomenon happen by just moving fast. First you have to establish a connection and unify yourself with your *uke* [training partner]. Then you can accelerate. It's not a matter of turning endlessly at the same speed. You make a connection and then accelerate . . . spiraling down in the center and then coming up suddenly, making changes like that. When water goes around in a circle, accelerates, and then stops suddenly, it may become mist, rising upward—like a cyclone, as it flies around and up. On a larger scale, O-Sensei frequently referred to the flowing interplay of fire and water. The phenomena of nature are inside us and can manifest in technique.

I often train with an image in my mind of the big spinning circle with the middle becoming empty. When it's happening, I'm not thinking of anything at all. And at the end, when there is a sudden change . . . how wonderful it would be to be transformed into the spirit of love at that moment.

Expand Your Spirit

Sensei, you emphasize the importance of moving expansively while training. When we are in a small space, how is it possible for us to practice moving in a big way?

It depends on how well you make use of the limited space you have. For instance, if you are in a small square, wouldn't it be good to extend your energy out to fill every corner of the square?

When you look at the technique I am doing, it may seem that the reach of my arm extends only to the tips of my fingers. You may think the pivoting turn of *tai no henko* [a blending movement] goes only so far. But what I feel is that I am sending out my ki, my breath, all the way to the opposite wall of the dojo. My body has turned only to a certain degree, but my energy is rotating expansively. As my hand moves upward, my spirit rises toward heaven.

If you look only with your eyes, you will not perceive everything. Human eyes are limited. A camera may actually see more. When I

Students of all levels practice *tai no henko* together at the Aikido Winter Intensive in Santa Cruz, 2008.

first saw the entrance to the house where I stayed in Seattle, I simply thought, "What a nice house!" The next day, I was amazed to see a beautiful, blooming hydrangea bush next to the front door. It had completely escaped my notice the day before.

Call out to your training partner, and send out your spirit . . . farther than you can see. Being in a small place does not limit the size of your spirit. No matter how small your physical movement is, you can put your heart into it.

Offer the Spirit of Love

What is the best position of the hands when I'm practicing an Aikido technique such as *tai no henko* [a basic pivoting blend]? Some teachers have instructed me to keep my fingers close together. Others have told me to open and relax the fingers. Which is the best method of practice?

Like you, I have often been taught to keep the fingers and thumb together. But it seems natural that they would open and separate. I don't think much about the question of whether the fingers should be open or closed. I don't want that to be my focus in training. What I focus on is the feeling of carrying what I treasure most in the palms of my hands. My intention is to carry what is most dear to me in the palms of my hands and offer it to my partner in the course of training.

About three years ago, I began a new phase in my training. Until that point I would end a throw like *irimi nage* with my hands turned down. This is a common hand position in Aikido. But I came to dislike the feeling of throwing "down." I decided to change my form at the end of the throw into a palms-up position, expressing an uplifting feeling. These days I try to express that feeling in every technique. I would like to envelop everything with the spirit of love, then reach out and offer it to my partner.

When O-Sensei stood holding a sword in his hands, the feeling of his stance was awe-inspiring. You could say it was frighteningly intense. But within that intensity there was a clear feeling of love. When I was on the receiving end of O-Sensei's techniques, they were amazingly powerful. He could have destroyed me easily, yet I never experienced the slightest injury. Inside the power of O-Sensei's technique was love. I want to realize the heart of love that O-Sensei demonstrated. That is why I continue my practice.

It is important that we develop strong technique. But it is essential that we develop the heart of love as well. We started out talking about hand positions, and look where we ended up—with everyone wrapped up in the spirit of love.

More Heart

Our world is changing more and more rapidly, and our lives are changing rapidly as we rush toward the future. I have the feeling that as we are hurrying forward, we've lost track of where we are going. How do you see Aikido as fitting into that future world and making a contribution?

When you lose track of where you are and where you are going, it's natural to feel as if things around you are going too fast. Anyone would feel that way.

I love Aikido training. If you have something you love in your life, if you have health, friendship, and heart, there's no reason to be in such a rush. Through Aikido, we experience being together in harmony, in connection with others. Developing more of the feeling of "being together" can eliminate some of the feeling of rush—or of competition with others, which may be causing the feeling of being in a hurry.

O-Sensei told us over and over that the essence of Aikido is not winning over an opponent, but realizing truth and accomplishing

186

one's own mission in life. In this, there is no strong or weak, no fast or slow. If you rush through the technique to get to the throw, Aikido practice loses its delicious flavor. If you just come to class, practice technique, and leave right away without taking the time to communicate with others, something is missing. The heart is missing. I feel that human society is suffering from a lack of heart. Through our Aikido practice we need to develop more heart, both on and off the mat.

A young Aikido student enjoys training with her instructor in Santa Cruz, 2012.

A Sign of Progress

I know Aikido is a path of harmony, but sometimes I become discouraged with my practice on the mat. Perhaps I am tired, or I feel that my body just can't do it. Things don't go smoothly, and I find it difficult to relax. I get so frustrated that I decide to take some time off, and then I stop coming to class. How do you deal with frustration and discouragement?

When things don't go smoothly, when training is not enjoyable, it is understandable that you want to stop. I've experienced frustration countless times. I imagine I always will. But in my mind, it's the opposite. When things are not going well, I feel I need to train more.

Recognizing that things are not going well is a sign of progress.

At first, you don't understand Aikido at all. Then, you feel you've got it. Then you feel you don't understand it anymore. When you become aware that your practice is not going well, that's when you are attempting to take the next step. Let's say that there are ten things you are studying, and you've already learned the first one. Usually what you are frustrated about is the next one. So that implies progress. You are reaching beyond what you can do right now.

Sometimes I have the feeling that I don't understand *anything*. It seems to me that when I truly feel I know nothing, even though I have learned many things to get to that point, I don't understand what the next step is. The next level in my training.

When you encounter something difficult, it takes time to resolve it. Things don't just go smoothly. In Japan we have an expression, *Kabe ni ataru:* "Hit the wall." What should you do when you hit the wall? Train!

Perhaps if you practice more slowly, you will become aware of what the problems are. You'll see your own shortcomings. You will understand what is causing the problems that are decreasing your joy in training.

On the other hand, taking time off from training can be important, too. Pause and reflect on your own practice. Take some time to think about it. How about watching classes? If you watch other people training, you may feel motivated to get on the mat again.

If you take time off from training, you may come to understand how precious it is to be able to practice. At this point in my life, I feel a sharp regret for the times I stayed off the mat. I wish I had that time available to me now, the time that I chose not to train. Give me that precious time back! This time, I would train.

"The source of *bu* is the love of *kami*. It is the spirit of love and protection for all. The training of *budo* forges in our minds and bodies the power of divine love, which produces, protects, and nurtures all things in the universe. The techniques of *budo* are signposts, pointing the way which leads to this."[40]

～ MORIHEI UESHIBA O-SENSEI

Receiving Instruction

I've noticed that each Aikido technique can be done in a variety of ways. And each teacher has a different "flavor." How can I receive instruction from multiple teachers?

Every single person is unique. We all have different faces. In the same way, each person has his or her own way of thinking and approaching Aikido. When you look at different teachers, the most important thing to ask yourself is this: What are they aiming at? Then learn and absorb the good points of each teacher. If you observe bad points, reflect on yourself. Try to see if you have any of those bad points. If you do, focus on eliminating them in yourself.

Robert Frager Sensei teaches a special class as part of a celebration of forty years of Aikido in Santa Cruz, 2010. Frager Sensei brought Aikido to Santa Cruz in 1969.

Commitment

You had the experience of being O-Sensei's *uke*. You attacked him and received his techniques many times. What state of mind did you have when you went in to strike O-Sensei?

In the early years with O-Sensei, around the time I received my black belt, I was often asked by O-Sensei to attack him, or to push or pull him. But I was often criticized by O-Sensei for my poor *ukemi* [skills of attacking and receiving]. O-Sensei would sometimes get so frustrated with all of us students for our lack of good *ukemi* that he would exclaim, *"Keiko ga dekin!"* ["I can't train with you!"]. Then he would walk off the mat and disappear into his room for a while.

O-Sensei clearly wanted us to strike fast. I would think I had done my strike with everything I had ... but it wasn't the complete commitment O-Sensei wanted. When I was told to strike with a *bokken* [wooden practice sword] for real, as if holding a live blade, I found it difficult to do. Maybe if I had believed that I had the ability to handle such an intense attack myself, I would have been able to provide that kind of attack for others. But I didn't have that level of self-confidence, so I worried that others might have trouble as well, and that feeling inhibited my ability to strike in a fully committed way. Even when I would try to strike as fast as possible, O-Sensei would tell me I was too slow.

When O-Sensei expressed his exasperation with us, I believe that he was telling us to train harder and with more focus. To practice swinging the sword, and to improve our *ukemi* so that we could strike cleanly and quickly.

It is essential to continue to make progress both as *uke* [the one who attacks and receives] and as *nage* [the one who throws].

Anno Sensei demonstrates Aikido with wooden swords in California, 2011.

The Intention of *Uke*

What should your intention be when you are *uke*, the person who attacks and then receives an Aikido technique? Is your intent to defeat your partner, or simply to strike?

The intention of *uke* is not a matter of competition; it is a matter of improving one's own practice. When you are the person who attacks, you can concentrate on increasing the speed and precision of your attack. But you need to take into consideration the level of the person you are training with. It wouldn't be appropriate to give a new student your fastest attack. That would not result in good training. You must ask yourself, "How can I do my very best training as *uke* in each different situation?"

Personally, I think the practice of *uke* [one who receives] is more difficult than that of *nage* [one who throws]. To be able to truly receive the technique means, in my opinion, you have accomplished something even greater than the ability to perform the technique as *nage*. I feel it is actually best to begin your practice in the role of *uke*, by receiving the techniques. In the old days there was a saying: "*Ukemi* [receiving] for three years," but these days, people want to start out by learning to throw.

It is the same in any traditional study. You start at the beginning, and learn the basics first. People who have really mastered a craft have immersed themselves in the basics and laid a good foundation. They haven't rushed to get to the end. In my view, the level of *uke* and *nage* increase together. When you learn a throw, you learn how to receive it. If you can receive a throw, then you understand its essence.

Non-Resistance

Aikido is said to be the principle of non-resistance, but how should I apply that to the practice of *ukemi* [the art of receiving]? When I am *uke*, I often find myself either resisting my partner, or giving the technique away and falling down on my own.

In my opinion, it is neither wrong to resist nor to fall down easily. I do both! There isn't just one single way to do the *ukemi* correctly. I think it is fine to practice in a variety of ways.

Sometimes it is good to resist each other. Then you can develop the ability to complete your technique even when you encounter resistance. There will be times when you work with hard grabs and fast strikes, and other times when you practice in a more relaxed manner. In my opinion, the most important thing is that you train in a mutually agreeable way. You can communicate with each other and work it out. You can suggest, "OK, now let's give each other a bit of resistance." It can be seen as a kind of cooperative resistance.

But on the beginning level of Aikido practice, I would encourage you not to focus on resisting your partner. That's an element you can explore later, after you have learned more. At first, it is better for you to take the fall voluntarily, even though it might feel like you're falling for no reason. That's the way you learn how to take the falls. I believe it is not good practice for new students to focus on resistance. After you have developed more skill and confidence in your *ukemi*, then you can explore the practice of constructive resistance. You can invite your partner to resist. You can have an agreement to resist. Then you train in order to become able to do the technique despite the resistance.

Anno Sensei teaches at the 2010 Santa Cruz Aikido Summer Retreat.

"The journey through life is beset by many hardships. Success comes to those who resolve their difficulties with the flexibility and open-mindedness of *ukemi*."[41]

~ MORIHEI UESHIBA O-SENSEI

On the Same Team

What is the relationship between *uke* [one who receives] and *nage* [one who throws]?

When I first began to practice Aikido, I heard O-Sensei say, *"Bu wa ai nari:* The martial essence *[bu]* is love." At that time, all I thought about was getting strong, so O-Sensei's words were inexplicable to me. I had no idea what he meant. I thought that *budo* was about being strong and defeating others. Gradually, as I experienced the connection between *uke* and *nage,* I began to understand that Aikido, born of *budo,* had evolved past its martial origins. As O-Sensei said, "Aikido is love."

The relationship of *uke* and *nage* is similar in feeling to the relationship of pitcher and catcher, in baseball. They must be completely attuned to each other and be able to communicate without words. I feel it is important for *uke* and *nage* to become unified in spirit.

In baseball, the pitcher and catcher are on the same team, but they feel the other team to be their enemy. Aikido training leads to a feeling of oneness with everyone, not just your own group. The warmth and brightness of day is wonderful, but nighttime is also essential. It would be strange to say that day and night oppose each other. We need to grasp the feeling of being unified with everyone. O-Sensei had reached a state of being that enabled him to do that. He was already unified with the other person. He had reached that level.

The Meaning of *Ukemi*

What is the importance of *ukemi* in Aikido?

When we practice *ukemi,* we are studying O-Sensei's teachings. Studying Aikido is taking *ukemi*—receiving—from O-Sensei. You are studying what O-Sensei taught, and you are seeking to receive it, aren't you? You are *uke:* the receiver. When you ask what attitude you should have as *uke,* that's it. To reach a level of true *ukemi,* we need to train until we completely perceive and understand what our partner is doing.

Ukemi—receiving—is of utmost importance. How wonderful it would be if I were able to receive, right now, the totality of the spirit O-Sensei left with us. But I have only begun to understand a small part of O-Sensei's teachings.

I say that *ukemi* is of utmost importance, because I believe *ukemi* means cultivating in ourselves the kind of heart that can receive the heart of nature, of the universe. It is the same as receiving your partner's technique on the mat, when you are *uke.* If you are able to receive your partner's throw freely and naturally, then you have nothing to fear.

Ukemi, to me, means *satori:* enlightenment.[42]

Jack Wada Sensei (kneeling) teaches at his dojo, Aikido of San Jose, in California, 2009.

Let Go of the Throw

Aikido students—especially beginning students—love to do the throws. Their goal is often to throw, and throw hard. When they see their partners take the fall—boom!—they feel they have accomplished something, so that becomes their aim in training. It seems to take a long time to shift to the next level of aspiration.

Yes. I find it quite a challenge, too.

What I want most at this point is to eliminate the concept of "throwing." Let go of the intention to throw someone down. When I absorb my *uke* [training partner] completely, then I have the feeling that my *uke* is simply moving of his or her own accord. I want the technique to occur without the feeling that I have thrown my *uke*. That's my aspiration, but it is not easily accomplished.

The timing is important. For instance, in *kokyu nage* [breath throw], my aim is to draw my partner in as my arm rises, so he or she falls naturally. If *uke* is already falling, there is no need to throw. This depends on the timing, or you could say the harmony, between *uke* and *nage*. But whether it is *shiho nage* [four directions throw] or *irimi nage* [entering throw], I'd like to get rid of the "throw"!

Anno Sensei teaches in California, 2012.

198

No Competition

I occasionally experience challenges from people who practice competitive martial arts. They want to compete with me and have me show them how Aikido works as a martial art. What do you recommend that I do in that situation?

To deal well with that kind of situation, you have to have polished yourself by training long and hard. If you speak of Great Love and Great Harmony but cannot show it, people may not listen to you. We need to retain our awareness of Aikido as *budo,* even as we are taught to let go of winning and losing. If we focus exclusively on the spiritual aspect of Aikido, then what we do becomes something more like a religion. It is essential to train hard, to thoroughly understand Aikido as *budo,* and then to transcend any sense of competition. O-Sensei definitely forbade competitions *[shiai]* in Aikido.

When I first started training, I simply wanted to be able to throw people hard—to be stronger than other people. Gradually, as I continued to practice, I came to feel it was impossible for me to be strong in the way I had imagined. No matter how strong you become, there will always be someone who is stronger. Even if you are incredibly strong as a young person, when you grow old, someone will definitely be stronger . . . like a new "champion" who defeats and replaces the previous one. No doubt it is a wonderful feeling to be the champion, but it's a temporary thing. Surely there is something much more valuable than that to pursue.

As we get older, we become unable do the kind of fast and strong training we did before. We experience aches and pains in the body, and diminishing physical strength. That awareness leads us to a new level of Aikido practice. O-Sensei originally trained in martial arts that focused on strength and speed, but at some point he shifted to an emphasis on cultivating love through training.

Back in the early days of our training, we students weren't thinking about Great Love or Great Harmony. We focused more on becoming strong and doing strong techniques. That was when people occasionally came to challenge us. I believe that if you train hard and you also focus strongly on spiritual development in Aikido, a natural resolution begins to occur. The challenges fade away.

Polishing the Spirit

You often speak of polishing and purifying the spirit. What is it that we are polishing away?

Selfish desire. The important thing is to let go of desire. Desires, such as the desire to amass increasing amounts of wealth or to defeat others, can be selfish and even harmful. One desire leads to another, on and on.

In Aikido, it is important to develop skill, but it is problematic if we harbor the desire to defeat an opponent. That is the desire we must eliminate. However, the desire to become one with another person and to do beautiful technique—that is a good desire! If you throw away all desires, you will stop training. Put forth your full effort, and over time, your desires will naturally dissipate. If you don't apply yourself fully, you won't be able to fully eliminate those desires.

It is important to reflect on the nature of the desire to become strong. Do you want to advance in the direction of Aikido, or is your desire to become strong ... stronger than others? Is your aim at *Aikido* ... or is it directed at other people? If you train with wholehearted commitment and aim at Aikido itself, then you will progress in that direction.

I find it helpful to try to improve myself one little step at a time. For instance, I polish myself by gradually increasing the size of my movement. If I am practicing a complete rotation, and I want to increase my capacity to turn, I increase the amount of rotation gradually. I'll start with one complete turn, then add a tiny fraction of a turn to my movement each time. This builds up my skills, step by step.

Then, if I have polished myself consistently and expansively, a decrease in size naturally occurs. Extraneous things are polished away until they may completely disappear. What remains after that is small, but radiant with light. How wonderful to practice expansively, and then to continue to polish and purify yourself until you become so small that you become light itself. At that point, the techniques of *budo* will spontaneously emerge.

Even a small light has power. No matter how big your technique may be, it still needs to catch fire, to shine. No matter how long you train, if you practice only to become skillful or to defeat another person, your technique may never actually become Aikido. Polish and purify yourself so that what comes out of you is not ego, but a good light that is in alignment with the principles of nature.

Connection

Sensei, in your initial interaction with the *uke*, when the other person is about to attack you, you have already connected with them. It's noticeable. It seems to happen as they are approaching you, before they have a chance to touch you. How are you able to make that connection?

O-Sensei said that Aikido is *inryoku no tanren* [a process of forging the "power of attraction"]. You draw the other person to you. It is a connection of harmony and love.

It is more difficult to connect with someone who is very different from yourself. Don't you find that to be true with beginning students? You may feel you have a tremendous "power of attraction" in Aikido, but just try to draw in a beginning student . . . they stand there unmoved! When you ask them to come and grab you, they may not respond. Even when you know someone well, it can be difficult to establish a real connection. It may look as if you are connected, but if there is still a gap between you, that is not a true connection.

People in Shingu were drawn to O-Sensei's practice from the moment they would hear the news that he was coming down from Tokyo to teach. They felt powerfully pulled in to train at the dojo, to get ready, and to practice their *ukemi*. We were attracted by O-Sensei from the moment we heard he was coming. But for some reason, as soon as we saw O-Sensei's face, we became confused and wouldn't know what to do. Suddenly I'd be called upon as *uke*. When I was thrown by O-Sensei, I didn't understand what was happening. The feeling was, "Ahhhh!" and then it was over. I can't describe it in words. Was it fast? Strong? Painful? I couldn't tell. I would be thrown before I had any thoughts or impressions. That's about all I can say about *inryoku no tanren:* forging the power of attraction!

As you continue your training, follow your *senpai:* people who have more experience and have preceded you on the path. Your *senpai* need to be training as well as they can and trying to approach the mystery that O-Sensei expressed. I think about *inryoku:* the power of attraction. What is it? How can I cultivate it? That is what I'm exploring.

We can talk endlessly about levels of technical skill, but I feel the only real difference is "age." That's the only thing that can't be changed—how long and how well you have lived your life. Your understanding deepens as you experience life's ups and downs, and as you have many different experiences in training. You understand what you have experienced; but what you haven't experienced, you don't understand.

There's an old saying in Japan: "Seek out hardship, even if you have to buy it." Don't avoid things that are hard, or that you haven't experienced yet. Go out of your way to find things that are challenging, especially when you are young, so that you learn the most, and deepen your understanding.

What O-Sensei taught was not simply "love" [*Ai*] . . . he spoke of "Great Love" [*Dai Ai*]. There is a difference of level. Think about it.

202

What is the difference between love and Great Love? Between harmony and the Great Harmony that O-Sensei spoke of so often?

When I'm doing an Aikido technique, my partner's role is crucial. If I concentrate solely on expanding my own movement, my partner will not follow along. But if we join together, if our level of training mutually rises, we will produce a Great Harmony. And a sense of gratitude will naturally arise.

Black belt students training together at Aikido of Santa Cruz, California, 2011.

Embrace Your Partner

Once when I went in to take *ukemi* from you, it was as if I were just levitated. It was the lightest feeling, and I landed as if I were on a cloud. It was an extraordinary sensation, as if something had opened up. All I wanted was to do it again! Later that night, when I asked you about it, you told me you had been concentrating on what O-Sensei may have meant by "standing on the Floating Bridge of Heaven." What you were trying to do in your practice had mirrored my experience completely. How does that happen?

I believe that kind of phenomenon can happen when the ki of two people becomes unified, and they are no longer thinking. I'm not thinking about lifting my partner in a technical way. Instead, I have the feeling of embracing my entire partner and lifting them up from below, as if carrying a baby. I don't have the sense that I'm pressing them down during the fall. I feel as if I am holding them in my arms, and then setting them down. That's a feeling that is growing in my practice. I want to have the feeling that I am holding something precious in my hands all the way through the technique, from the beginning to the end.

When I am doing an Aikido technique, I sometimes imagine that I am moving a large container that is filled to the brim with water. Or that I am carrying a delicate paper globe in the upturned palm of my hand. I need to move smoothly in order to keep it from spilling or falling. I would like to be able to move naturally and discover what kind of speed is possible. I am impressed by the way food servers can walk while carrying trays of glasses filled with liquid. They move quickly and naturally, without spilling. In Aikido, we train with many different kinds of people, of different sizes and shapes. Transporting each vessel without spilling is a challenge.

The Summit of Aikido

If Aikido is a mountain, what is the summit?

Attaining the summit of the mountain is not my greatest desire. I'm happy to give my full effort to the climb, but my goal is not to arrive at the summit. My pleasure is in the process of the journey.

O-Sensei himself did not say he had reached the summit of Aikido. O-Sensei told us his journey was far from over. He said, *"Ima kara da*—It begins now."

Even though I am certain I cannot go as far as O-Sensei did, I will make a good effort in the climb. But what is most enjoyable to me is the pleasure of making the climb with others, establishing a mutual rapport, and conversing with each other about the beauty of the places we encounter along the journey.

There must be a beautiful view from the top of the mountain, but it's not the summit that I want. How wonderful it is when everyone makes the climb together! That is my goal.

A Constant Inquiry

What should we focus on as we continue to practice Aikido?

"Bu [the martial essence] is love," said O-Sensei. "Humanity is one family." I hold O-Sensei's words as a continuous refrain in my mind as I train. Constantly asking myself, How can we make O-Sensei's teachings live in the techniques of Aikido? O-Sensei taught, "Aikido is not a matter of winning and losing, of competing with one another." If this isn't clear to everyone, then it should be communicated more frequently. Aikido instructors need to make sure everyone knows.

In O-Sensei's Aikido, there is no opponent. You don't create an opponent. You become one with the other person right from the beginning, as soon as you face them. And beyond that, you become one with nature. I believe that was O-Sensei's way of thinking.

So, in my opinion, you should train hard and throw people a lot! It is an enjoyable practice, and it is good to become strong. But while you are practicing Aikido technique, reflect on O-Sensei's words. Throw each other vigorously and remember that O-Sensei said, "Aikido is not a matter of creating an opponent nor of contending with others." Keep that always in your mind.

O-Sensei told us, "Aikido is the form and the heart of *kami.*" Throw, throw, throw, *and* simultaneously think about O-Sensei's words. Then you will perceive if what you are doing is Aikido. Train with the constant refrain—a constant inquiry: "Aikido is love."

There are many kinds of love. O-Sensei spoke of *Dai Ai:* "Great Love." I don't fully understand what Great Love is. So I continue my practice of Aikido.

Go Deeper

I recently received a black belt in Aikido, and I hope to continue my training. You have practiced Aikido for over fifty years. What is your advice for keeping one's Aikido practice fresh after getting a black belt?

O-Sensei gave us *dan* [black belt] ranks quickly. He gave me *shodan* [first degree] after a year of training, *nidan* [second degree] after another year, and *sandan* [third degree] a year after that. About the time I received *sandan*, O-Sensei began to use me as *uke*. He would let me grab on to him and then send me flying.

When I met O-Sensei, I was so amazed by him, I felt as if I were seeing someone who lived on a cloud. His appearance was very kind and gentle. I was always surprised by the way he would initiate respectful greetings—even to his students. When I entered the dojo, O-Sensei would bow to me and say *"Gokurosama"* ["Thank you for your hard work"]. He would extend a greeting before his students did. That was startling. I felt a tremendous respect for him, which continues to this day. When O-Sensei was on the mat during classes in the dojo, his presence was truly awe-inspiring.

One time when I attended an Aikido demonstration in Tokyo, I heard O-Sensei say something that I will never forget. It was a big gathering, and many instructors gave demonstrations. At the end of all the demonstrations, O-Sensei spoke. He declared, "Even those of you who have high-level black belts don't yet understand Aikido. What you are doing has not yet reached the level of Aikido."

I have thought about his words ever since that time. I wasn't able to ask him what he meant that day, but now I have the feeling that I may understand. O-Sensei's way of thinking was expansive and centered on the universe. By contrast, we tend to focus on throwing people, taking pride and pleasure in doing technique. That's quite a difference. When O-Sensei watched his students demonstrating Aikido, I'm sure he saw into their hearts. Were they doing the techniques of Aikido with the hope that all people in the world would be in harmony? Or was it with a competitive feeling, with a sense of "look at me"? O-Sensei would have clearly understood the level of training that each person demonstrated that day. When O-Sensei said, "Even the high-level black belts don't understand Aikido yet," I believe he was trying to motivate all of us to go deeper into our practice of Aikido.

So we need to dedicate ourselves to our training. Practice Aikido techniques over and over until you reach a place of saturation, where

there is nothing left undone. Then I believe you will be able to express the spirit of Aikido freely. Practice with an expansive spirit at all times, regardless of whether you are making a big physical movement or you are sitting still. Train so completely that you integrate Aikido in yourself.

As you continue to practice, things evolve. It's a natural process, like the seasons changing in nature. The view of training I held last year will naturally shift to a

Anno Sensei teaches at the Summer Retreat in Santa Cruz, California, 2011.

new perspective this year. So I'll have to keep going! If you want to make your love bigger, train more. You won't develop further if you conclude, "This is all the love there is," and stop training.

I never heard O-Sensei say that he had finished his training. Towards the end of his life, he said, "*Now* I am starting to understand Aikido."

Motomichi Anno Sensei invites a Western student to train with a wooden sword on the high cliff of Onigura, in the Kumano mountains, 1979.

The Kumano River, part of the network of ancient pilgrimage routes that were designated a World Heritage Site by UNESCO in 2004.

The Kumano Hongu Shrine, one of the three Grand Shrines of Kumano. The large *shimenawa* rope indicates a gateway to a sacred area.

Top: Motomichi Anno Sensei offers a formal demonstration of Aikido at an international gathering at Oyunohara, former site of the Kumano Hongu Shrine, 2008.

Bottom: Anno Sensei in the Kumano mountains, overlooking the Nachi waterfall, 2005.

Top: Anno Sensei and Linda Holiday visiting the Kumano Hongu Shrine, 2006.

Bottom: Three generations of Aikido are represented at an international seminar in Japan, 2008. Anno Sensei (standing) directs two young Aikido students, one Japanese and one American. Linda Holiday translates; senior teachers from various countries observe.

Anno Sensei instructs a group of international students at the Kumano Juku Dojo, 2012. The calligraphy on the wall is by the founder of Aikido: *Hikari* ("Light"); signed (on right) "Morihei."

Anno Sensei and Linda Holiday after a morning class in the Kumano
Juku Dojo, 2012. The large wooden structure is the dojo shrine,
in which the spirit of Aikido's founder was ceremonially enshrined
after his passing in 1969.

Top: Motomichi Anno Sensei teaches a class at Aikido of Santa Cruz, 2012.
His *uke* is a senior black belt from Shingu, Japan.

Bottom: Anno Sensei sends a student flying at the Santa Cruz Aikido Summer
Retreat, as Linda Holiday translates, 2012.

Anno Sensei leads a vigorous Aikido class at the age of eighty-one, at the Santa Cruz Aikido Summer Retreat, 2012.

Linda Holiday leads a seminar at Vanadis Aikido Dojo in Stockholm, Sweden, 2012.

Anno Sensei instructs a class at the Santa Cruz Aikido Summer Retreat with Linda Holiday as his *uke*, 2011.

Linda Holiday demonstrates the beginning of a technique with one of her students, at the Santa Cruz Aikido Summer Retreat, 2012.

Motomichi Anno Sensei in California, 2012.

"Aikido is a way of taking off the layers that cover up what is inside.
If each of us could shed those layers, we would all shine with the same
light. If you keep training, you will shine."

—Anno Sensei

Did You Remember?

During the classes you teach, I hear you say many wonderful things that I want to keep in my heart. But one minute after starting to train with my partner, my mind has gone blank! After the training period ends, you ask us, "Did you remember?" And I think, "I forgot, again!" Do you have any suggestions for how not to forget what we've been taught?

I think you should forget! Forget it, and then train and train. Study O-Sensei's words, hold them as much as possible within yourself—and keep training. From time to time, spontaneously, you will actually realize something within yourself, with your own body.

Aikido is not something you are taught. It is something you realize.

Ki no miwaza / tama no shizumeya / misogi waza / michibiki tamae / ametsuchi no kami: "Sacred techniques of ki / Calm the spirit / Acts of purification / Please guide me / Spirits *[kami]* of heaven and earth!" (A poem by the founder of Aikido.) Calligraphy brushed by Motomichi Anno Sensei.

~6~

AIKIDO and the PRACTICE of PURIFICATION

"Aikido is *misogi* [purification],"[43] said O-Sensei. In Chapter Six, Anno Sensei reflects on the meaning of *misogi* and the role of purification in the philosophy and practice of Aikido. His definition of *misogi* is broad and accessible to all, transcending bounds of culture. He conveys his personal experience of the esoteric purification practice of *Chinkon Kishin,* which he learned from O-Sensei in Kumano and still practices every day. Anno Sensei offers a rare view inside the spiritual exercises of *shin kokyu, torifune,* and *furutama.* He invites you to include them in your own practice, while reflecting on the deepest purpose of *misogi.*

In 1973, Anno Sensei kindly guided me through my first experience of traditional, cold-water *misogi* purification in Japan (as described in Chapter One). After I returned to California, I began to lead groups of Western Aikido students into the cold waters of the Pacific Ocean, to do the *misogi* practice I had been taught in Kumano. I have found that the invigorating renewal of *misogi* has a universal appeal. On the first day of any year, you will find crowds of people gathered on the beach in Santa Cruz, rain or shine, to participate in a collective act of *misogi.* The water is fiercely cold, but the energy flowing through us is exhilarating, as we remember once again that we are an inseparable part of the "breath" of Great Nature.

—Linda Holiday

O-Sensei Said, "You Must Practice *Misogi!*"

When I first started Aikido training, I heard O-Sensei say, "Do *misogi!* You must practice *misogi!*" At that time, my concept of *misogi* [purification practice] was that you stood under waterfalls and tormented yourself with cold water. I didn't understand why someone would do that.

Ni-no-taki, a waterfall and natural pool used for purification practices, located upstream from sacred Nachi Falls in Kumano, Japan.

I questioned a friend of mine at the dojo, who was the head priest of a small Shinto shrine. He told me that all Shinto priests do the practice of purification under waterfalls. Young Shinto priests go together in small groups to do these ascetic spiritual practices in various places, and they receive professional recognition for doing so.

I wondered what it would be like to experience the waterfall *misogi* myself. I asked my friend the priest if he would take me along with him when he went out to do *misogi*. He took me with him five or six times, to local waterfalls such as Asari and Takimoto. My friend chanted the *Norito* [Shinto prayers]. Then we went in the river, where we did the practice of *torifune* ["the rowing exercise"] while chanting a rhythmic "Ei-ho! Ei-ho!" in unison.

The waterfall *misogi* was fascinating. What I remember most is that it was cold! It was tough. It was wonderful! I had a feeling of awe—the awesomeness of nature. I thought it would be an amazing thing to be able to sustain a practice of *misogi*.

Why Practice *Misogi*?

Misogi—the practice of purification—is necessary, because we naturally accumulate impurities from the world around us. Think about your house. Even if you do nothing to it, dust accumulates in your house and it gradually becomes dirty. Doing the practice of *misogi* is like cleaning your house. The more consistently you do this internal housecleaning, the more you will be able to sustain a clean, clear heart.

Misogi practice is a way of restoring our minds and bodies to a state of purity. No matter how correct we think we are, we inevitably develop some impurity in our thoughts or feelings. This doesn't mean we have done anything wrong. But we might, for instance, entertain negative thoughts about someone. Negative feelings just appear, even if we don't act on them. Through the practice of *misogi*, we can gradually develop a more consistently pure state of mind. In my opinion, that purity is the true, original heart of humankind. You could call it the mind of *Mu* [emptiness].

The heart of a baby is the purest of all. Anybody who looks at a baby feels love. A baby is truly *Mu* at birth, and it is lovable because it knows nothing. When you are born, you don't have

Linda Holiday Sensei leads a group practice of *misogi* in the Pacific Ocean in Santa Cruz, California, New Year's Day, 2012.

much of an ego-self. But as you study and learn, and go through trials in life, the individual self emerges. You accumulate both positive and negative aspects of self. The question is how to sort through them—how to let go of the negative parts and retain the positive ones. We need to learn many things, and then return to the pure heart of an infant.

The practice of *misogi* [purification] develops a heart that is able to endure suffering. In human life there are many misfortunes. You need courage to deal with them. And you need courage if you want to help those weaker than yourself. *Misogi* is undertaken to cultivate that strength of spirit. To develop an undefeatable heart.

Purification in Aikido Training

O-Sensei told us, "Aikido training is the process of cleansing yourself." He would exclaim, "The dojo is a washing machine! You put yourself inside the dojo to purify body and mind." It makes sense to bring yourself back to the dojo [training hall] over and over, to "do your laundry." Aikido technique is also like a washing machine. We polish and purify our hearts in the process of practicing technique. As we repeat this process, gradually we become less likely to be sullied by what we encounter in the world, and more able to sustain a clean, clear state of being.

In Aikido, we polish many parts of ourselves by practicing in a variety of ways. If you always practice slowly, you won't understand speed. If you always practice fast, you won't understand the heart of slowness. By training in all sorts of techniques, from the front and from the rear, stepping forward and stepping back, you are polished and purified through practice. And through that process, your whole being begins to shine.

I believe that Aikido training purifies us as we engage in the exchange of energy with a variety of people. There are inevitably some individuals whom you dislike, and with whom you don't want to train. It is important to think about why it is that you feel that way. Reflect also on the fact that some people may dislike you as well. When you practice letting go of the heart that dislikes others, you are able to polish and purify yourself, and develop further.

In order to forge steel, to eliminate the impurities in the metal, you need to heat it up and cool it down many times. That's how you temper it. People are like that, too. A warm heart is essential, but if you engage in *shugyo* [intensive spiritual training] with the spirit of *misogi*, even a sharp scolding from your teacher can benefit your practice. As we are treated kindly and sternly by turns, our true hearts emerge.

Studying and learning are also forms of *misogi* [purification]. When a glass is empty, it can be filled with ease. When it is full, it has no room for anything new. When students have a deep desire to receive instruction, they are able to fully absorb what a teacher offers them. But if a student is already full, nothing more can go in. A successful transmission depends upon a student's ability to receive it.

Through the practice of *misogi*, you empty your mind—make it *Mu* [empty], make it pure white. Then when you receive something, you can perceive it clearly. If you're trying to write a message, it is best to write on a blank white piece of paper, isn't it? If the paper has a lot of writing on it already, it's hard to perceive the message.

Acquiring knowledge can be preparation for *misogi*. For instance, we do one form of purification by going into rivers and waterfalls. Some people simply go in without formal preparation, and experience *misogi* in the coldness of the water. Others memorize the *Norito* chants, study what others have done before, and do the *misogi* practice with that knowledge. There are many ways to approach the practice of purification. Each person does it differently.

You can develop *mushin*, the mind of *Mu* [emptiness], through Aikido training. But the mind may also become fixated while training. A fixated mind is filled with thoughts: "I want to defeat my opponent," "You have to do it this way!" or "This is scary." Thoughts like these become obstacles. The opposite of a fixated mind is *mushin* ["no-mind": a clear, empty mind]. The practice is to let go of each thought as it arises. Then your understanding grows through your own experience.

215

My practice is in the moment. My intention is to become one with my partner in a natural way. Without thinking, "*I* want to do a certain form." But we do think. We direct our practice with our thoughts. Then, at some point . . . we become one, and the technique manifests without self-consciousness. You could call that experience *Mu*.

We need to hold firmly to the purpose of Aikido training, and the purpose of *misogi*. We practice *misogi* purification in order to improve our lives. *Misogi* is what you do in order to become your best self.

Anno Sensei demonstrates Aikido with wooden swords in California, 2011. The calligraphy in back is by O-Sensei, and reads "True victory; victory over oneself" (left), and "Aikido" (right).

Everything Is *Misogi*

I believe that human life, from birth to death, is a process of purification. Each and every day of our lives is *misogi*. As we live, we are cleansed and purified. We are polished by what we do each day.

Whatever you do, if you do it for the purpose of becoming your very best self, then it is *misogi*—purification. This is not a matter of becoming better than others. We practice *misogi* in order to cleanse ourselves, to increase our own beauty. If an activity worsens you or dirties you, it is not *misogi*. When I say, "Everything is *misogi*," I'm thinking of polishing myself, improving myself, moving toward the light.

A trip you take to the mountains could be *misogi*, or not, depending on what you are thinking and feeling at the time. If you play *pachinko* [Japanese pinball] every day for entertainment, thinking of it as a way to win prizes and money, it won't be *misogi*—if you lack the intention to purify yourself. But if you tried playing *pachinko* and then realized it was a waste of time, then you could say that even playing *pachinko* could be *misogi*, a process of purification.

Isn't it all *misogi*? Even trying to become strong in Aikido training?

What you see, what you hear, what you touch . . . you can experience it all as *misogi*. Don't think that *misogi* consists only of certain purification practices we do in the river or under a waterfall, or the practice of Aikido in a dojo. The purpose of the practice of *misogi*, in my opinion, is to discover what is true. To find the truth of oneself.

The present moment is *misogi*.

The founder of Aikido performs solo movements with a wooden staff at the old Aikikai Hombu Dojo in Tokyo, around 1965. His solo movements were sometimes referred to as *misogi* (purification), or as *kaguramai* (a sacred dance offering).

The Second Opening of the Stone Door

According to the *Kojiki* [a collection of sacred myths of ancient Japan], the first *kaguramai* dance was performed by a female deity, *Ame no uzume*, at the time of the "Opening of the Stone Door" *[Iwato Biraki]*. As the story goes, the sun goddess *Amaterasu omikami* had withdrawn into a cave and closed the stone door at the entrance, plunging the world into darkness. *Ame no uzume* called all the deities together and performed a dance—the first *kaguramai*—thereby helping to draw the sun out of the cave. The Stone Door opened, and light returned to the world.

O-Sensei described Aikido as the "Second Opening of the Stone Door" *[Nidome no Iwato Biraki]*.[44]

—Linda Holiday

O-Sensei often performed solo movement with a wooden sword or staff. People referred to this movement as his *kaguramai* [sacred dance offering]. Perhaps they began to call it *kaguramai* because O-Sensei sometimes presented it as an offering at Shinto shrines. His movement definitely had the feeling of an offering done in a sacred place.

When O-Sensei held a sword, he was one with the sword. He would say that he had drawn the entire sword inside his body, inside his heart. That was his way of expressing it. When O-Sensei performed his *kaguramai*, the feeling was that the sword or staff he held in his hands had become one with his spirit.

In the *Kojiki*, the very first *kaguramai* dance was performed at the time of the "Opening of the Stone Door" *[Iwato Biraki]*. O-Sensei often spoke of the "Second Opening of the Stone Door."

The Second Opening of the Stone Door is purification. If we look at the world today, we see it is full of impurity and political chaos. To open the Stone Door a second time means to purify our world and the heart of humankind. To brighten a world that has become dark. I believe that is the purpose of Aikido. The spirit of O-Sensei's *kagura-mai* was one of purification, in order to bring a new world into being.

If you are in a leadership or teaching role, it is essential that you, too, become able to do *kaguramai* as a purification. Holding a sword, holding a staff, or simply using your body, you need to be able to purify the hearts of everyone and everything. In order to do that, as O-Sensei said," Purify yourself first."

Aikido is not about the ability to do impressive techniques. O-Sensei was not focused on specific ways to perform techniques. Whether he was performing *kaguramai* or Aikido techniques, O-Sensei said that he was not actually doing the techniques himself. He felt instead that Great Nature was doing Aikido through him. I believe that shows how purified O-Sensei had become. O-Sensei offered his practice of Aikido as a prayer for the establishment of a world of love.

A "Poem of the Way"

Sanzen sekai	In three thousand worlds
Ichido ni hiraku	The plum blossoms
Ume no hana	Open all at once—
Nido no iwato wa	The stone door will
Hirakare nikeri	Open a second time.[45]

     ∼ MORIHEI UESHIBA O-SENSEI

The founder of Aikido holds a wooden staff in the old Aikikai Hombu Dojo in Tokyo, c. 1965.

Breathing and Purification Practices with Anno Sensei

In the following sections, Anno Sensei shares firsthand knowledge of the breathing and purification practices that O-Sensei often led at the beginning of Aikido classes. After discussing the deep meaning of breathing, Anno Sensei offers his personal interpretation of *Chinkon Kishin,* the esoteric practice of purification that is still performed daily in the Kumano Juku Dojo and in various Aikido dojos around the world. Anno Sensei offers a rare window into his own experience of the multifaceted spiritual exercises of *shin kokyu, torifune,* and *furutama,* and invites you to include them in your practice of Aikido.

As you read Anno Sensei's inspired descriptions, you may wish to refer to the detailed instructions for the practice of *Chinkon Kishin,* which are provided in the appendix.

—Linda Holiday

Shin Kokyu: The Breath of *Kami*

When I was a child, I was taught to do *shin kokyu* at school. What my schoolteachers meant by *shin kokyu* was "deep breathing." They would tell us, "Inhale through your nose, and breathe quietly and deeply." People often say that when you breathe deeply, you receive fresh oxygen and it's good for your health. But what O-Sensei would say is that with a single breath, you absorb everything sacred and wonderful in the universe and make it a part of you.

When O-Sensei would say to us, "Let's start class with *shin kokyu,*" he was using a different term than my schoolteachers did. *Kokyu* means "breath" or "breathing." The first word, *shin,* is commonly written with the Chinese character [*kanji*] signifying "deep." In that case, *shin kokyu* means "deep breathing." But *shin* can also be written with the Chinese character which means *kami* [spirit, divine nature]. For O-Sensei, the term *shin kokyu* meant "the breath of *kami*."

O-Sensei's teaching about breath was profound. It was more than the specific instructions he gave us: "Breathe deeply, passing the breath through the brain, through the spinal cord, into the deepest part of your *hara* [belly]." His teaching was larger than that, and more essential.

I think of *shin kokyu* as the breath of nature, the kind of natural breathing that allows us to become one with everyone and everything. That doesn't mean that everyone's breath is the same. Each person has a unique way of breathing. But *shin kokyu*—the "breath of *kami*"—begins with the intention to breathe in a way that connects you to everyone else. To breathe in harmony with nature, with all people, and with *kami*. This is essential for human life, for our ability to survive.

Motomichi Anno Sensei in the Kumano Juku Dojo in Shingu, Japan, 2012. In back of him is the dojo's *shinden* (shrine).

Ordinarily you might think of *kokyu* as the physical breath you perform in order to ensure your own survival. You could say that the activity of cellular respiration is *kokyu*. Breath sustains life. But for what purpose do we live? When you reflect on that, you realize the value of *kokyu* in Aikido.

In Aikido, to live means to live in the finest possible way, with the desire for the whole world to live together in harmony. That is the philosophy of Aikido. That is Aikido's *kokyu-ho:* our practice of breathing.

Breathing In, Breathing Out

When O-Sensei led us in the practice of *shin kokyu*, he would often talk about *uchu no myosei* [the marvelous nature or spiritual essence of the universe]. He would say, *"Su-iki wa uchu no myosei o kotogotoku jiko no tainai ni osame:* As you inhale, draw in all of the spiritual essence of the universe and settle it inside your own body."

O-Sensei told us, "When you exhale, in your heart you must reflect on the way your breath goes out into the world. In your mind's eye, see how your breath spreads out and circulates." What I think O-Sensei meant by this is "Reflect on your actions." Exhalation is not just the out-breath. It is behavior—our words, our acts. How do our actions impact the world?

When you exhale, how does your "breath" go out into the world and circulate in human society? How do you conduct yourself? How are your actions received by other people? If your behavior is not correct, it will come back to you. And what is not correct will diminish over time.

I often heard O-Sensei say, "Examine yourself with the eyes of the heart. While examining yourself in this way, do the breathing practice of *shin kokyu.*"

Natural Breathing

O-Sensei clearly meant the breathing practice of *shin kokyu* to be the breath of nature. If it is the breath of nature, it will be neither forced nor excessive. But I believe that to get to the level of truly natural breathing, it is important to apply oneself to the practice of breathing deeply.

Over the course of my years of training, I have explored various methods of breathing, including extreme methods of breathing deeply into my *hara* [belly] with long, slow inhalations and exhalations. Now, my approach is to breathe naturally, inhaling and exhaling without strain ... without thoughts of strength or weakness, without trying to make the breath long or deep. My intention is to breathe in a natural way.

Gradually, as you continue to train, and especially as you get older, there must be no physical strain. For instance, in *torifune* ["the rowing exercise"], it is important to do the movement with speed and power. But you can't keep up that pace forever. I have done intensive *torifune* practice, but at this point I feel it is no longer necessary. Now I relax my arms and practice moving my spirit.

Anno Sensei demonstrates the position for the practice of *shin kokyu* ("the breath of *kami*").

However, it would be a mistake to take that approach from the beginning. The result would be shallow, maybe even useless. You would end up taking it too easy, without actually strengthening and polishing yourself.

Shin kokyu—the breath of spirit, of *kami*—will mean something different to each person. What is important is for each of us to apply ourselves to this study of breathing. And also, at times, to practice breathing that is deep, expansive, and powerful. I feel that truly natural breathing is possible when you have previously practiced deep, intentional breathing—and it is not possible without that experience.

When I practice *shin kokyu*, I don't completely shut my eyes. I keep them partially open, with the feeling of gazing at the entire world . . . seeing both outside and inside, simultaneously. O-Sensei often said, "See with the eyes of the spirit." Not with the physical eyes, but with the eyes of the spirit, the heart. Polish your true spirit; find your true heart. This does not mean thinking solely of yourself, but of your true life—the life you have been given. Breathe while you reflect on your true self.

Begin with *Shin Kokyu*

As we begin the practice of *shin kokyu* ["the breath of *kami*"], we breathe in the sacred essence [*myosei*] of earth and the sacred essence of heaven. I believe that all of nature, including both heaven and earth, is the universe of which O-Sensei spoke. He often used the word *myosei*: mysterious, marvelous nature or essence. We could say "the breath of the Great Universe."

During the practice of *shin kokyu*, we envision the entire universe. If it is difficult to focus on the whole universe, you can envision nature. As we breathe, we absorb the *myosei*—the essence—of Great Nature, of the Great Universe. When O-Sensei used the term *kami*, I believe he was referring to the entire universe.

Technique is, to an extent, explainable. Matters of the spirit are not as easily explained. I believe it was quite difficult even for O-Sensei to explain. So he would say, "Become one with *kami*." I think O-Sensei was talking about becoming one with the movement of nature. About completely unifying with your partner, and moving naturally, without

226

strain. But to "become one with *kami*" is not an easy thing to under-stand. How can we do that?

O-Sensei told us, "First, begin with *shin kokyu*." After the practice of *shin kokyu* ["the breath of *kami*"], we next practice *torifune* ["the rowing exercise"; a rhythmic solo movement], in order to take that breath into movement. Then we take that energy into the practice of technique with another person. This brings the breath of *shin kokyu* into the rest of your practice.

Left: Anno Sensei demonstrates the extending-out position for the practice of *torifune*, with the weight shifted forward.

Right: Anno Sensei demonstrates the torifune drawing-in position, with the weight shifted back.

The Practice of *Torifune*

I believe *torifune* ["the rowing exercise"] has been practiced in Japan since ancient times, but there is still little understanding of its importance. You could say that *torifune* is the foundation of movement and technique. When we practice *torifune*, we train our hearts and our bodies. We breathe well and become more healthy. *Torifune* develops your ability to transfer weight, to turn the hips, and it cultivates *kokyu ryoku*: breath power. The "Ei-ho, Ei-ho" sound we do with the movement of *torifune* also cultivates breath power.

The essence of the *torifune* practice is the breath. Breathing out, and breathing in, while strengthening and stabilizing the hips. "Breath power" is more than your own individual breath. O-Sensei's teaching was about becoming one with *kami*—one with nature. You can cultivate breath power in conjunction with others, and with Nature. When you breathe in, you absorb everything. You become one. Then you exhale with a feeling of love. This feeling, of love for everything, is the foundation.

Whether you are inhaling or exhaling, ultimately it is the same feeling: gratitude. Isn't it natural to feel thankful as you absorb all the wonders of the universe? And as you return, with the out-breath, all that you have received, that is also a feeling of gratitude.

The most important thing is the state of one's spirit. I feel that my spirit resides in the center of my *hara* [belly]. The navel is where we were all originally connected to our mothers. It is the place of origin, the source of my life; I feel it as my center. My intention is to become one body with nature, with the universe . . . with *kami*.

The Practice of *Furutama*

To begin the practice of *furutama* ["spirit-shaking"], you inhale deeply, unite your left and right hands together, and bring them down in front of your center *[hara]*. With your hands firmly clasped together, you shake them vigorously up and down, while silently concentrating on three *kami*, beginning with *Amaterasu omikami* [the *kami* of the sun].

When O-Sensei did the *furutama* practice, he joined his hands together in front of his center, and shook them up and down. The right hand was underneath, and the left hand was on top. But the visible part of the *furutama* practice is not the important part. Your *spirit* must become unified. The reason to do this practice is to concentrate the ki of Great Nature in yourself. To become one with nature. The feeling is one of spiritual focus.

It is important to become consistently relaxed and natural in the practice of *furutama*, as well as in the practice of Aikido technique. Relax, and don't force things. This is an important study. If you cultivate a feeling of oneness, your techniques will tend to have that same feeling. As you come to understand many aspects of the *furutama* practice, including the spiritual ones, that understanding will be present in the way you do Aikido techniques.

The feeling I have as I practice each day varies with my state of mind. It is not an easy

Anno Sensei demonstrates the position—the visible part—of the *furutama* practice.

practice to rid oneself of the concepts of "strong" and "weak." Some days the feeling is better than others. I practice with the desire to able to train well and communicate from the heart. I would like to develop a consistent feeling of oneness with nature ... with *kami* ... with the universe. That is why I do this practice every day.

Envisioning the *Kami*

As we do the three sections of the *furutama* practice, in each section we envision a different *kami*: first *Amaterasu omikami*, then *Oharaido no okami*, and finally *Ame no minaka nushi no okami*.

The first one, *Amaterasu omikami*, is the name of the sun goddess in the *Kojiki* [ancient book of Japanese stories and myths]. *Amaterasu* means to shine *[terasu]* from heaven *[ama, or ame]*. The sun sustains human life. It sustains all life. When we clap four times, that represents heaven, fire, water, and earth: the sun in heaven, and water on the earth. The great origin. The power of the sun causes the water to rise up as vapor. Fire and water interact in a mutual exchange.

Amaterasu omikami is the love in nature. Humans are one part of nature, but the love of *Amaterasu omikami* is much bigger than the love between two people. I always imagine the light of the sun, and a bright, warm heart that is nurturing to everyone and everything. If there were no sun, nothing would grow. The sun nurtures and supports everything in nature. When I think about *Amaterasu omikami*, that's what I envision.

"In short, Aikido is a method of purification *[misogi]*. Through the technique of *misogi* you continually forge the spirit of love and protection for all things."[46]

↜ MORIHEI UESHIBA O-SENSEI

The *kami* of the second *furutama* section is *Oharaido no okami* [the "great *kami* of purification"]. I believe this represents the function of cleansing in nature . . . the process of cleansing your own heart. In the natural world, rain and wind exemplify this process. When I do the *furutama* practice and chant *Oharaido no okami*, I often imagine the purification of rain. I envision water, wind, and all the functions of nature. You could even think of a typhoon as a kind of purification. In this *furutama* section, I don't think specifically of the sun, but without the sun, water would no longer rise from the earth. Without the heat of the sun, there would be no wind, and no rain would fall.

I feel the meaning of *Oharaido no okami* is to make your own heart clean and beautiful. Forget your self, your ego. Where is your true heart? Where is the life that you received from *kami*? If you focus on that while you chant *Oharaido no okami*, you purify your heart. When your heart has become cloudless, it is like a mirror; it reflects things as clearly as the water of a calm lake reflects mountains. When your own heart is clear, you reflect and receive the universe. You become one with the heart of *kami*.

If you ask, "What kind of *kami* is *Oharaido no okami*?" no one will be able to give you a precise answer. *Oharaido no okami* represents the processes of nature, and all the processes of nature are interconnected.

"Understanding that all the functions of the universe are inside yourself is true *budo*."[47]

∿ MORIHEI UESHIBA O-SENSEI

All of nature—trees, water, earth, the entire planet—has come into being through the power of *kami*. We have human form, but we are a part of *kami* [divine nature]. We can shine, like the sun. With that intention, our hearts become warm and loving, and we can naturally develop the capacity to nurture others. In order to do that, we must become firmly centered. We must have a heart like the *kami* of the final *furutama* section: *Ame no minaka nushi no okami* [the "*kami* of the center of the universe"].

For me, *Ame no minaka nushi no okami* is the easiest to imagine. I think about the center. I can't literally imagine where the center of the whole universe is, but when I ask myself, "Where is the center of the universe?" I feel something. I ask myself, "Where is my own center? Where am I centered?" It is important to become firmly centered in your own self, and not to allow yourself to become sidetracked into judgmental thoughts about other people. O-Sensei taught that the essence of Aikido is to become one with the center of the universe. To study the whole universe and come to understand the answer to the question, "What is the very center of *everything*?"

When I silently chant *Ame no minaka nushi no okami,* I imagine the center of the entire universe, or the *kami* that was born from that center. It may not be possible to become the center of the universe when we are such a tiny part of the whole. But perhaps we can come to comprehend the whole.

As we practice, we envision the *kami.* It seems to me that each *kami* contains the whole. When I think of *Ame no minaka nushi no okami,* I imagine the entire universe. And *Amaterasu omikami* [the sun] is not just one point in space, not just the function of fire . . . it gives light to the whole universe. When I envision the sun and its immense power, I feel deeply grateful. If you imagine it this way, each *kami* expands to include everything.

If we become able to think of the whole universe as one, peace will be born. If one person after another comes to understand the heart of gratitude and the truth of interdependence, humanity will be able to live in peace. That was O-Sensei's teaching. We must become peaceful. I continue my practice of Aikido with that intention.

Keep the Spirit of Harmony Strong

After the final *furutama* practice, when we voice the *kiai* [focused shout] *"Ei!,"* it is with the feeling of complete commitment to the goal of being in harmony with all people. Through this practice, we are cultivating an unshakable, unbreakable feeling of harmony with the entire world. Of course, it is easy to lose the feeling in the very next moment. But we must never give up on the spirit of harmony. As you voice the *kiai*, set a strong intention, "I will not allow things to deteriorate. I will keep the spirit of harmony strong." In this way, you are sending a message to your own spirit to remain strong.

Then, moving circularly, send out the heart of gratitude. We send out the heart of Aikido, in all directions, at all times. Moving left and right, above and below, and to all sides, the circles represent the all-embracing consistency of spirit that is our aim in practice. The feeling is one of deep, expanding gratitude—*okagesama*—toward everything in the universe.

The truth of *okagesama* [deep gratitude] has been forgotten in modern society. People mistakenly feel that their lives are powered by their own efforts. We seem to have forgotten that our lives are sustained by a power far greater than our individual strength. Everything in this universe is engaged in a process of mutual assistance. Our lives are dependent upon this mutual interaction and exchange. That is why we must understand the importance of *kokyu:* breathing.

Motomichi Anno Sensei in the Kumano Juku Dojo, 2012.

Physical movement goes only so far. Your vibration expands through breath and sound. I believe your breath, spirit, and body all grow into a larger movement, and breath power comes to be integrated in your practice of technique. It is infinite and boundless.

Chinkon Kishin: Return to the Origin

Chinkon kishin is an ancient term. The practice of *chinkon kishin* is a part of the training *[shugyo]* undertaken by Shinto priests.

I remember O-Sensei saying, "*Chinkon kishin* is done for the purpose of becoming one with *kami.*" In Aikido, the purification practices of *shin kokyu, torifune,* and *furutama* are methods of doing *chinkon kishin.*

The first part of the term, *chinkon,* means "to calm or settle the spirit." It is similar in meaning to "unify" *[toitsu].* You concentrate, or unify, your feelings, thoughts, and spirit. *Kishin* means "to return to *kami.*" You unify your spirit with Great Nature, with *everything.*

Bring together the heart of the sun, the heart of the moon, the heart of wind, the heart of water—bring all the processes of nature together inside yourself. The heart of harmony, love, sincerity—concentrate all of that in your center, first, before you engage in physical technique. If we lack that spiritual concentration, if we study only technique, our practice will have a fundamentally different result. It is essential to begin in that place of spiritual unification.

To me, *chinkon* means to become calm and natural. To return to the original, natural state of one's spirit: to the heart of *kami.* But we don't understand what that natural heart is. Even if we think it is important to develop a natural heart, we may still get caught up in many other things and in our ego-selves. We need to go back to the origin.

O-Sensei said, "*Kamiyo no mukashi ni tsukimodosanakereba naranai: We must return to ancient age of kami.*" By that, I believe he meant to develop this original state of mind.

In ancient times, people were content if they had enough to eat. They didn't hoard food for themselves, or make a business of selling it to other people. They didn't have that kind of attitude. People shared resources. They took care of each other and the earth. Now, we have become accustomed to living with many luxuries. We need to have electricity, and we can't do without our air conditioning! Scientists understand that the temperature of the earth is rising, and we've reached the point at which we may go on to destroy nature. Having developed such a high level of materialism, it is difficult to turn back.

Human beings and nature share the same origin. Our lives depend on the power of all things, together. We must learn this truth. Take good care of nature. Take good care of each other. That is the spirit to which we must return. Stand in the state of *Mu* [emptiness]. Allow yourself to stand on the Floating Bridge of Heaven. Take your spirit there, and express that state in everything you do.

We must return to the origin. For me, that is the essential meaning of *chinkon kishin*.

Ame no uki hashi [ni] tatasarete, "Standing on the
Floating Bridge of Heaven"; calligraphy brushed by
Morihei Ueshiba O-Sensei, founder of Aikido.

~7~
The FLOATING BRIDGE of HEAVEN

In this chapter, Anno Sensei invites us to contemplate the Japanese concept of *kami* (divine or sacred spirit), along with the Floating Bridge of Heaven and other mysteries at the heart of life. His simple, profound interpretation of *kami* illuminates the universality of the teachings of the founder of Aikido. Anno Sensei speaks to the need of the modern world to realize the truth of interdependence and to reconnect with the heart of Great Nature.

The Floating Bridge of Heaven, a central concept in the teachings of O-Sensei, Aikido's founder, refers to an ancient Japanese story of creation. It is often described as a bridge between heaven and earth, and it is sometimes associated with rainbows. Mysterious and insubstantial, the Floating Bridge is a place of generative power, where complementary opposites unite in a pure act of creation. O-Sensei declared, "To practice Aikido is to stand on the Floating Bridge of Heaven."[48]

—Linda Holiday

The founder of Aikido in Iwama, Japan; 1962.

The Meaning of *Kami*

The word *kami* was frequently used by O-Sensei, the founder of Aikido. It refers to a mysterious, unknowable power. I believe what O-Sensei meant by *kami* was the mysterious power of nature. And what is that? It is the power that sustains life and nurtures all things.

Because *kami* is not easily explained, I often use the word *shizen:* nature. It is easier to explain to someone that a plant is nurtured by the energy of nature, and that we humans are the same. Plants are visible, and readily available for study. Plants, animals, and people have all been brought into being by the power of nature. Human beings are a part of nature, of *kami.* Things that are made by human beings, such as buildings or electronic devices, even if they seem mysterious to us, are not thought to be *kami.* I believe that *kami* is nature.

Our relationship to nature is profound. It is the relationship of macrocosm and microcosm. There is Great Nature, and we are Small Nature. We are One. This means that everything, and everyone, coexists. Even the sun has not come into being independently. A tree is alive with the energy of the universe. Human beings are the same. We borrow the energy of all things in the universe. A mysterious power sustains our lives. *Kami* is something you *feel.* There is no way to fully express it in words.

When we see something natural and amazing, we call it *kami.* Deep in the mountains of Kumano there is an ancient shrine, *Tamaki Jinja,* which was founded over 2,000 years ago. You can hike up the mountainside behind the shrine buildings to see a sacred rock. The rock is called *goshintai:* the sacred body of *kami.* A massive *sugi* tree at the shrine, thousands of years old, is revered as *goshinboku:* the sacred tree of *kami.* The power of *kami,* of nature, inspires a feeling of gratitude toward the mysterious power that is invisible to the eye, inaudible to the ear, and inexpressible in words.

World of Connection

O-Sensei taught, *"Shin jin go itsu: Kami* and humanity are one." I believe that to be one with *kami* means to understand the essence of *kami* and to unify with that mysterious power. We must understand clearly that a single blade of grass, a tree, or a person, is connected to the whole. Your own life is not separate. You are not only connected to your father and mother, or to your friends. Your life is inseparably connected to plants, to rain and wind . . . to everything. When you have let go of selfish desires, when there are no thoughts clouding your mind, you become one with a mysterious, nurturing energy, which brings joy to others. It is a natural process.

Kami is the power of mutual assistance. Our lives are sustained by this power of mutual cooperation. Whether you think of plants, trees, or a single stone, there is a relationship of reciprocity. There is a relationship between large and small, between stone and stone. A relationship with water, with fire. Everything is mysteriously connected. When I look at any one thing, I feel, "How wonderful!"

Humanity is one part of the whole. I believe we need to think more deeply about that connection. Male and female join together to make children, but it's more than that. We are connected to the whole universe. The power of that relationship is what I call *kami*. I'm not speaking of the connections that I create as an individual, but of the relationships existing in nature. This world of connection is the power of *kami*.

It is urgent that we come to understand the heart and the power of *kami*. There have been wars all over the world since ancient times, and the danger of war is increasing. When you understand who you are, when you understand the heart of *kami*, you can't make war. It's inconceivable.

When you truly understand what has led to your being alive today, here and now, you experience a feeling of gratitude. Our lives are dependent upon air, on water, and on the heat of the sun. Plant life is dependent upon all of this, and we depend on plants for food. Humans are truly supported by nature in its entirety. To understand the power of nature—of *kami*—is to experience natural gratitude.

When we live in the midst of material abundance, we forget the necessity of this spirit. If you have to search desperately for food to eat, you know what gratitude is. Perhaps you aren't worried about being able to eat today, and are content to sit back and relax. But the natural truth is that everyone working together is what makes it possible for us to have food. Gratitude is born from that realization.

"My dojo is nature; it is the universe. It is truly a dwelling, a dojo, and a temple built by Kami. If you look with the eyes of your heart, it is the teacher that possesses the scientific and spiritual truth which will lead you to enlightenment."[49]

~ MORIHEI UESHIBA O-SENSEI

A Japanese Shinto priest bows to an ancient *sugi* tree at the Tamaki Shrine, deep in the Kumano mountains; 2008. The white paper *shide* and the rope encircling the tree indicate sacredness.

"I Did Not Create Aikido"

O-Sensei trained himself for many decades, and he integrated all the things he studied into Aikido. However, he often said that he did not personally create Aikido. After all his years of training, near the end of his life, O-Sensei said, "I'm just now beginning to understand Aikido." What a very different state of mind that is from someone who boasts about being strong, or declares, "I'm the only one who knows this!" O-Sensei's extraordinary statement "I did not create Aikido" will stay in my heart forever.

"I did not create Aikido; I learned it from *kami*," O-Sensei told us. This seems clearly true. O-Sensei learned from animals, birds, plants, and trees . . . from all of the workings of nature. It is logical, then, to say that he was taught by *kami*. It is not reasonable to think that a human being could create nature. I feel that O-Sensei's statement shows a true humility.

"Completely absorb the sacred nature of the universe within your own body," said O-Sensei. I believe what he meant by that was to study the universe: Observe it, understand it, and incorporate that understanding into your own body. What emerges from that process will be the true techniques of Aikido.

O-Sensei on a riverbank in the mountains of Kumano, with his wife, Hatsu (left); Hikitsuchi Sensei (right); and a young Aikido student in Shingu (standing), 1955.

243

Izanagi and *Izanami* on the Floating Bridge of Heaven

The *Kojiki* [Records of Ancient Matters] is a collection of stories from the prehistory of Japan, first written down in 712 CE. The stories recount the creation of the universe and its evolution through time. According to the *Kojiki,* the Floating Bridge of Heaven is the place where two *kami* engaged in a mythological act of creation.

The creation of the universe is described in numerous stages. First, a point appears spontaneously in the original void; the *kami* of that first point of existence is called *Ame no minaka nushi no okami:* "the *kami* of the center of heaven." Following this spontaneous manifestation, seven generations of singular or paired *kami* appear sequentially, representing a long evolutionary process.

The seventh generation consists of a male *kami* by the name of *Izanagi* ["He who invites"] and a female *kami* by the name of *Izanami* ["She who invites"]. Together, *Izanagi* and *Izanami* descend from the High Plain of Heaven to stand upon the Floating Bridge of Heaven. On the Floating Bridge, they unite and begin the process of creating the first land—the islands of Japan.[50]

Said the founder of Aikido, "The myriad gods and all the wonders they can perform are in fact within each one of us. The divine animates us. We are the universe. *Izanagi* and *Izanami* are eternally interacting inside our bodies. We are an integral part of creation."[51]

—Linda Holiday

The Floating Bridge of Heaven

When O-Sensei led us in purification practices at the beginning of class, he would say, "First, stand on the Floating Bridge of Heaven." I would wonder, "Where is the Floating Bridge of Heaven? How do you stand on it?" I didn't understand what he was talking about.

I feel that the way O-Sensei chose to express himself was essential to what he was trying to teach. What O-Sensei was trying to convey is inexpressible in ordinary words and concepts. It's something else. If O-Sensei had said, "Stand on the mat, put your left foot here, and your right foot there," people would have taken it literally and received only that. He would have conveyed something very different about Aikido that way. Instead, O-Sensei spoke to us about things like the Floating Bridge of Heaven.

All the words of O-Sensei are wonderful to hear and to reflect upon. As I study the words of O-Sensei, I feel that I am just now starting to understand some of what he said. I have my own feeling about it, but I can't say to you, *This* is the exact meaning of the Floating Bridge of Heaven. I am continuing to study and learn. So let's say that our practice starts now. Let's imagine that we are all lined up, together, ready to begin our studies.

What might it mean to stand on the Floating Bridge of Heaven?

"The Floating Bridge of Heaven is the *koryu* [mutual exchange] between fire and water," said O-Sensei. "It is the manifestation of the heart of *Izanagi* and *Izanami*." When I think of the Floating Bridge of Heaven, I imagine an exchange, a flow of energy, between heat and water. Something insubstantial, like air. Steam rising from water.

I believe that the function of *Izanagi* and *Izanami* refers to the breath. O-Sensei often spoke of the breath of *kon-paku a-un. Kon-paku* implies the combined power of the spirit and the power of the physical body. In Aikido, we must unify spirit and body—both are essential.

A-un [Japanese transliteration of the Sanskrit *aum* or *om*] represents the totality of the breath: exhalation and inhalation.

To *stand*, I believe, indicates a state of being. It doesn't mean to take a physical stance, although the same word can be used in that way. I feel that to stand on the Floating Bridge means to be in a state of oneness with nature, with the whole universe.

To me, the *floating* part of the Floating Bridge of Heaven implies freedom. A freely moving mind. Naturalness. And since it is the floating *bridge* of heaven, I imagine a bridge connecting heaven and earth. A natural flow. Nothing stuck in one place. No awareness of self. *Mu* [emptiness].

O-Sensei clearly said that Aikido begins when you stand on the Floating Bridge. I believe this means that Aikido begins when you stand with a feeling of emptiness. Stand on the bridge between, in the space between, heaven and earth. Stand where there is nothing to stand on, in the midst of a flow of energy. Let your mind become empty. O-Sensei taught us to begin with the process of emptying.

The founder of Aikido, Morihei Ueshiba O-Sensei.

The Practice of *Norito*

When O-Sensei taught in Shingu, he sometimes chanted the *Norito* [Shinto prayers] at the beginning of class. He would chant for a long time, while we all knelt on the mat in *seiza*. I was young then, and I didn't have much interest in the *Norito*. I wondered what O-Sensei was doing. My legs would start to hurt from kneeling so long, and perhaps it would be cold in the dojo. I remember thinking, "Why doesn't he just start class and get into active training right away?"

Now I have come to appreciate the *Norito* that O-Sensei chanted. The chants contain meaningful teachings on how to live one's life as a human being. For instance, the word *makoto* [sincerity] is found in the *Norito*, and O-Sensei would frequently speak of this concept. In Japanese, the word "sincerity" is written with a *kanji* composed of two parts, a part that means "word" on the left side and a part that means "become" on the right: "Words come into being." This means that a person of sincerity puts his or her words into action. The *Norito* chants are full of many words that are teachings like this.

All the *Norito* chants expound the principles of nature. They refer to the names of the *kami*. They speak of spirit and heart, of the four souls, and of five kinds of love. The words of the *Norito* chants remind us to bloom like a flower, to become radiant, and to remember the spirit of gratitude toward nature. I think this is our true spirit. We are born with this purpose, but we lose our way. We become disconnected from nature and from other people, and we come to believe that we are separate. I believe this is a mistake.

The *Norito* chants tell us to engage in self-reflection and to purify our hearts. They remind us that in order to do the right thing, we need courage and strength of heart. We need to set our intentions every day, so that we don't lose our way . . . so that each of us can fulfill our mission in life and bring joy to others. All of that is written in the *Norito* chants. Even the purpose of Aikido can be found in the words of the

247

Norito. The chants tell us that all human beings are children of the divine—of *kami*—and we must learn to get along with one another.

Sometimes people focus on chanting the *Norito* in a certain, proper way, or on memorizing the words of the Buddhist sutras. But these are not just things to memorize. They are spiritual practices, devised as methods for us to realize the essential heart they contain.

After O-Sensei chanted the Norito at the beginning of class, he would talk to us, for half an hour or more, about *kami.* Then he would often lead us in *shin kokyu* [a purification practice]. That was the way he began our Aikido training.

If you develop an understanding of these important matters, your Aikido practice will advance in that direction. If you don't think about these things, and instead practice only physical technique, you will go in a different direction. One could say that through the practice of *misogi* purification and *Norito* chanting, O-Sensei gave birth to the principles of Aikido. I do these practices in turn, while remembering O-Sensei, in order to understand what Aikido is.

Kototama: Words of Spirit

We need to develop the ability to explain the techniques of Aikido to others. Not simply to explain the physical aspects, but to convey the spirit of harmony and love within Aikido techniques. The ability to explain and convey the spirit can be called *kototama* ["word-spirit"; words of spirit]. If a conversation is truly something wonderful, it is *kototama.* If it goes no farther than ordinary conversation, it has not reached the level of *kototama.*

When the desire for everyone to be in harmony is present in what you say, I feel your words are *kototama.* If the heart of love and gratitude permeates every word, that is *kototama.* I felt that spirit consistently present in what O-Sensei said. I admired that. He didn't waste a single word. Whenever O-Sensei spoke, he gave us something to be treasured.

When O-Sensei chanted the sounds A...O...U...E...I...and other *kototama*, he would say that the sound had to emerge naturally, of its own accord. "A" [ah]... is a feeling that wells up and comes out naturally in a sound. While O-Sensei was sounding the *kototama*, he would say, with "A" the sound emerges naturally, and with "ME" [meh] the sound goes out and circulates. The sound *a-me* means "heaven," as in *Ame no uki hashi*, the Floating Bridge of Heaven.

The way I understand it, the sound expands and moves circularly, naturally, like the movement of the universe. The movement of the Great Universe is expressed in sound, as a small universe. Then, moving with the feeling of oneness with all things, that feeling is expressed in the techniques of Aikido. It is natural movement, expressing yin and yang, *Izanagi* and *Izanami,* water and fire. O-Sensei often said, "*Suika musunde, tate yoko o nasu:* Uniting water and fire, create vertical and horizontal." Vertical and horizontal—this forms the "cross" of *Aiki.*

O-Sensei showed his *kototama* to us, but he did not teach us specifically how to do it ourselves. We understood that his *kototama*, what he voiced, was the expression of the spirit; and we simply watched and listened. As I reflect back, it seems to me that O-Sensei's *kototama* was neither mind nor heart, but rather something that welled forth from O-Sensei's spirit, as a result of the severe training of mind and heart that he had undertaken over the course of his life.

O-Sensei composed many poems. Some of them are important to the understanding of technique. One particular poem is my favorite. You could say that an ordinary poem is written by thinking of something, and then adding your personal feeling to that thought. This is not an ordinary poem. It is a *kototama* that emerged from O-Sensei, words which came out of his spirit.

The founder of Aikido speaks to a group of people at Sakaguchi Ryokan, a Japanese inn where he sometimes stayed when he came to Shingu to teach Aikido. The large ceramic pot in front of him is a *hibachi* used for heating in winter.

Aiki ni te	In Aiki,
Yorozu chikara o	Activate
Hatarakashi	Every power
Uruwashiki yo to	To harmonize peacefully
Yasuku wa subeshi	With this beautiful world[52]

~ MORIHEI UESHIBA O-SENSEI

In *Aiki*—through training in Aikido—use every power you possess, the strength of every part of your being—to construct a world of beauty and peace, filled with the spirit of love. Aikido cultivates a heart that can do this.[53]

A Larger Perspective

As I watched O-Sensei over the fifteen-year period that I knew him, it seemed to me that O-Sensei completely manifested *kami no kokoro:* the heart of *kami.*

O-Sensei was focused on *kami.* He thought about Great Nature. O-Sensei's level of thinking went beyond ordinary consciousness. He seemed to look at everything from a larger perspective. This is a difficult thing to do even when we try. When I'm having a conversation with someone, what is central in my mind may be myself and my own concerns. I may be speaking on an ordinary interpersonal level that is easily understood. But O-Sensei had gone beyond that. When O-Sensei spoke, the object of his focus did not seem to be the individual or group of individuals with whom he was speaking. I felt that O-Sensei's attention was on something else. He would speak of Great Nature. What O-Sensei said, and the feeling with which he said it, were extraordinary. It was as if he were engaged in conversation with the universe.

As far as I saw him, O-Sensei was consistent. Even when he became ill at the end of his life, he did not seem to resent his illness. He lived with a feeling of gratitude. I would like to develop a consistent feeling of gratitude. But there are times when I find myself thinking, "Why do I have to suffer like this?" In an ordinary state of mind, when we experience pain, we ask, "Why me?" We don't say "thank you" to the pain for teaching us something. O-Sensei seemed to be completely receptive. How incredible it would be to receive everything, and turn it into gratitude and joy.

"This universe is composed of many different parts, and yet the universe as a whole is united as a family and symbolizes the ultimate state of peace. Holding such a view of the universe, Aikido cannot be anything but a martial art of love."[54]

⌁ Morihei Ueshiba O-Sensei

Divine Technique

O-Sensei spoke frequently and at length about matters of the spirit. Many wonderful people listened to him. But he could not cause them to feel things the same way he did. Many of the people who heard O-Sensei say repeatedly, "Aikido is the divine technique of *kami*," viewed Aikido primarily in terms of physical technique. That was how they received and interpreted O-Sensei's teaching.

If you tell people *"This* is the answer," or *"This* is the meaning of *kami* [spirit, divine]," they will find it difficult to accept. Each person's understanding is unique and evolves over time. Even the teachings of Christ and Buddha have been subject to the process of personal interpretation.

We who practice Aikido must ask ourselves, how much of its spirit has been incorporated into our own personal training? We train hard, learn technique, and throw each other. If we are busy with these endeavors, we may find it difficult to integrate even a small percentage of the spirit of Aikido. I believe this is a challenge we all share.

O-Sensei said that Aikido is the *shingi* [divine technique] of *Ame no murakumo kuki samuhara ryu-o* [a powerful dragon-king *kami*, a purifying force in the universe]. O-Sensei would frequently refer to this dragon king spirit. I believe *Ame no murakumo kuki samuhara ryu-o* represents the essential form *[sugata]* and all the movement and energy of nature, and that O-Sensei referred to all of the workings of Great Nature as *kami.* What would it mean to integrate that into your practice of Aikido?

It is important to study and practice the techniques of Aikido thoroughly, so that they become a part of you. Then you can "forget" the techniques. You can relax and let go of your physical power. When you do Aikido techniques without resorting to physical strength, you are able to move in harmony with another person. You become one. That leads to the heart of deep gratitude *[okagesama],* harmony, and love. I feel it is our practice to integrate harmony, love, and sincerity into the techniques of Aikido.

When you practice the Aikido technique of *shiho nage* [four directions throw], it must become *shingi:* the "divine technique" of *shiho nage.* Every technique must become *shingi:* a divine technique. This is not a matter of strength versus weakness, but of becoming one. When you have become one with another person, and beyond that, one with nature, I feel that your technique has then truly become "Aikido."

We need to train hard in technique, and develop our hearts as well. It's not enough to talk about Great Love, and say we want to get along with people. This spirit must be expressed in *waza* [technique]. Otherwise it will be something other than Aikido—a religion, perhaps. In Aikido, the word *waza* refers to behavior. What you do must be congruent with what you say.

O-Sensei said, "Aikido is the sacred form and spirit of *kami.*" The techniques of Aikido express the form and spirit of *kami*. And what is the form of *kami*? It is not strength. It is not winning over others. The spirit of *kami* is the heart of Great Love.

Ame no murakumo kuki samuhara ryuo no shingi, "The Divine Technique of the Dragon King Who Purifies the Universe" (a frequent reference by O-Sensei to a dragon-king guardian spirit); calligraphy brushed by Motomichi Anno Sensei.

Born of Mystery

I believe everything is One. Ultimately we are all One. In order to perceive this oneness, we train in Aikido, do various forms of meditation, chant the *Norito* and Buddhist sutras, and so on. I think we all want to reach the place where everything is One, but we stop before we get there.

I was born in a place where nothing exists. Of course I had a mother and a father, and other circumstances that contributed to my birth. But my parents did not "make" me. I am not something that can be made like that. It is the same for all of us. We are born of a mystery. And we die into mystery. No matter how much other people may try to help you, you die in a mysterious place unreachable by the assistance of others. When you realize that, how do you live your life?

We are all born of mystery, of a power far greater than our parents. O-Sensei said, "A human being is a child of *kami*." If you are a child of *kami*, it makes sense that you could come to be like *kami*. But we have a human ego *[ga]*. If you let go of your ego, you become *kami*. The ego, the "self," is the difference.

Your sense of self comes from your parents and the other people around you. When you are born, you know nothing. People educate you, and you learn many things. Your individual self is important in order to live and work in human society. But sometimes it gets in the way. The ego-self is desire. It is the lazy mind. A mind that thinks in terms of winning and losing.

We all want to live in the spirit of love and harmony, but we end up fighting with each other. If we understood what makes us fight, we could stop fighting. We devote ourselves to Aikido training in order to understand the heart of love and harmony, and to live bright and joyful lives. Meditators come to know this heart through their practice of meditation. Musicians make music that brings people together in harmony. Buddhists realize this spirit through chanting the sutras and putting their faith in the Buddhist way. It's just a question of how far we choose to go in the development of our understanding.

Although I'm not personally a Christian, I feel Jesus Christ must have been truly incredible. So much light has come from his teachings, over such a long time. When people have put forth the effort and reached the light, they radiate light forever, even after they die. But we risk staying here in the shadows if we don't apply ourselves to our practice. I believe if we give our full effort, we can reach the light. O-Sensei journeyed all the way to the light and became an inspiration to others.

It is an incredibly precious opportunity to be born as a human being. We are gifted with the ability to grow indefinitely, if we study and apply ourselves. Humans have rapidly developed the power to make computers and to travel into space. Once you've reached this wonderful state of being human, you might as well take the opportunity to train and develop yourself fully. And as long as we live, we are all helping each other and being helped by others.

Doesn't everyone want to have joy, and give joy to others? For example, you plant a big garden in front of your house. Gardening is hard work, but you want to give everyone the pleasure of seeing its beauty. You prepare food and serve it to others, or eat food that has been prepared by others.

O-Sensei often said, *"Kami ni ikasareteiru:* Our lives are sustained by *kami."* If we reflect deeply, we realize that all of our food comes from nature. Our parents raised us, but if we think deeply, we understand that we are nurtured by all things in nature. We owe our existence to all things. If we continue to reflect, we will reach the inescapable conclusion that we are born of nature—of *kami*—of mystery.

Return to the Heart of *Kami*

O-Sensei frequently said, "Through Aiki, we must return to the age of the *kami*." I feel this is an important mission of Aikido. The *kamiyo*— "the age of the *kami*"—refers to a time in the ancient past in which Spirit was primary. But with the passage of many generations, this spiritual principle has been usurped by the principle of selfish desire, and a materialistic civilization has been the unfortunate result. By focusing on material things, humanity has lost its heart to greed, and this has brought about strife and war. Instead of ending this selfishness, humanity has continued its focus on the prosperity of a materialistic civilization. We have now reached the frightening prospect that the great earth, our mother, may be destroyed.

O-Sensei understood this. He taught that all people must quickly awaken to the path of becoming a true human being, and must revive the spiritually centered "age of the *kami*." For this reason he founded Aikido, a path in alignment with the age of the *kami*.

In the first lines of the book *Maki no Ichi*, O-Sensei wrote: "*Aiki* comes from the sacred form and heart of *kami*; it is the infinite, absolute spirit of the world's creation and organization, which is truth, goodness, and beauty."

Aiki is born from the form *[sugata]* of *kami*. When you look around you, what you see is *sugata:* things that are manifest in form. Trees in the mountains. People. Everything is made of the mysterious power of *kami*. And *Aiki* is born from the heart *[kokoro]* of *kami* ... which is Truth, Goodness, and Beauty.

When I say *kami*, I am not thinking of the kind of *kami* that humans have created. *Amaterasu omikami* [the sun goddess] and many other *kami* are described in the ancient stories in the *Kojiki*. But the *kami* I am thinking of is the form and heart of nature. It is true, and good, and beautiful. *Kami* is greater than any single thing. It is infinite. It is the absolute power that created the world.

257

To give birth to the heart of gratitude, we must study how the world came into being and return to the heart of *kami*. That spirit—that heart—is *Aiki*. That was O-Sensei's ideal. You will make no mistake if you make this the foundation of your training.

Shin Zen Bi, "Truth, Goodness, Beauty"; calligraphy brushed by Motomichi Anno Sensei.

Standing on the Floating Bridge

When O-Sensei taught class in Shingu, he would bow and pay his respects to the *kami*. Then he would often begin with *shin kokyu* [a purification practice]. He would say, *"Mazu, ame no uki hashi ni tatasarete:* First, stand on the Floating Bridge of Heaven."

O-Sensei frequently used the word *tatasarete* for "stand." A more common word for "stand" is *tatte*. There is a vast difference in meaning between *tatte* and *tatasarete*. *Tatte* means simply to stand, on your own, of your own volition. But *tatasarete* expresses the concept of "being made to stand." *Tatasarete* means that something else, or someone else, causes you to stand. O-Sensei often used the word *tatasarete*. It is a very interesting and difficult concept. I like to think about the meaning of *tatasarete*.

O-Sensei didn't set about intentionally to create Aikido. Aikido came into being naturally. You could say that Aikido was created by *kami* [spirit, nature]. Or that *kami* caused O-Sensei to create Aikido. "Caused to create" *[tsukurasarete]* is the same kind of wording as "caused to stand" *[tatasarete]*. It's the same feeling. It is not something you attempt to do yourself, through personal volition. It happens naturally. I believe that *tatasarete*, being "caused to stand," means becoming completely unified with nature.

It is difficult to give a precise definition of *tatasarete*. But I feel that all Aikido technique has this aspect. Perhaps everything is like that. Music, for example. If you are playing a musical phrase, how much emphasis do you give to each note? How long do you linger on the last note? There is no one set way to play music. Each person feels it differently, and may find it difficult to explain exactly how they do it.

I believe O-Sensei used the term *Ame no uki hashi*—the Floating Bridge of Heaven—because it refers to heaven *[ame]*, the highest state of your own spirit. You have to realize this on your own, through training yourself and through *misogi*. You stand on your own in order

259

to purify yourself, starting with *shin kokyu* ["breath of *kami*" purification practice]. You purify yourself, and come to your own understanding that you are born into this world and you will die. Gradually you come to understand what it means that you are alive in this world.

When we think it is our own personal power that sustains our lives, we end up doing selfish things. But our lives are sustained by food, by everything in the universe. In order for you to live, something else must give its life. Nature—*kami*—can sustain humanity if this is kept to a minimum. If we don't understand this, we will cease to exist.

No matter how much you come to understand, you still don't know. But the level of your understanding changes. At first, no matter what, it is *tatte:* standing on your own. Ultimately, it evolves into *tatasarete:* being "caused to stand."

Toward the end of his life, O-Sensei said, *"Shizen ni tatasarete iru:* I have been 'made to stand,' by nature." You don't have to be literally standing up to have the feeling of *tatasarete:* being made to stand. Being in a natural state. It is important to stand with the feeling of unity with the heart of *kami*.

Stand naturally. Without conscious intention. Stand in a pure place, a place without any pollution or impurities. Stand without self-consciousness, in total clarity. We are already standing there. We have already been made to stand there.

Right here, right now, I am standing on the floating bridge. I have been caused to stand on the floating bridge—that's the feeling. When you go to a beautiful place in nature, a feeling comes over you, doesn't it? You become inspired. This is *tatasarete:* you are "caused to stand."

I would like to be able to sustain that feeling continuously—to stand on the floating bridge wherever I go. Whether I am downtown, or in the mountains, or at home . . . wouldn't it be wonderful to be able to sustain the same marvelous state of being? I want to develop that ability, but I have a ways to go. When I'm facing a sword attack in the dojo, I become aware that I am not consistently in that wonderful state of mind!

To me, the dojo is sacred, so I go to the dojo to cultivate the state of being on the Floating Bridge of Heaven. As you accumulate more experience in training, you become able to return more quickly to that state, don't you? You have the intention to re-experience the feeling that inspires you, for instance the awesomeness of nature that moves you when you are in the mountains. You develop a greater ability to return to that state of being. I want to stand on the floating bridge in the dojo, and be able to sustain that feeling wherever I go.

What is the Floating Bridge of Heaven? Where can it be found? In heaven . . . in an unknowable place . . . the state of *Mu* [emptiness]? To stand on the Floating Bridge of Heaven is to understand the heart of Great Nature.

Anno Sensei in the high Sierra Nevada mountains of California, 2000.

Aiki O Kami, "Great Spirit of *Aiki* [Harmony]"; calligraphy brushed by Morihei Ueshiba O-Sensei, founder of Aikido.

~ 8 ~

AIKIDO in the WORLD

O-Sensei described Aikido as a path of peace. It was his dream that Aikido would make a profound contribution to the evolution of human society. He taught, "All of us in this world are members of the same family, and we should work together to make discord and war disappear from our midst."[55] The founder also explained, "I teach this art to help my students learn how to serve their fellow beings."[56]

In this chapter, Anno Sensei reflects on numerous aspects of Aikido in the world and "off the mat." He speaks from a lifetime of Aikido that stretches from studying with O-Sensei in postwar Japan to teaching Aikido internationally as a practice of peace. Responding simply and openly to questions from Westerners, he shares his thoughts about the relationship of Aikido to peace, leadership, integrity, and a sense of service. Anno Sensei offers encouraging advice to teachers and students alike, and urges all of us to cultivate what is most important—the heart.

The founder of Aikido was fond of exclaiming, *"Sekai wa hitotsu!*—The world is One!"* Anno Sensei reminds us that the founder's vision of peace and unity is still very much alive.

—Linda Holiday

Aikido and the Spirit of Peace

The true spirit of Aikido is the spirit of peace. Through Aikido training, grasp the principles that O-Sensei espoused, and cultivate in yourself the spirit of peace. Then convey that spirit to at least one other person. Teach the principles of Aikido and share them with other people. That will lead to peace.

There is a fighting spirit that naturally arises, in all of us. If you have a fighting heart, it will tend to bring out a fighting heart in other people. The philosophy of Aikido is "to win correctly and to win over oneself," in the midst of conflict. It is through actual training that you learn to resolve the fighting spirit.

I'm not just thinking about the fighting spirit inside everyone else. This is my own practice. I feel that I have plenty of fighting spirit left inside of me. It's still there, in my heart and in my technique. I have accomplished only a fraction of what I would like to accomplish in my training. And so I continue my practice.

Why do people fight? How can we eliminate fighting? You could say that *budo* is a study of conflict. By practicing *budo* [the martial way], it is possible to understand conflict and its resolution. As you continue to train, you come to understand that *not fighting* is the better alternative. This understanding gives birth to the heart of love. Aikido teaches love. In Aikido, through the martial art training, we come to understand the spirit of peace.

Training is essential. Train into yourself the wonderful principles of Aikido, which leads to *kami,* to nature. Strengthen your own center so that your partner can be close to you. Find your own balance in the midst of movement. In this turbulent world, find what is true. Through training in a variety of situations, you can develop a natural, sustainable posture that will not deteriorate. Training is the way.

Over the years, as I have kept O-Sensei's principles in mind, my training has gradually moved in the direction of love and of peace.

If you study O-Sensei's Aikido principles and philosophy and keep them in mind, then Aikido training itself will lead you from technique to the development of spirit.

The process of Aikido training is a mutual polishing. I still have much to polish and purify in myself, so I would like to train myself along with you. It's important to keep training and polishing each other. I believe that was O-Sensei's dream: for all of us to train, to become more radiant, and to bring that increasing light into the world.

If you focus your efforts in that direction, you will grow in a way that other people will naturally appreciate. As you continue to train and polish yourself, other people will be drawn to the practice of Aikido. Then Aikido itself will grow. If many of us practice sincerely in this way, that will have a good effect in the future.

As the world goes forward, we need to become people who can convey the way of *Aiki* to others. Develop the spirit of peace, and then take it into the world.

Anno Sensei leads a group bow, a gesture of respect and gratitude, at the beginning of an Aikido class in Santa Cruz, California; 2010.

The Possibility of Cooperation

What we need in the world now is the spirit of cooperation, of help-ing each other. Competition is no longer useful. Fifty years ago, O-Sensei said this change would come. I remember very clearly hear-ing O-Sensei say, "The martial arts [budo] of the past, based upon winning and losing, are no longer useful. For the age that is coming, they are unnecessary. We need Aikido: good relations between all people. What is essential now is budo that can bring people together in harmony." He encouraged people practicing Aikido to train hard in order to be of help in the coming transition, into a humanity infused with the spirit of love.

Aikido teaches the possibility of cooperation. When people first encounter Aikido, it is often a surprise for them to see that it is actually *possible* to blend forces together in a harmonious way. O-Sensei taught, "There is no opponent." This gives birth to the ability to cooperate.

However, it is also natural to feel that the attitude of loving oth-ers and not having opponents, though admirable, may be weak and lead to defeat. Many people feel that in order to get by in the world as it is, they need to set themselves up against others, to compete with opponents and defeat them. But in Aikido practice, you have the experience of harmonizing, or cooperating with others, without being defeated. Aikido shows us that it is possible to eliminate your concept of "opponent," as O-Sensei taught, without being defeated and without defeating someone else.

To see these principles of Aikido, and then actually feel them in your body, is a transformative experience. When people practice Aikido, they experience in their own bodies the feeling of blending and unifying with another person, of resolving an opposition, rather than one side forcefully prevailing over the other. Part of the useful-ness of Aikido is to show people that this is possible. To show that love, cooperation, and harmony are not weak, but have real power.

Future school principals and administrators enjoy learning useful applications of the Aikido principles of harmony, at an "Aikido for Educators" seminar taught by Glen Kimoto, senior instructor at Aikido of Santa Cruz; 2009.

And that to apply this approach in their own fields—politics, the military, business, or any other endeavor—is not to become weak, but to come into alignment with forces that are powerful.

Our function as we practice Aikido is to develop our training so that we can show the power of harmony and the possibility of cooperation. It's not easy at the beginning, but with practice, we can develop these abilities over time. Then other people can see them and be inspired by the possibilities. People who don't do the physical training themselves may still be able to glean useful ideas from what they see, and apply them in their own areas. If they are introduced to the principles of Aikido and appreciate them, those principles may prove useful in the future. If you plant the seed of Aikido, at some point it will sprout.

Cultivate Heart in Leadership

Ancient cultures emphasized a spirit of gratitude and a philosophy of oneness with nature. Reverence for nature has been strong in indigenous peoples everywhere. But in today's world, most of us don't live that way. Now we expect to have all sorts of material comforts and luxuries, and it has become more common to think only of oneself. I feel it is selfish desire, thinking only of oneself, which has led to the world we live in today. A true desire would be the desire for *everyone* to live a wonderful life, in harmony with nature.

It appears that many people are living the good life and having a pleasant time, but now that human society has gone too far in that direction, we will suffer for it. We have used our knowledge of science to develop various kinds of human-made power. We ride around in cars, and fly in airplanes from the United States to Japan. These are wonderful conveniences. But we are now experiencing global warming.

Leaders of the world are discussing how to deal with this threat to human survival. They are trying to hold mutual talks, but some of the people in power lack a spirit of cooperation. Their attitude seems to be, "How dare you say that to us? If you want to change what you are doing, fine—but we will continue on our present course." This is similar to people who focus exclusively on strength in techniques and believe that the most important thing is to "win." They may say, "It doesn't matter what fine words you use—they are worthless if you cannot put them into action. If you are defeated, you cannot accomplish anything."

If we want to be effective leaders, we must train ourselves long and well. If you lack skill in technique, if Aikido's mysterious power does not flow through you, your words may lack effectiveness as well. This is relevant not only to teachers, but all people—business leaders, for instance, and people who employ others in companies.

269

If the heart is not present, the lower-level employees won't want to follow. They will develop the attitude, "I'll just do what's best for me as an individual."

The more diligently you train yourself, the more energy and warmth will come through you. It is essential to train in such a way that light is generated. If it's dark around you, people will not follow you—they won't be able to see the way. What we need is to cultivate a heart that brightens its surroundings . . . a kind heart. This is important for everyone, not just people in Aikido. O-Sensei's hope was that we would all cultivate this kind of heart, and the people of the world would live together as one family.

I believe the mission of those who are leaders in Aikido is to convey to others—to even one more person—the true heart of Aikido. It is a mistake *not* to think about this, and to focus only on becoming "bigger" or stronger than others. All leaders need to reflect on this.

A "Poem of the Way"

Aiki to wa	Aiki is
Yorozu wago no	All the power
Chikara nari	Of harmony—
Tayumazu migake	Train ceaselessly,
Michi no hitobito	People on the Way! [57]

    ~ Morihei Ueshiba O-Sensei

One Common World

O-Sensei declared, *"Aikido ni wa jikan mo kukan mo nai:* There is no time or space in Aikido." When I heard O-Sensei say this, I did not understand what he meant. I remember the feeling with which he said it, but "no time, no space" is difficult to explain. As I reflect on O-Sensei's words, the meaning they have for me now is this: "The most important thing is the present moment."

No time. No fleeting temporal matters like "What time shall we start?" or "Shall we meet tomorrow?" The important thing is *right now*—that's how I interpret it. If you do Aikido, you can incorporate "No time, no space" in the practice of technique. No matter how fast his partner would strike, O-Sensei was able to take his time. He didn't rush. In his technique, he seemed to have transcended time. You can understand this in the context of martial arts techniques, or in the context of your whole life. When people of religious faith heard O-Sensei say, "There is no time or space," they, too, were amazed and moved by his words.

No space. No matter how far away we are from each other, we share one common world. It is not a matter of being near or far. It doesn't make sense to insist that Aikido is only Japanese, or that you have to go to a particular place in order to learn Aikido. Distance is irrelevant. Wherever you are in the world, you can practice Aikido fully.

Aikido is not only Japanese. I believe that Aikido belongs to the whole world.

IN DIALOGUE WITH ANNO SENSEI:
AIKIDO IN THE WORLD

In the following section, Anno Sensei responds to questions about expressing the heart of Aikido in the world.

Anno Sensei speaks at a seminar in California, 2010.

Teach to the Top

What do you think O-Sensei would have thought about the environmental problems now facing us? O-Sensei loved nature and wanted to protect the environment, didn't he? But perhaps he did not think much about political matters.

O-Sensei did think about political matters. He loved nature, and he believed that humans must live in harmony with nature. O-Sensei was concerned that if things didn't change, the world would end up in the situation we are now in. He frequently said it was essential to teach Aikido to people in power—to politicians, heads of companies, and leaders in other fields. O-Sensei felt it was important for the people "at the top" to come to understand Aikido. He said that we didn't have enough time to rely simply on change spreading upward from the base. We need to change the minds of governmental leaders. If we only teach Aikido to people who come to classes at the dojo, or only to people we know and like, it will be too slow a process.

When O-Sensei told us that we would need to teach Aikido to people "at the top," we didn't understand what he meant. We were still thinking of Aikido primarily as *budo,* as a martial art. So we didn't grasp the significance when O-Sensei said the leaders of society needed to understand Aikido. He told us we would need to get Aikido's message across to the people at the top, while there was still time. O-Sensei wanted us to realize that it was an urgent matter.

It was O-Sensei's ideal that Aikido would be helpful in bringing about a more peaceful world. He believed that given the direction the world was headed in, it was likely that the situation would gradually worsen. It was his hope that through making a deep study of the principles of Aikido and spreading them widely, we could stop war. I believe it is most important to convey the philosophy of Aikido: the necessity for people to live in harmony with nature and with each other. The spirit of Aikido is one of harmony and love—not a small love, but a great love, including the love of Great Nature.

Some people may come to understand a little bit of Aikido and then stop. Or they may forget what the goal of Aikido is and replace it with their own goals. But we have to try to convey Aikido. If we just wait around to see what happens, it may be too late. We need to take positive steps forward ourselves.

Anno Sensei instructs at an international Aikido seminar in Paris, 2010. His demonstration partner is Kuribayashi Sensei from Shingu. Swiss Aikido instructor Juerg Steiner stands behind Anno Sensei, interpreting into several languages.

Inryoku: The Power of Attraction

I heard the former chief instructor in Shingu, Hikitsuchi Sensei, say that the goal in Aikido is not actually to harmonize with the person attacking you, but to bring that person into accord with your movement, which is in accord with nature. How can we provide this kind of positive leadership, without simply agreeing or accommodating?

I agree with Hikitsuchi Sensei. It is a matter of leadership. We do harmonize with people, but we can't simply blend with whatever our partner does. It is futile to try to agree completely with others. Ultimately, in practice and in technique, the other person is coming to you, seeking something. As an Aikidoist, you train to develop something in yourself that other people will seek, and follow.

O-Sensei often talked about *inryoku no tanren:* forging the "power of attraction," the power to draw in and absorb others. It makes sense, doesn't it? Rather than merely blending with the other person, you draw them to you. Then, in order not to fight, you guide them in a better direction. For this to be possible, you need to become a person who is credible and trustworthy.

"Heaven and earth are perfect and complete. This is a beautiful, shining world. Only our spiritual awakening as human beings is awaited. All things will grieve if we do not straighten up."[58]

∽ Morihei Ueshiba O-Sensei

275

The Ability to Perceive

I've recently taken on a new leadership role at work. How can Aikido principles be used in leadership?

In Aikido training, we sometimes practice stepping back and allowing the other person to strike fully before we respond. This approach respects the fact that the other person, your partner, has a point of view. You let them express their point of view. You hear them out. If they have a good idea, that's great. If you don't think they have a good idea, you can respond, "Here's another idea, what about this one?" Once you are able do that, you can advise them and suggest an alternative more quickly the next time.

Linda Holiday teaches a class at her dojo in Santa Cruz, 2012.

AIKIDO in the WORLD

You have to listen first, in order to clearly understand. But you may come to understand how the other person feels even before they speak. You don't always have to hear someone to know where they are headed. Sometimes you've watched their behavior, or you feel what is happening. It's not just a matter of words. Aikido training develops the ability to perceive what another person is feeling.

If you are the head of an organization, you have to understand, quickly, what people are thinking about when you hear them speak. You need to see where people are headed, and sense what their intention is. For instance, are they thinking only of themselves? You have to be able to perceive these kinds of things in order to do your job successfully as a leader. Ideally, people will understand your true intention and support you on that basis. They need to understand the direction of your leadership.

A Sense of Service

How do the teachings of Aikido relate to leadership in government?

O-Sensei spoke of the fundamental principle of *saisei itchi*. This means that people who are in positions of power must govern with the proper intention. *Sai* [ceremonial spiritual affairs] and *sei* [government or administrative affairs] need to be conducted with the same spirit [*itchi*: unity]. People who govern must not be motivated by desire for money, position, or power. The fundamental principle must be to lead everyone in a good direction, and to express gratitude to *kami*—which means to be grateful to *everything*. It is a feeling of thankfulness. An attitude of giving. A sense of service is essential.

In my opinion, *saisei itchi* means that one's own spiritual path, as well as the path of public service, must stay true to the principle of a pure heart. We must conduct ourselves with sincerity in all spheres of action, aligning ourselves with nature, protecting nature, and living in harmony with the movement of the universe. A true spiritual path is not a self-centered one, but brings joy to all people.

I believe that inside each person there are two hearts: a heart that wants to be connected in a good way with others, and a heart that wants to be lazy. These two hearts are in competition. The selfish heart says, "I'm just watching out for myself." The other heart says, "I want to join with others." After people participate in Aikido training for a while, the feeling of wanting to cooperate with others may be strengthened. It is important for a dojo to have that function, to help people change in that way. Although it is easy to teach people who already have a good attitude, in Aikido dojos we also need to develop the capacity to bring about change in people who start out with a poor attitude.

A person could give lip service to peace, yet harbor selfish desire inside. We need the ability to distinguish between sincerity and falseness. To notice if a person is saying all the right things about peace and community benefit, but doing things in a selfish way. Since Aikido is a human endeavor, Aikido is not immune to that possibility. But it is the teaching of Aikido to change that attitude into the heart of sincerity. It is the responsibility of leaders and teachers to guide people in a better direction.

Put Ideals Into Practice

Aikido is the principle of harmony. But when we look at the world today, we see so many places of extreme conflict—for instance, the conflict between Israelis and Palestinians, Irish and English, the problems in Iraq. How can Aikido bring people together in harmony?

These are problems that people have created, so people should be able to resolve them. It is within human capability. But it's too difficult for any one person alone. If people join together, resolution is

Reunited at the 2012 Santa Cruz Aikido Summer Retreat (left to right): retreat co-instructors Jack Wada, Motomichi Anno Sensei, Mary Heiny, and Linda Holiday.

possible. The challenge is to develop the intention to resolve things. I believe that Aikido has a role to play. If, through our training, we cultivate the desire and the ability to resolve problems, we will draw closer to the Aikido principles taught by O-Sensei.

By the time he was in his twenties and thirties, O-Sensei already had a strong desire to work for the benefit of the community, and he put that into practice. For instance, he gathered together a big group of people and moved with them up to the island of Hokkaido, to settle that area and to establish a community there. He took responsibility as a leader. This was clearly something that he was doing in service to the community and not just for himself. By actually putting that spirit into practice, he became credible to others. When O-Sensei spoke about love, people listened to him. Because he had put his ideals into practice, his words had power.

Lead in the Direction of Peace

Why is it so difficult for leaders to work in harmony with each other?

The problem is that everyone thinks they are right. People who have a fighting heart are of the strong opinion that they are right and others are wrong. I believe we practice Aikido in order to develop the ability to discern whether something is good or bad. To understand whether it is beneficial to fight, or if there is something more important.

Leaders have immense responsibility. They can lead us in the direction of peace or of fighting. It is difficult to see the correct path and lead in the direction of peace. Those who influence the long-range direction of the world need to truly devote themselves to understanding which path the world should take. To be a leader you must become the kind of person who would inspire gratitude naturally. You must be absolutely believable. Otherwise people will feel that you may talk a good line, but your behavior is not congruent with what you say.

But people constantly fight with each other, arguing "My side is right!" It's strange, isn't it? That intelligent people in powerful leadership positions think like that and lead us to war. Even the teachings of Aikido, depending on how they are interpreted, could potentially lead to war. So we need to get a firm grasp of the true principles of Aikido, and then dedicate ourselves, through our practice of Aikido, to pray for world peace.

Universal Science

In Aikido, we train ourselves in the dojo and develop ourselves as best we can. Then we go to work, and to other places, where we interact with people who don't practice Aikido. How does the training in the dojo relate to the ways we apply Aikido in the rest of our lives? Isn't it important that we also express the teachings of Aikido "off the mat"?

Yes. The real meaning of Aikido lies in putting it into practice in the world. To express the heart of Aikido in the world—at work, at play, within interpersonal relationships—is, I feel, the ultimate significance of our practice.

O-Sensei said, "Aikido is *uchu kagaku* [universal science]." I believe Aikido is connected to everything. Doesn't any field of study lead us ultimately to understand the heart of *kami,* to an appreciation of the value of nature? Whether we study Aikido, science, or math, we are learning something that follows the laws of Nature and is in alignment with deep truth. We must not abuse this knowledge of nature for destructive purposes. Every true path has the core intention to brighten the world we live in.

I feel that people who farm, and people who do Aikido, are doing the same thing. Over and over, we nurture and cultivate. Our practice is repetitive cultivation. If you want to grow beautiful leaves, you can't just focus on the leaves. You have to till and prepare the soil, making good conditions for growth that will come later. This isn't something that can be accomplished immediately. You do things now that will make it possible for things to bloom next spring. You look at what is invisible, and cultivate the spirit.

When we practice footwork on the mat, it is like tilling the soil, so we can plant seeds from which something will grow. The movement practice we do in class one day will be "fertilizer" for later techniques. The practice of basic technique is a necessary foundation for the next phase of practice. All the practice we've done up until now will help us go deeper in our future development. Keep a wide view. Plant next year's seeds.

Undefeatable Love

I've always been intrigued by these words of O-Sensei: "Aikido is nonresistance. As it is nonresistant, it is always victorious." How could anyone make such a bold, confident statement?

If you became one with *kami*, if you reached the state of oneness with Great Nature, you, too, would be able to make that amazing statement.

Zettai fuhai means "always victorious" or "absolutely undefeatable." A Sumo wrestler who came to test O-Sensei's strength was defeated. People came from other martial arts and were unable to defeat O-Sensei. Many of them later became well-known students of O-Sensei. After other people heard those stories, it became general knowledge that O-Sensei was "undefeatable."

What impresses me most about O-Sensei is his teaching of love. In 1925, after he went to Omoto, O-Sensei had a spiritual experience in which he realized, *"Bu* [the martial essence] is love." It was an astounding change of consciousness, to a level at which there is no competition, no sense of winning and losing. After that realization, I believe what O-Sensei did gradually evolved from *bujutsu* [martial art techniques] into Aikido. It became a Way.

In that state of *"Bu* is love," with the complete disappearance of the fighting heart, I believe one would be able to say *Zettai fuhai:* absolutely undefeatable.

When you speak of being "undefeatable," I think about Gandhi. As far as I know, he did not practice a martial art or engage in self-defense, but he spoke of love and truth. He maintained his spiritual integrity even under attack, even in the face of death. Could Gandhi be an example of being "undefeatable"?

Yes. I would call that *shinnen kakuritsu* [the development of unshakable faith]. If we pursue our training with complete commitment, become one with *kami*, and establish complete faith—if we have firmly estab-

282

Instructors and students of all levels training together at the Santa Cruz Aikido Summer Retreat, 2011.

lished "love"—that kind of strength would appear. The power of the heart. No fear of death. No concern about victory or defeat.

It is important to ask ourselves how far we have gone in the development of "unshakable faith." What is the level of our effort? How much have we actually trained, polished, and purified ourselves?

Even people who seem weak can summon a tremendous power in extraordinary circumstances. I feel that Aikido is one of the Ways [michi] that develop in us a spiritual strength that transcends life and death. I believe that any true path, at its essence, must teach us how to live. How to go beyond thoughts of life and death to develop the capacity to love.

I believe that anyone can do Aikido. It's not a matter of talent. You don't have to be athletically or intellectually gifted to train joyfully in Aikido. I know this from personal experience. If you want to go into a musical field, you have to have at least a little musical talent, but anyone can practice Aikido. That is one of its greatest gifts.

It is wonderful to hear you say that anyone can practice Aikido if they put forth the effort. But people who have never tried Aikido, or who are in the first years of practice, may not share your perspective. Some people worry that their bodies are not strong enough. They may look at the physical practice of Aikido and think, "I just can't do that."

That is why leaders and teachers of Aikido need to make a deep study of O-Sensei's teachings. O-Sensei often said, "Aikido is not a matter of strength and weakness. The goal of Aikido is not to compete or to win." Leaders and teachers in Aikido must speak about this often. It will increase the responsibility and the sense of mission of those in leadership.

Each person's training is unique and wonderful. Each person can do Aikido in his or her own way. When you have reached a state of mind that is unconcerned with relative skill, then comparisons with other people are irrelevant. If you have no thoughts of winning or losing, what you have will be enough. If I fully develop the heart of love, giving it my full effort, then when I am completely committed, I too can say with O-Sensei, "*Bu* is love." It is a matter of unshakable faith.

I say anyone can do Aikido. I believe that is true. People will, however, practice Aikido for different amounts of time. They will do as much as they can. If they train sincerely and with commitment, I feel that is enough. No matter how much you apply yourself, there is still a matter of ability. We are all born with natural abilities. We need to apply ourselves fully. Then, if there is something you cannot do, you can accept that. The important thing is to put forth your full effort. Ask yourself, how am I choosing to use my twenty-four hours each day?

If you become frustrated with your progress in Aikido, reflect on your way of thinking. If you are training, but you feel as if you just can't do Aikido successfully, you can remind yourself that this is a time of invisible growth. Growth is happening in a place you cannot see. If a plant doesn't establish strong roots, if it only sends out branches, it won't be able to withstand the winds of the next typhoon. Tell yourself, "This is a time when my roots will grow stronger."

If you keep practicing with commitment, your heart will be strengthened, too. You will have a feeling of success: "I did it!" The important thing is to be able to sustain your practice despite feelings of frustration or competition with others. You may not be able to do everything, but if you put forth your full effort, you will be able to say *Zettai fuhai:* "Absolutely undefeatable."

A Mysterious Power in the Universe

I am going to be leading a therapy group for men who have been violent. I think the teachings of Aikido would be helpful to these men. But because they have committed violence, I won't be able to teach them any martial arts techniques. How would you recommend I approach this?

I imagine that the kind of people who commit violent crimes don't have many friends to talk with, heart to heart. They must feel lonely. When these men use violence, they appear to be strong, but actually their hearts are weak. It is because their spirits are weak that they resort to violence.

In recent years, crime has increased in Japan, too. These days, we even hear about children who commit acts of violence. To me, violence indicates a lack of real, mutual, heart-to-heart communication.

In Aikido training, we learn from everyone. We learn from the most experienced people, but we also learn from new students. Everyone is connected through the heart and develops a mutual understanding. It is important to create a place where that can happen. You'll need to lead the therapy group in a way that facilitates a mutual heart-to-heart understanding. It would be interesting if the group members could talk with each other and reflect on questions such as "Why are we alive?" and "What allows us to live?"

It is good to reflect on the fact that we are not separate and alone. We are naturally connected to others. Each person has a father and a mother, and lines of ancestors stretching back into history. If we go back far enough, we find that *everyone* is connected. That is why we must all live in harmony.

There are some couples who desperately want to start a family but find they are unable to have children no matter how hard they try. Others who feel they have enough children already become pregnant again. People who are praying for a daughter give birth to a son, and others who hope for a son receive a daughter. Why do these things happen? What brings these things about? We don't know. It's not under our control. As I go through each day, I have no idea how long I will live. And everyone else is in the same situation. We humans simply do not have the power to control these things. There is *something else* at work.

There is a mysterious power in the universe. We need to honor that fact. And things become more interesting when we do. It's good for everyone to reflect on this. When you come to realize that there is a power in the universe that supports us all, I believe you are not likely to want to hurt or kill another human being. In my view, Aikido training is a way to realize the truth of the mysterious power that sustains all our lives.

Thank you. That's helpful. I frequently wonder what I have to offer this group of offenders that I am supposed to lead. When I hear you speak, I realize that I have the opportunity to treat these men nonviolently. Making a connection from the heart is something I can offer them, and that is a capacity I've developed through Aikido training.

You have a big responsibility. It's important for you to train hard and well. I believe the men in your group must have committed violence because they didn't understand a fundamental truth. If they understood this truth, they probably wouldn't commit crimes. Even people on death row may not understand. Even when they face death, they may not understand.

It is easier to talk with someone if you have the feeling that you could die with them. One time, I had to deal with a person who was threatening someone in the dojo in Shingu. This man was armed and ready to be violent. I interceded and spoke with him alone. I wouldn't have been able to talk with the man if I had felt afraid or if I had been trying to defeat him. But I wasn't thinking about victory or defeat. In that moment, in that state of mind, I didn't even care if I was killed. Of course I do want to live. But sometimes, in a frightening situation, you find yourself able to detach from life and death. So I was able to speak naturally with the man and resolve the situation.

To approach someone like that, I feel it is best to avoid any thought of straightening the other person out or guiding him in a good direction. It's better to go in with the feeling of learning from the other person. Find out how things got to be the way they are. If you speak with that kind of feeling, it's easier to be relaxed. Instead of urging, "Come this way," or "This is what you should do," you can ask, "How did it happen?" I think seeking to learn from the other person is a good approach.

Remember the Goals

What advice would you give to us as teachers of Aikido?

Look to the advice that O-Sensei has given us already. That's the advice that I am giving to myself, every day.

Ask yourself, what were O-Sensei's goals for Aikido? In one of the very first books on Aikido, O-Sensei wrote, "The purpose of Aikido is to develop people of sincerity." Teachers need to reflect on this. O-Sensei emphasized the cultivation of harmony and love—good relations between all people. As teachers of Aikido, it is important to focus on these goals.

If you study mathematics, you begin with the number "1." Then you go on to the number "2." After that, you study how to add, subtract, multiply, and divide. You learn how to use numbers in many ways. But what is the goal of your study? Is your goal to make money, to gain a position of prestige? Or are you studying math in order to bring people together in harmony? Of course, you can't get by in

Young students of Aikido contribute to a discussion led by their instructor; Santa Cruz, 2012.

life on ideals alone. You need to make a living. But in any field of endeavor—math, business, Aikido, or anything else—the most important thing is what you actually do with what you learn. Ask yourself, "What is my goal?"

And, of course, you need to continue your training and your study of technique. Train hard and well. Your technique will gradually change and evolve to different levels. But as O-Sensei would often tell us, "If you want to learn technique, study the heart." As a teacher, as a leader, it is important to remember the primary goals of Aikido and to share them with others. If you do that, I believe that students will come to you and want to learn.

Reflections for Teachers

Two years ago I started a new dojo. I find it's quite a responsibility to be the chief instructor. Are there any particular principles you feel would be helpful for me to reflect on as a new teacher?

Here is a motto that I have found useful for many years, in life, in work, and in technique as well: "Eliminate *muri, muda,* and *mura.*" To eliminate *muri* [strain] is to eliminate stress and excessive force. To eliminate *muda* [waste] is to refrain from useless words or actions. To eliminate *mura* [inconsistency] is to avoid the pattern of going strong and then suddenly slacking off—even within a single technique. In other words, to develop a consistent flow. Ridding oneself of *muri, muda,* and *mura* means to develop naturalness, focus, and consistency.

I'll share with you another set of principles that I often use as a guide: *Yasashiku, hiroku, fukaku.* This means "Gently, expansively, deeply." *Yasashiku* means "gently" or "easily." Be kind to others. As a teacher, teach in a way that is easy to understand. *Hiroku* [expansively] indicates an expansive, broad state of mind. Think big ... keep the big picture in mind. And *fukaku* [deeply] means to go deep, to avoid staying on the surface of things. In Aikido, we need to aim at what is in the depths.

When I watch people instructing Aikido classes, it often seems that they want their students to focus on what the instructor is doing and to imitate the instructor. But in my opinion, that is a poor approach to teaching Aikido. Rather than focusing on what you yourself can do, I suggest you try to convey what O-Sensei did. As a teacher of Aikido, even though I don't have a complete understanding, I attempt to convey the teachings of O-Sensei. If you consistently direct students to aim at O-Sensei's Aikido rather than your own, I believe those students will make rapid progress.

I remind myself of these principles, and I practice them. The advice I give to you is advice I try to follow myself.

Spread the Way of Harmony in the World

When you travel from Japan to other countries to teach Aikido, do you feel that we are making progress towards O-Sensei's goal of spreading "The Way of Harmony" in the world? As Aikido grows internationally, are we going in the direction of the ideals that O-Sensei expressed?

Things often go well at the beginning. I would say that people who are relatively new to Aikido seem to be clearly advancing in the right direction, toward the goals of Aikido. But after students continue to train and reach a certain level of skill, it is possible to forget what the real goals of O-Sensei's Aikido are. They may end up thinking only about technique. Or perhaps they feel they have completed their study. In Japanese this is called *manshin* [pride, conceit]. We are taught that it is not good to be *manshin* [prideful]. But what if the people giving this message are *manshin* themselves? It is a problem if leaders and teachers become self-satisfied. That can happen anywhere, at any time.

Morihei Ueshiba O-Sensei, founder of Aikido, contemplating a
blooming cherry tree at the Kumano Hongu Shrine.

Promotional testing in Aikido can be a difficult matter. I imagine that O-Sensei must have experienced problems in this area, too, with people asking him to give them black belt ranks [grades]. I remember that O-Sensei used to say, "It would be better if we didn't have any rank in Aikido. But if there were no rank, people might not be as motivated to train." I heard O-Sensei remark, "Black belt ranks should be presented to people at the Kumano Hongu Shrine."

What O-Sensei said has many levels of meaning. I believe O-Sensei meant that we need to go to a "place" where we are not fixated on things like black belts. Rather than focusing on rank, we need to focus on developing in ourselves the heart of *kami*. O-Sensei said that the goal of Aikido is to cultivate people of sincerity. Isn't it Aikido's goal, then, to develop people whose minds are not fixated on things like rank? The most important thing is developing the right attitude.

If you want the people in your country to consider Aikido, you need to train and polish yourself steadily. If you want people all around the world to be drawn to the practice of Aikido, model a high level of behavior. Otherwise, people will think you are just acting in your own self-interest, and they will not be satisfied with what you are saying to them. I think about Kobo Daishi, the founder of Shingon Buddhism, who went into solitary retreat in the mountains in order to understand the heart of *Mu* [emptiness]. That level of personal commitment is inspiring. If we just sit around and take it easy, we can't expect to persuade people that way. We need to apply ourselves sincerely and take another step forward.

"We must dedicate ourselves to our mutual and thorough study of the laws of the universe, and progress quickly to the completion of our understanding. We must respect and honor the universe, respect the divine spirit *[kami]* of the universe, respect each and every person, and also respect and love ourselves. By doing this, we show the real existence of the spiritual culture of Aikido."[59]

~ MORIHEI UESHIBA O-SENSEI

Future Generations

The first generation of Aikido teachers consists of people like you, Sensei, who had direct experience of O-Sensei and who teach from that experience. We are learning as much as we can, now, from O-Sensei's direct students. But when that is no longer possible, what is your advice for the next generation of teachers and leaders as we try to convey Aikido?

While I am here, it is my intention to convey everything I understand to others. But it is important to remember not to look at *me*. I haven't mastered Aikido. I can't move like O-Sensei. My goal is to encourage everyone to study the teachings of O-Sensei one by one and reflect on them. O-Sensei is no longer physically here, but he clearly left his teachings behind for us to study. O-Sensei clearly taught, "Aikido is love." That teaching is here. Now.

Everyone has his or her own way of doing Aikido. The techniques of Aikido vary quite a bit from person to person. If you want to spread Aikido and keep it going into the future, focus on its most fundamental goals: harmony between people and cultivating the heart of love. Transcend winning and losing as you polish your technique. We need to have skill in technique, but it is even more important to remember that Aikido's purpose is to bring people together in harmony.

Instructing hundreds of students at the 2011 Santa Cruz Aikido Summer Retreat, Anno Sensei directs the group's attention to the message in the calligraphy of Aikido's founder: "True victory; victory over oneself."

Teaching Aikido technique to others is an incredible challenge. One day I think I am doing something good, but the next day something new and different will start to happen. We have to teach basic form to beginning students—right, left, up, down—without knowing if it is ultimately correct. O-Sensei used to say, "Technique changes every day."

These days, there are standardized forms of Aikido techniques, formalized by the second Doshu, Kisshomaru Ueshiba, the son of

O-Sensei. But O-Sensei himself, in his era, did not teach that way. You could say he used an old-style teaching method. Things were always changing. That's why all of O-Sensei's direct students are different from each other. We each viewed O-Sensei from a slightly different angle, and took in O-Sensei's teaching in our own way.

Please study Aikido together, learn from each other, and carry Aikido forward in the best possible direction.

The Heart of Aikido

Sensei, as you look at the world today, what do you feel is the most important thing we can do as people on the path of Aikido?

I believe it is most important to teach Aikido to as many people as possible, and widely spread an understanding of the heart of Aikido. The mission of Aikido is to spread the awareness that we need to be concerned about *everyone's* welfare and happiness, and to spread an understanding of how people can get along with one another. That is a difficult task, but it was O-Sensei's hope that Aikido would be helpful to the world in that way. He frequently said it was essential to teach Aikido to people in positions of power and authority. People "at the top" *need* an understanding of Aikido. We must learn to think of everyone. To spread the teachings of Aikido widely, and to think about the whole.

All people are born the same. Our lives are sustained by air, water, the heat of the sun—all the powers of nature. When people in Japan perceive Great Nature, they describe it as *kami,* or the heart of Buddha. In other countries, it's natural to use other terms. In my opinion, when O-Sensei used the word *kami,* he was applying it to the whole universe. O-Sensei spoke of Great Nature, of sincerity and truth. It is important to consider how to interpret the truth so that it can be comprehended in each country.

Every person practicing Aikido is a leader, an example for those who come later. We all need to develop our ability to lead. O-Sensei used to say that each person was an angel [*tenshi*], serving the *kami* and conveying the spirit to others. Please persevere in your Aikido training and become *kami no tsukae*—a divine servant. I believe that each one of us can do that.

I feel that my function is to convey to you the words I heard from O-Sensei. As you hear them over and over and absorb them into your body, they will gradually become a part of you. As we absorb the spiritual teachings of O-Sensei, we will advance together on the path of Aikido and develop as true human beings. Then Aikido will have a bright future.

Now is the most important time. The world today is chaotic—you know this. But the age of the heart will come. O-Sensei emphasized that we must return to the heart. Firmly grasp O-Sensei's philosophy—the heart of Aikido—and integrate it into your technique, into your own body. Train hard and well, until, like O-Sensei, light shines out from your heart. Then what comes out of you naturally will be Aikido.

Please understand the heart of Aikido, and spread it widely.

AFTERWORD
THE JOURNEY CONTINUES
Linda Holiday

When Anno Sensei first traveled to Santa Cruz to teach Aikido in 1999, several instructors from my dojo and I took him into the high country of the Sierra Nevada mountains, as he had introduced me long ago to the mountains of Kumano. Though Anno Sensei was nearly seventy at the time, he walked all day in the alpine mountains, greeting the leaping cascades, the trailside flowers, and the granite boulders as if they were family members. We climbed up steep rocky slopes and practiced *misogi* in a snowmelt lake. This image of Anno Sensei, transported from Japan to the mountains of California, in harmony with nature and sharing with Westerners the teachings he had received from O-Sensei, brought to mind the truly remarkable expansion of Aikido in the years since the founder's lifetime.

From his early classes with O-Sensei in the 1950s, Anno Sensei recalls the founder articulating a profound vision of Aikido as a practice to be shared with the whole world. This vision has now become a solid reality. Beginning with O-Sensei's personal students in Japan, the Aikido community has grown into an enormous tree with branches reaching around the entire globe. Over the last four decades of my own practice, it has been thrilling to take part in Aikido's expansion in the West, from a few isolated clubs taught by Aikido pioneers to the vast, vibrant network of dojos and Aikido-derived practices in existence today. Whatever country, city, or village you visit, chances are there will be an Aikido dojo in the vicinity. There is a rich diversity of approaches to the art, with numerous organizations and teachers that specialize in various aspects of Aikido. As the tree of Aikido has expanded, its branches have grown large, abundantly populated, and at times far apart from one another.

Aikido no Kokoro: "The Heart of Aikido"; calligraphy brushed by Motomichi Anno Sensei

Yet all of the branches of the Aikido tree grew from the same root and can find common vision and purpose in the fundamental teachings of the founder. "The *Aiki* path is infinite," declared O-Sensei. Any major field of study—be it physics, music, sociology, or Aikido—contains diverse areas of research and expression that complement and complete one another. O-Sensei himself explored many areas of practice over the course of his life. If we look underneath the organizational and stylistic diversity in Aikido, we find the foundational teachings of O-Sensei. When we honor that common root, it can nourish and inspire all of us. I believe that the spirit of harmony, collaboration, and mutual respect will enable the practice of Aikido to thrive in successive generations and make its full contribution as the path of peace that O-Sensei envisioned.

Much has happened since I first invited Anno Sensei to Santa Cruz and followed an instinct to ask if I could create a book from his teachings about Aikido and O-Sensei. When Anno Sensei arrived at my dojo, he was in his late sixties. This year he turns eighty-two. He has crossed the Pacific Ocean to teach in California almost twenty times. His warm, humble wisdom has been an essential presence in the lives of a whole generation of Aikido students on the West Coast of the United States and beyond. Each of the last several years, Anno Sensei has made the long journey "one more time," arriving in Santa Cruz accompanied by his wife of more than fifty years, one of his dedicated students from Kumano, and stacks of freshly brushed calligraphy to give away as gifts to students and friends. Anno Sensei's seminars have drawn together teachers and students from many branches of the Aikido tree, as he has encouraged all of us to search for the heart of Aikido in the teachings of O-Sensei—and in our own lives.

These years have been precious ones, full of milestones and passages. A few years ago I marked forty years since I took my first steps on the Aikido path, and last year my dojo celebrated its thirtieth anniversary. Training with the generations of sincere students flowing through the dojo and working with other senior teachers to nurture our Aikido community has immeasurably enriched my life and deepened my sense of purpose. It has been a particular joy to see my son, now grown up and towering cheerfully over his mother, earn his own black belt in Aikido. I've taken many students and colleagues, as well as my son, on pilgrimages to Kumano. Sharing my Aikido practice with a widening circle of friends around the world has been a delight and an inspiration. Through it all, it has been my great honor to study with Anno Sensei, to organize his seminars in the United States, and to have his support as I worked to create *Journey to the Heart of Aikido.*

The river of time flows steadily on. This year, after six decades at the historic Kumano Juku Dojo, and after serving for the last nine years as its chief instructor and director, Anno Sensei has formally transferred the responsibilities of dojo leadership to the next generation of instructors. This is one of many similar transitions of great poignancy happening throughout the Aikido world. It is a reminder to treasure the irreplaceable gifts of the generation of Aikido teachers who learned directly from the founder, O-Sensei.

More than half a century ago, O-Sensei expounded a big vision of Aikido spreading throughout the world and playing a role in the development of peace in human society. The founder offered a paradoxical practice of love emerging out of the heart of the martial arts, and a pragmatic method of cultivating harmony and integrity in action, for a world facing serious challenges. This is our world now, and our challenge.

"Aikido is for the entire world," said O-Sensei. "Train ceaselessly for the good of all."

Our journey to the heart of Aikido continues.

—LINDA HOLIDAY
   APRIL 2013

APPENDIX:
INSTRUCTIONS FOR *CHINKON KISHIN NO HO*
As learned at the Kumano Juku Dojo in Shingu, Japan
by Linda Holiday

The following detailed instructions are based on directions given to me by Anno Sensei and Hikitsuchi Sensei, who learned the practice from O-Sensei, the founder of Aikido.

This exercise, which combines meditation, breathing, visualization, and movement, is a purification practice that O-Sensei often did at the beginning of class. Its purpose is to develop a state of unity with the spirit of the universe *[kami]*. The term *kami* refers to the divine spirit(s) of the universe, to nature, or more broadly, to that which inspires in us a sense of awe and mystery. Developing a state of unity with *kami* implies a transformation of consciousness, and an integration of body and spirit, which are fundamental goals of Aikido training.

A formal name for the whole purification practice is *Chinkon Kishin no Ho*: "a practice of calming the spirit and returning to *kami*." We often refer conversationally to the practice by using the name of its first section: *shin kokyu*, which means "the breath of *kami*."

Sequence of the Sections of *Chinkon Kishin No Ho*:

1. *Shin Kokyu:* "The Breath of Kami"
2. *Torifune:* "The Rowing Exercise" (first time)
3. *Furutama:* "Spirit-Shaking" (first time)
4. *Torifune* (second time)
5. *Furutama* (second time)
6. *Torifune* (third time)
7. *Furutama* (third time)

8. *Otakebi no gyo* (optional section)

9. Conclusion

1. *Shin Kokyu:* "The Breath of *Kami*"

Stand relaxed and straight, with your feet about shoulder-width apart. Place your hands, palms together, in a low position and breathe in the ki of earth while drawing your hands upward along your center line (Figure 1a). Breathe in the ki of heaven as you continue to raise your hands together toward the sky (Figure 1b). Exhale as you lower your hands. Repeat the inhalation. With your hands in the uppermost position, clap sharply four times (Figures 1c–1d). The four claps represent heaven, fire, water, and earth *(ten, ka, sui, chi):* the elements that make up the dynamic order and harmony of Nature.

〜 Figure 1a. Breathe in the ki of earth. 〜 Figure 1b. Breathe in the ki of heaven. 〜 Figure 1c. Clap four times: heaven, fire, water, earth. 〜 Figure 1d. Clap with the left hand slightly above the right.

Bring your hands down to your center, just below the navel, and form a circle there. The left hand rests palm up on the right, and the thumbs are lightly touching (meditation position) (Figures 1e–1f). Close your eyes (or leave them slightly open) to facilitate an internal focus. Breathe deeply, slowly, and completely, in through the nose and out through the mouth. When you inhale, imagine that the breath, the essence of the universe, is drawn in through your nose, up through your brain, and down through your spine into the deepest part of your center *(hara)*. When you exhale, be aware of your breath expanding and spreading out, and follow the breath to the farthest reaches of the universe. As you breathe out, reflect on the quality of your own presence and behavior in the world.

〜 Figure 1e. Standing position for *shin kokyu*. 〜 Figure 1f. Hand position for *shin kokyu* (left hand on top of right).

A traditional part of *shin kokyu*, as O-Sensei taught it, is the practice of silent chanting. In this section, you can silently chant the syllables I-KU-MU-SU-BI, with one syllable for each breath. Start by exhaling with "I" (pronounced "ee" as in "meet"). Continue with KU ("koo," while inhaling), MU ("moo," exhaling), SU ("sue," inhaling), and BI ("bee," exhaling). Then inhale without a syllable, and repeat the whole sequence at least twice more, or as long as you like. *Musubi* is an ancient Japanese term that refers to the powers of creation and harmony. (The more modern word *musubi* or *musubu* means connection, literally "to tie together," or "to form a relationship.") *Ikumusubi* further refers to the *kami* (spirit; energy) that increases and "vivifies" the creative processes of life.

During *shin kokyu*, breathe fully and continuously, and concentrate on the ceaseless circulation of energy in the universe. At the end of this section, open your eyes and breathe in the ki of earth and heaven again, twice, while raising your hands along your center line (same as in the beginning) (Figures 1a–1b). Clap four times to invoke heaven, fire, water, and earth (Figures 1c–1d).

2. *Torifune:* "The Rowing Exercise" (first time)

Step into left *hanmi* (stand with your left foot forward). Shift your weight forward, extend your arms, close your hands into fists; then shift your weight back while pulling your hands strongly to each side of your hips (Figures 2a–2b). Move from your center while keeping your hips stable and your upper body straight and relaxed. Repeat in a continuous motion. Imagine that you are grasping the fabric of the earth and pulling it into your center, then pushing it away again in a powerful motion. This is sometimes called "the rowing exercise." A more esoteric name for this practice is *ame no torifune no gyo:* the ascetic practice *(gyo)* of the "heavenly bird-boat." This refers to the "boat" which traveled back and forth between Heaven and Earth during the process of the creation of

〜 Figure 2a. Begin *torifune* with left foot forward. Shift weight forward and extend arms. 〜 Figure 2b. Shift weight back and pull hands to hips. Extend forward again and repeat the motion continuously.

the universe, according to the stories in the ancient Japanese texts that O-Sensei studied.

When you do *torifune*, you can accompany your movements with the *kiai* (focused shout) *"EI-HO."* When you shift back and draw strongly into your center, shout *"EI"*; when you shift forward and extend outward, shout *"HO."* Do the *torifune* "rowing" motion for a short or a long time. As you sustain this powerful movement, absorb inside yourself the raw, unrefined power of nature. (This is called *aramitama*.) Finish with a strong pull into your center and step back into a natural, balanced stance with your feet about shoulder-width apart.

3. *Furutama:* "Spirit-Shaking" (first time)

Place your hands together and breathe in, while raising your hands along your center line (as in the beginning of *shin kokyu*). Then clasp your hands together and lower them as far as they will go, in front of your abdomen. Left hand (representing heaven) is on top of right hand (representing earth). Close your eyes, or leave them slightly open, to facilitate an internal focus. Shake your united hands vigorously up and down, and sustain an energetic vibration while breathing deeply (Figures 3a–3b).

~ Figure 3a. Clasp hands together and shake them vigorously at your center. ~ Figure 3b. Clasped-hand position for *furutama* practice (left hand on top).

3a

3b

Furutama literally means "spirit-shaking." Through the practice of *furutama,* the raw natural power *(aramitama)* generated in the *torifune* practice is digested and transformed into a power that is peaceful and harmonious *(nigimitama).* Energy circulates throughout the body, we become more centered, and the energies of yin and yang are balanced. In addition, during each of the three *furutama* sections, we focus internally on a particular spirit or energy *(kami).* O-Sensei instructed students to chant silently, inside their hearts, the name of each of three *kami.* You can also visualize or invoke each type of energy in your own way.

The *kami* (spirit, energy) of the first *furutama* section is AMA-TERASU OKAMI. This literally means "the great spirit shining in the heavens" and refers to the sun, with its generative powers of *musubi.* With its warmth and radiance, *Amaterasu okami* (or *Amaterasu omikami*) represents a powerful nurturing energy sustaining all life, an infinite love shining equally upon everyone and everything. Concentrate on embodying a radiant spirit of love. Set a clear intention and then let the practice develop naturally.

4. *Torifune* (second time)

Repeat the *torifune* exercise in the right *hanmi* (standing with your right leg forward) (Figures 4a–4b). Finish with a strong pull into

∾ Figure 4a. *Torifune* with right foot forward. Shift weight forward and extend arms. ∾ Figure 4b. Shift weight back and pull hands to hips. Extend forward again and repeat the motion continuously.

your center and step back again into a natural, balanced stance with your feet about shoulder-width apart.

5. *Furutama* (second time)

Breathe in again the ki of earth and heaven, close your eyes, and repeat the *furutama* practice (Figure 5). In this second section, concentrate on *OHARA-IDO NO OKAMI*. This means "the great spirit of purification." Purification, or *misogi,* is often associated with the element of water, especially flowing and cascading water. This represents the principle of movement in nature, of change and renewal. Breathe deeply and with a continuous flow. As you shake your hands vigorously up and down in front of your center, invite the spirit of purification into your practice, and strengthen the desire to purify your heart.

~ Figure 5. Clasp hands together and shake them vigorously at your center.

6. *Torifune* (third time)

Repeat the *torifune* exercise in the left *hanmi* (left foot forward) (Figures 6a–6b). Finish with a strong pull into your center and step back again into a natural, balanced stance with your feet about shoulder-width apart.

~ Figure 6a. *Torifune* with left foot forward. Shift weight forward and extend arms. ~ Figure 6b. Shift weight back and pull hands to hips. Extend forward again and repeat the motion continuously.

7. *Furutama* (third time)

Breathe in the ki of earth and heaven, and repeat the *furutama* practice for the third and final time (Figure 7). This time concentrate on center: *AME NO MINAKA NUSHI NO OKAMI*. This literally means "the great spirit of the center of the universe." It refers to the very first, original energy of the universe, the single point from which everything has emerged and evolved. Find your own center, breathe deeply, and sustain the *furutama* vibration. Find a sense of unity within yourself, and with everyone and everything in the universe.

~ Figure 7. Clasp hands together and shake them vigorously at your center.

8. Optional section (see page 311)

9. Conclusion

Open your eyes, and breathe in the ki of earth and heaven again, twice, as you raise your hands up your center line from earth to sky (just as you did at the beginning) (Figures 9a–9b). Clap sharply four times: heaven, fire, water, earth (Figures 9c–9d). Clasp your

~ Figure 9a. Breathe in the ki of earth. ~ Figure 9b. Breathe in the ki of heaven. ~ Figure 9c. Clap four times: heaven, fire, water, earth. ~ Figure 9d. Clap with the left hand slightly above the right.

〜 Figure 9e. Interlock fingers and rise up onto the balls of the feet.
〜 Figure 9f. Drop down onto the heels; pull hands towards heart while shouting the *kiai "EI."*

hands together and rise up onto the balls of the feet; then shout the *kiai "EI"* as you drop down onto your heels and pull strongly toward your heart (Figures 9e–9f). Clap four times once again.

With your hands clasped together (left over right), inscribe large horizontal circles, first counter-clockwise, then clockwise (three each). Then inscribe vertical circles, three counter-clockwise, then three clockwise. Follow the person who is leading, as he or she makes expansive, harmonious circles (Figures 9g–9n). Send out the spirit of harmony and gratitude in all directions. When you are finished, sustain this feeling and spirit as long as possible!

〜 Figures 9g–9i. Make horizontal circles with hands clasped.

~ Figures 9j–9l. Make vertical circles with hands clasped.

~ Figures 9m–9n. Swing clasped hands left and right, with sense of a circle going around you.

Optional section: Otakebi no Gyo

After the third *furutama,* there is a section that O-Sensei frequently did, but is not always practiced with the other parts. It involves calling out the name of various *kami,* and your own name as well, in a declaration of unity with the spirit(s) of the universe. *Otakebi no gyo* means "the spiritual practice of calling out strongly." A detailed explanation of this practice is not included here. What follows is a list of the *kami* that O-Sensei called upon in this section, and very simple instructions.

Hook your thumbs into your *obi* (belt), rise up on the balls of your feet, then come down firmly on your heels as you call out the name of each *kami: Iku musubi; Taru musubi; Tama tsume musubi* (one at a time); then *Iku tama; Taru tama; Tama tomari tama.*

Then call out your own name, followed directly by *Tokotachi no mikoto* (for men, a male *kami*); or *Tokotachi no hime* (for women, a female *kami*). (For instance, O-Sensei would have said "Ueshiba Morihei, *Tokotachi no mikoto!*") Call the names out strongly, with the faith and conviction that you will achieve unity with the spirit of the universe.

Finish with the breathing, four claps, *kiai,* four more claps, and expansive circles, as described above in "Conclusion."

"Aikido is *misogi*, purification of body and mind, a way to reform and transform the world. I show my techniques to encourage those of little faith."[60]

～ MORIHEI UESHIBA O-SENSEI

A NOTE ON TRANSLATION

I originally conceived of this book as a collection of conversations with Motomichi Anno Sensei. From his first visit to Santa Cruz in 1999, it was clear that Anno Sensei conveyed the teachings of Aikido warmly and eloquently in a conversational mode. Even in formal settings, he managed to communicate the feeling of a heart-to-heart conversation. I served as Anno Sensei's personal interpreter, conveying his words and teachings during classes on the mat, and in quickly flowing verbal interactions as he spoke with people individually or in small groups. I got into the habit of carrying a recording device with me at all times and letting it run whenever Anno Sensei was speaking about Aikido. In this way I was able to preserve many beautiful expressions of Aikido teachings in a variety of settings.

Most of the translated material in *Journey to the Heart of Aikido* has come from my collection of hundreds of hours of audio and video recordings of Anno Sensei speaking in Japanese. Organizing, reviewing, and selecting excerpts from these recordings, and translating them into smooth and accurate English, has been an immense undertaking that I have pursued for more than a decade. In order to convey most effectively the heart and intention of Anno Sensei's words and the essential body of teachings he has offered over the years, I have rearranged the order of some of Anno Sensei's remarks, combined similar material that was recorded at different times, and eliminated conversational digressions and most of the remarks of other people. Over time, I have shaped this material into a clear narrative that works well in English, while remaining true to the meaning of the original Japanese. As Anno Sensei does not speak or read English, he has given me complete freedom and trust in the translation and organization of the material. Therefore, although the words and teachings of Anno Sensei

313

in this book are entirely his, the organization, editing, and translation are all mine. It is my sincere belief that Anno Sensei's teachings are faithfully represented in *Journey to the Heart of Aikido*, but any errors of fact or interpretation are, of course, completely my responsibility.

Translating from Japanese to English is universally recognized as a challenge. Japanese is a unique language, belonging to none of the major language families of the world. Japanese grammar, vocabulary, and ways of communicating are so different from English that a strictly literal translation is not possible. The translator must inevitably make her or his own interpretation, and choose words and sentence structures in English accordingly. For instance, many sentences in Japanese do not have subjects or objects in the way that is considered necessary in English. Japanese communications utilize context and implication to convey meaning that would typically be more explicit in English. In addition, the almost complete absence of plurals, pronouns, and other common elements of English present a constant challenge for the conscientious translator. You could say that the original Japanese communication has to be actually *reconstructed* in English, based on one's understanding of the context and the intention of the speaker. I can't claim to have a complete understanding of Anno Sensei's teaching—or, of course, of the teachings of Aikido itself. But my study of this material, and my attempt to understand it deeply, has been the focus of my adult life, through both academic and personal studies. It has been a profound education and honor for me to engage so intensively with Anno Sensei's teachings, to transform them into English, and now to share them with the world in *Journey to the Heart of Aikido*.

In this book, I have chosen to render Japanese names in "Western order" for clarity and flow in English. For instance, I identify the founder of Aikido as "Morihei Ueshiba O-Sensei." Morihei is his personal name, Ueshiba is his family name, and O-Sensei is a title of respect, meaning "great" or "venerable" teacher. In the Japanese language, family names precede personal names, as in "Ueshiba Mori-hei," but throughout this book I have used the Western order. And in the case of the founder, I have most often referred to him simply as "O-Sensei." This is the way Anno Sensei and most of my teachers have referred to him, conveying both respect and warm regard with that short term. Other writers and translators have made a variety of valid choices in how to refer to the founder, and the term "O-Sensei" itself can be spelled in various ways.

I have used the modified Hepburn system of writing Japanese words in Roman characters, as it is the most common Romanization method in use today, and the most intuitive one for English language readers. In the interest of simplicity, I've chosen not to indicate the presence of long vowels (in Japanese words) by the use of macrons or additional letters.

Certain words in Japanese have no exact equivalents in English. Some of these words, such as *ki* (vital energy, spirit), *dojo* (training hall), or *tatami* (Japanese straw mat), have been widely adopted into modern English, so I have chosen to leave them as Japanese words in the text of this book. *Kami* is an important word with no exact English translation. Its meaning in Japanese ranges widely to include "spirit(s)," "nature," "the divine," or a multitude of Shinto deities, and it can refer to anything that inspires a feeling of awe or sacredness. *Kami* is sometimes translated into English as "God" or "the Lord," unfortunately adding a Judeo-Christian connotation that is absent in the original Japanese. Since the founder of Aikido frequently used the word *kami*, it is essential to become acquainted with its range of interpretation in order to attempt an understanding of his spiritual philosophy. In this book, I have left the word *kami* in Japanese, sometimes accompanied by a brief, simple rendering into English (such as "spirit, nature") to indicate to the reader the kind of meaning that Anno Sensei favors. (His interpretation of *kami* is explained in more depth in Chapter 7 of this book, in the section entitled "The Meaning of *Kami*.")

I well remember how exciting it was in the early 1970s to see the first books on Aikido come out in English. How moving I found it to be able to read the teachings of O-Sensei himself in my own language. I would like to express my appreciation to all of the translators who have applied themselves assiduously since that time to the great challenge of translating the teachings of Aikido, and particularly the teachings of O-Sensei, from Japanese into English. The fruit of their labor, presented in so many books and articles, has been a truly invaluable gift to the Aikido community in the West. Each translator contributes a slightly different perspective and enriches our collective understanding of this marvelous and challenging material. In this book, I have intentionally included a number of short quotations from O-Sensei's teachings that have been rendered into English by a variety of excellent translators.

I encourage anyone interested in Japanese to undertake the study of this unique and fascinating language. The experience of reading the words of Aikido's founder in his original Japanese, hearing them spoken aloud in audio recordings of his teachings, and hearing O-Sensei being quoted directly in teachings by his personal students has been a lifelong inspiration to me and has informed my translations in *Journey to the Heart of Aikido.*

— LINDA HOLIDAY

GLOSSARY OF JAPANESE TERMS

Many of the terms in this list have multiple meanings that depend on context and personal perspective. This glossary provides brief translations for your convenience as you read *Journey to the Heart of Aikido*.

Agatsu 吾勝   Self-victory; victory over oneself; personal integrity.

Ai 愛   Love.

Ai 合   Harmony.

Aiki 合氣   Harmony; blending or joining of *ki* (energy).

Aikidō 合氣道   A martial art and spiritual path founded in twentieth-century Japan by Morihei Ueshiba, known as "The Way of Harmony" or "The Art of Peace" (lit. "Harmony-Energy-Way").

Amaterasu ōmikami 天照大御神   (also: *Amaterasu okami*) The sun goddess in Japanese mythology; the primary heavenly *kami* among Shinto's many deities.

Ame no minaka nushi no ōkami 天の御中主の大神   The first *kami* that appears in the Shinto stories of the origin of the universe; "the spirit of the center of the universe," representing the single origin of all existence.

Ame no murakumo kuki samuhara ryu-ō 天の村雲九鬼さむはら龍王   A "dragon-king spirit that purifies and sets things right in the universe." A frequent reference by the founder of Aikido, who believed the dragon-king was a guardian spirit, of Aikido and of himself.

Ame no torifune no gyō 天の鳥船の行   Often abbreviated as "torifune" and called "the rowing exercise," its full name means "the ascetic practice *(gyo)* of the heavenly bird boat [a mythological reference]." An exercise often done at the beginning of Aikido classes as a physical and spiritual warm-up.

Ame no uki hashi 天の浮橋   The Floating Bridge of Heaven; a mythological reference to a bridge between heaven and earth, where the male and female deities *Izanagi* and *Izanami* united to bring the material world into existence.

Aramitama 荒御霊   "Rough spirit": the raw, fierce, powerful, wild aspect of spirit. One of four essential aspects of spirit *(mitama)* in Shinto.

Atemi 当て身   In Aikido training, a strike delivered to show an opening (vulnerable spot), or to create an opening to apply a technique.

Bokken 木剣   A wooden practice sword used in Aikido and other martial arts.

Bu 武   Often translated as "martial," as in "martial arts," O-Sensei used this word with a deeper meaning of martial virtue, declaring "*Bu* is love," and "The source of *Bu* is the spirit of loving protection of all things."

Budō 武道   The martial path or way; martial art(s) practiced with an emphasis on spiritual development as well as physical technique.

Bujutsu 武術   Martial arts or techniques; implies more emphasis on physical technique and less on spiritual aspects.

Chinkon kishin 鎮魂帰神   Various forms of meditative, ascetic, and spiritual exercises practiced in Shinto or related disciplines (lit. "Calm the spirit and return to *kami*").

Dai shizen 大自然   Great Nature—encompassing humankind, the environment, and the totality of the universe.

Dai-ai 大愛   Great love; divine love.

Dan 段   Black belt ranks (grades) in Aikido, such as *shodan* (first-degree black belt), *nidan* (second-degree), *sandan* (third-degree).

Dō 道   Also pronounced "michi": Path, or Way. The "Do" of Aikido.

Dōjō 道場   Martial arts training hall (lit. "Place of the Way").

318

Dōshu 道主　The family heir and living successor of the founder of Aikido, and head of the Aikikai Foundation in Japan; currently Moriteru Ueshiba, O-Sensei's grandson.

Furutama 振魂　An exercise of spiritual concentration, utilizing a vibrating motion of hands clasped together (lit. "spirit-shaking"; also "furitama" or "tamafuri").

Ga 我　Ego, self. As a spiritual concept, *ga* implies a sense of separation or self-centeredness, considered to be an error and obstacle to spiritual realization.

Gi 着　(or *keiko gi* 稽古着) Training uniform worn in Aikido or other martial arts.

Gokurōsama 御苦労様　Expression of gratitude for another's efforts on your behalf, as in "Thank you for your hard work."

Haiden 拝殿　Prayer hall (of a Shinto shrine).

Hakama 袴　Traditional divided skirt worn in the practice of Aikido and many traditional Japanese martial arts, such as Kendo and Naginata.

Hanmi 半身　A basic stance in Aikido training, with one foot forward.

Hara 腹　Physical and energetic center in the human body, in the lower abdomen.

Honden 本殿　Main sanctuary hall of a Shinto shrine, where the *kami* is ceremonially enshrined and thought to dwell.

Hōnō enbu 奉納演武　Martial arts demonstration done as an offering at a Shinto shrine.

Ikkyō 一教　The first foundational technique in Aikido repertoire.

Ikumusubi 生産霊　Generative power of *kami* that vivifies and increases the flow of energy in all living things.

Ikutama 生魂　"Living spirit"; an esoteric Shinto term used by the founder.

Inryoku 引力　The power of attraction; gravity. O-Sensei described Aikido training as a method of "forging the power of attraction."

Irimi nage 入り身投げ   Foundational Aikido technique utilizing the principle of "entering."

Iwato biraki 岩戸開き   "Opening of the Stone Door"; a reference to a myth in the *Kojiki*, in which light returned to the world after a period of darkness.

Izanagi (no mikoto, no kami) 伊邪那岐(の尊・の神)   The male *kami* who united with a female *kami (Izanami)* on the Floating Bridge of Heaven to give birth to the first land (the material universe), according to Japanese mythology.

Izanami (no mikoto, no kami) 伊邪那美(の尊・の神)   The female *kami* who united with a male *kami (Izanagi)* on the Floating Bridge of Heaven to give birth to the first land (the material universe), according to Japanese mythology.

Kaguramai 神楽舞   Sacred dance offering performed at Shinto shrines.

Kami 神   Spirit(s); the divine; sacred nature; specific deities of Shinto; *kami* can refer to anything that generates a feeling of awe or sacredness.

Kami no tsukae 神の仕え   One who serves the *kami;* servant of the divine.

Kamisama 神様   Honorific reference to *kami* (sacred spirits, Shinto deities).

Kanji 漢字   Ideographic Chinese characters used to write the Japanese language.

Kansha 感謝   Gratitude, thankfulness.

Ki 氣   Vital force, life energy.

Kobudō 古武道   Traditional Japanese martial arts schools that have preserved their ancient mode of training, handed down from generation to generation.

Kojiki 古事記   *Records of Ancient Matters:* a collection of myths and stories from oral accounts in the prehistory of Japan, first written down in 712 CE.

Kokoro 心   Heart; mind; spirit.

Kokyū 呼吸   Breath, breathing; a central term and deep concept in Aikido practice that refers to more than the physical breath.

Kokyū hō 呼吸法   Exercise to develop "breath power" in Aikido.

Kokyū nage 呼吸投げ   "Breath throw" in Aikido, utilizing movement, timing, blending, and "breath" to throw, with infinite variations possible.

Kokyū ryoku 呼吸力   "Breath power"; related to the power of *ki*.

Kon-paku 魂魄   Two complementary aspects of soul or spirit. *Kon* is more purely spiritual; *Haku (paku)* is more connected to the body and the material world.

Kongōkai 金剛界   Buddhist "Diamond" World or Mandala, a representation of metaphysical space in Japanese Shingon Buddhism; associated with the Yoshino area of Japan, north of Kumano.

Kotegaeshi 小手返し   A basic Aikido technique, utilizing a wrist lock.

Kototama 言霊   "Word-spirit": the spiritual power in words, names, and sounds. "Kototama" can be a general term; it also refers to various complex systems of studying the spiritual meaning of Japanese sounds and syllables.

Kū 空   Emptiness, the void, insubstantiality. Written with the *kanji* for "sky."

Kū no ki 空の氣   The *ki* (energy) of *Ku* (emptiness); a teaching of the founder.

Kumano 熊野   The ancient name of the southern part of the Kii Peninsula; known as the spiritual heartland of Japan. Birthplace of the founder of Aikido.

Kumano Kodō 熊野古道   A network of ancient pilgrimage routes in Kumano, Japan, designated an UNESCO World Heritage Site in 2004.

Makoto 誠   Truth, sincerity, integrity.

Masakatsu 正勝   True (correct) victory.

Matsuri 祭り　Festival, sacred ceremony.

Michi 道　Path, way. Also pronounced "Do," as in Aikido.

Misogi 禊　Purification or cleansing of body, mind, and spirit; can also refer specifically to Shinto purification rites, often utilizing cold water on the body.

Mitama sai 御霊祭　Spirit ceremony (in Shinto).

Mu 無　Nothing; nonexistence; emptiness. An important teaching in Buddhism, especially Zen Buddhism.

Mushin 無心　An open, clear state of mind that can move freely and is empty of intrusive thoughts or emotions. A Buddhist term, in general use (lit. "No mind").

Musubi 結び　Joining, connection, tying together.

Musubi 産日　Powers of creation and harmony (ancient Japanese term).

Nage 投げ　Person executing an Aikido technique or throw (lit. "throw").

Nigimitama 和御霊　"Peaceful spirit": the refined, harmonious, peaceful aspect of spirit. One of four essential aspects of spirit (*mitama*) in Shinto.

Nihonshoki 日本書紀　Japan's first official written history, completed 720 CE.

Nikyō 二教　The second foundational technique in the Aikido repertoire, utilizing a wrist lock.

Norito 祝詞　Shinto ritual prayers and ceremonial words, chanted aloud in elegant, poetic language.

O-Jizō-san (Jizō Bosatsu) お地蔵さん (地蔵菩薩)　One of the most beloved of Japanese Buddhist divinities; guardian of children, travelers, and suffering souls.

Oharaido no ōkami 御祓戸之大神　"Great *Kami* of Purification." This refers to numerous spirits (*kami*) of purification, and also to cleansing processes in nature.

Okagesama おかげさま   Expression of gratitude to others; "Thanks to you."

Omote, ura 表・裏   Front and back; terms used to describe different versions of Aikido techniques. Also: the surface and what is underneath or inside.

Onegai shimasu お願いします   "(If you) please" or "I ask a favor." An expression used in Aikido practice to ask for instruction or to begin training with someone.

Otakebi no gyō 雄叫の行   The practice (*gyo*) of uttering loud shouts or calling out words strongly, as part of a purification ritual.

Saisei itchi 祭政一致   Among many interpretations, Anno Sensei favors this one: "The integration of spiritual principles into daily life and public service."

Sakaki 榊   An evergreen tree considered sacred in Japan. *Sakaki* branches are used as offerings in Shinto ceremonies.

Seiza 正座   Formal upright seated posture with one's legs folded underneath.

Senpai 先輩   One's senior (in school, work, martial arts, etc.).

Sensei 先生   Teacher.

Shiai 試合   Competitive match in martial arts.

Shide 紙垂   White folded paper streamers used in Shinto rituals, and to designate sacred objects and spaces.

Shihan 師範   Teacher; model. A master teacher who is a model for others. In modern Aikido, an honorific title for high-level instructors.

Shihō nage 四方投げ   Foundational Aikido technique (lit. four directions throw).

Shimenawa 注連縄   Sacred rope made of rice straw, used for purification and to indicate a sacred or pure space; often encircling objects or placed in a gateway.

Shin jin gō itsu 神人合一 "*Kami* and humanity are one."

Shin kokyū 神呼吸・深呼吸 1."Breath of *kami*" purification breathing practice. 2. Deep breathing exercises (using the *kanji* that means "deep," not "*kami*").

Shin kū no ki 真空の氣 The *ki* (energy) of true emptiness *(shin ku); a* teaching of the founder.

Shin zen bi 真・善・美 Truth, goodness, and beauty.

Shinden 神殿 Shrine.

Shingi (also read kamiwaza or kamuwaza) 神技 Divine (heavenly) technique or act.

Shinken 真剣 "Live blade (sword)." Sincerity; seriousness; committing heart and soul to an endeavor.

Shinken shōbu 真剣勝負 Live-blade battle; a serious struggle or life-or-death situation.

Shintō 神道 "The Way of *Kami*": the indigenous spiritual practices and religion of Japan, originating in prehistory.

Shizen 自然 Nature, the natural world.

Shizentai 自然体 Natural, neutral stance.

Shō chiku bai no ken 松竹梅の剣 Sword work of "pine-bamboo-plum."

Shodō 書道 Japanese brush calligraphy; the practice of writing calligraphy.

Shōmen uchi 正面打ち Frontal strike to the head.

Shugyō 修行・修業 Rigorous spiritual or ascetic training undertaken to learn a martial art or other practice, for personal development and spiritual awakening.

Sugata 姿 Form, shape.

Suki 隙 Opening, gap; a moment's inattention; vulnerability in a martial sense.

Sunao 素直　Sincere, humble, open-minded.

Susano-o no mikoto 須佐の男の尊　The storm god, a major *kami* (deity) in Shinto. Younger brother of *Amaterasu omikami,* the sun goddess.

Tai no henkō 体の変更　A turning and harmonizing movement that forms the basis for many Aikido techniques.

Taizōkai 胎蔵界　Buddhist "Womb" World or Mandala, a representation of metaphysical space in Japanese Shingon Buddhism; associated with the sacred mountains of the Kumano region of Japan.

Take Musu Aiki 武産合氣　A phrase often used by the founder of Aikido, referring to the spontaneous generation of technique and the experience of love, harmony, and unification with the universe at the highest levels of Aikido.

Tamashii 魂　Spirit, soul.

Tenshi 天使　Angel, heavenly being.

Uke 受け　The person who attacks and then receives an Aikido technique, usually taking a fall (lit. "receive").

Ukemi 受け身　The practice of attacking, receiving a technique, and falling.

Waza 技 (業)　Technique; can also refer to action or behavior.

Yamabushi 山伏　Practitioners of Shugendo: strenuous ascetic, mystical practices in sacred mountainous areas of Japan such as Kumano, since the seventh century CE.

Yatagarasu 八咫烏　Mythological three-legged crow, symbol of the *Kumano kami.*

Yokomen uchi 横面打ち　Diagonal strike to the side of the head.

Yū 有　Existence, being.

ENDNOTES

1. The founder of Aikido wrote numerous *do-ka,* "Poems of the Way." These are short poems expressing essential teachings of Aikido, composed in the traditional Japanese *waka* form, with syllables arranged in a 5-7-5-7-7 pattern. O-Sensei's *do-ka* were first given to me in handwritten calligraphic form by Anno Sensei in 1973. I have translated the five *do-ka* poems in my book from the original Japanese. Various collections of O-Sensei's poems have been published in books, in Japanese and in translated form (see the two books listed below).

   Kisshomaru Ueshiba, *Aikido,* under the supervision of Morihei Ueshiba (Tokyo: Kowado, 1957), 169–173.

   Morihei Ueshiba, *The Essence of Aikido,* compiled and translated by John Stevens (Tokyo: Kodansha International, 1993), 39–76.

2. Morihei Ueshiba, quoted in a radio interview (c. 1962), in the DVD *The Way of Harmony,* published by *Aikido Journal,* www.aikidojournal.com, 2005. My translation from the original Japanese.

3. Ueshiba, *Aikido* (1957), 51.

4. Kisshomaru Ueshiba, *Aikido,* translated by Kazuaki Tanahashi and Roy Maurer Jr. (Tokyo: Hozansha Publishing Co., Ltd, 1978), 181.

5. Allan G. Grapard, "Flying Mountains and Walkers of Emptiness: Toward a Definition of Sacred Space in Japanese Religions," in Buddhism: Critical Concepts in Religious Studies, Vol. VIII, ed. Paul Williams (New York: Routledge, 2005), 147–151.

6. Information about the history and faith of Kumano, and Kumano's designation as a World Heritage Site by the United Nations Educational, Scientific, and Cultural Organization, can be found on the following websites:

   "Sacred Sites and Pilgrimage Routes in the Kii Mountain Range," UNESCO. http://whc.unesco.org/en/list/1142

   "Sacred Sites and Pilgrimage Routes in the Kii Mountain Range," Wakayama World Heritage Center. www.sekaiisan-wakayama.jp/english/index.html

"Kumano Kodo Pilgrimage Routes (World Heritage)," Tanabe City Kumano Tourism Bureau. www.tb-kumano.jp/en/kumano-kodo

"The Kumano Field Museum: Its Meaning and Purpose," Kumano Field Museum. http://kumano-world.org/english/kfm_eng.html

Alison Tokita, "Performance and Text: Gender Identity and the Kumano Faith," in *Intersections: Gender and Sexuality in Asia and the Pacific*, Issue 16 (March 2008), http://intersections.anu.edu.au/issue16/tokita.htm, accessed December 20, 2012.

7. John Stevens, *Invincible Warrior* (Boston, Shambhala Publications, Inc., 1997), 76.

8. Jean Herbert, *Shinto: The Fountainhead of Japan* (London: George Allen & Unwin Ltd, 1967), 35. This is a 600+-page scholarly reference book on all aspects of Shinto, including its mythology. A detailed explanation of the land-creation of *Izanagi* and *Izanami* on the Floating Bridge of Heaven is found on pages 234–251.

9. Ueshiba, *Aikido* (1957), 201. "No opponent" was a central, frequent teaching of O-Sensei, and is found in numerous sources as well as oral accounts.

10. "Welcome to Aikido Hawaii," words of Morihei Ueshiba O-Sensei regarding his visit to Hawaii in 1961. http://www.aikidohawaii.org

11. The first full-length book published on Aikido was by Kisshomaru Ueshiba, under the supervision of his father, Morihei Ueshiba: *Aikido* (Tokyo: Kowado, 1957). This book was first published in Japanese, and was later published in English as part of Kisshomaru Ueshiba's *Aikido* (Tokyo: Hozansha Publishing Co., Ltd, 1978).

12. The fascinating life of Aikido's founder, Morihei Ueshiba, has been examined in detail in numerous publications, including these full-length biographies in English:

Kisshomaru Ueshiba, *A Life in Aikido: The Biography of Founder Morihei Ueshiba*, translated by Kei Izawa and Mary Fuller (Tokyo: Kodansha International, 2008).

John Stevens, *Abundant Peace: The Biography of Morihei Ueshiba Founder of Aikido* (Boston: Shambhala Publications, Inc., 1987).

A wealth of historical information about the founder's life can also be found in numerous articles and books published by Stanley Pranin of *Aikido Journal*.

My intention in this section of *Journey to the Heart of Aikido* is to provide only a brief overview of the life of the founder, with an emphasis on his spiritual pursuits, and on the development of Aikido in the Kumano region, where Anno Sensei studied with him. My account of this history is distilled from many sources that have been available to me over forty years of study, including oral accounts from Anno Sensei and other people who were personally acquainted with the founder.

13. Ueshiba, *A Life in Aikido*, 84.
14. Ueshiba, *A Life in Aikido*, 86.
15. Ueshiba, *Aikido* (1957), 203. This interview with Morihei Ueshiba and Kisshomaru Ueshiba was later translated into English, by Stanley Pranin and Katsuaki Terasawa, and can be found on the *Aikido Journal* website. http://members.aikidojournal.com/members-home/interviews-3/
16. Ueshiba, *Aikido* (1978), 5.
17. Susan Perry, editor, *Remembering O-Sensei: Living and Training with Morihei Ueshiba, Founder of Aikido* (Boston: Shambhala Publications, Inc., 2002), 89–90.
18. Mitsugi Saotome, *Aikido and the Harmony of Nature* (Boston: Shambhala Publications, Inc., 1993), 11. I had the honor of working with Saotome Sensei to translate early drafts of his brilliant first book. This excerpt, along with much of the first chapter of *Aikido and the Harmony of Nature*, was originally translated from Japanese as part of my senior thesis (Honors) at the University of California, Santa Cruz, 1979.
19. Ueshiba, *Aikido* (1957), 50. My translation from the original Japanese.
20. Stevens, *Abundant Peace*, 49.
21. Ueshiba, *Aikido* (1957), 219. Translated by Pranin and Terasawa, *Aikido Journal*.
22. Ueshiba, *A Life in Aikido*, 285.
23. Ueshiba, *A Life in Aikido*, 288.
24. Ueshiba, *A Life in Aikido*, 306.
25. Susan Perry, "Interview: Motomichi Anno Sensei," trans. Mary Heiny and Linda Holiday, Aikido Today Magazine #69 (2000): 9–11. (The

last paragraph in this section ("A Lifelong Practice") has been slightly adapted from the interview.)

26. Stanley Pranin, "Interview with Seiseki Abe (1 & 2), *Aikido Journal* #114 (1998). http://members.aikidojournal.com/private/interview-with-seiseki-abe-2/

27. Laurin Herr and Tim Detmer, "Michio Hikitsuchi Sensei," translated by Aya Nishimoto and Laurin Herr, *Aikido Today Magazine* #79 (December 2001), 7,10.

28. Herr and Detmer, "Michio Hikitsuchi Sensei," 10.

29. Susan Perry, editor, *Remembering O-Sensei*, 82–83.

30. Ueshiba, *A Life in Aikido*, 316.

31. Ueshiba, *Aikido* (1978), 179.

32. Ueshiba, *Aikido* (1978), 169.

33. Ueshiba, *Aikido* (1978), 181.

34. Ueshiba, *Aikido* (1957), 219. Translated by Pranin and Terasawa, *Aikido Journal*.

35. Ueshiba, *Aikido* (1978), 179.

36. Kisshomaru Ueshiba, *The Spirit of Aikido*, translated by Taitetsu Unno (Tokyo: Kodansha International, 1984), 75.

37. Perry, "Interview: Motomichi Anno Sensei," trans. Heiny and Holiday, *Aikido Today Magazine*. (The last two paragraphs of the section "A Paradox" have been adapted from the interview.)

38. Morihei Ueshiba, *The Essence of Aikido: Spiritual Teachings of Morihei Ueshiba*, compiled and translated by John Stevens (Tokyo: Kodansha International, 1993), 39.

39. Ueshiba, *Aikido* (1978), 178.

40. These words of O-Sensei were passed on to me by Motomichi Anno Sensei in the form of hand-brushed calligraphy, in Shingu, 1973.

41. Mitsugi Saotome, *The Principles of Aikido*, translated by William Gleason and Paul Kang (Boston: Shambhala Publications, Inc., 1989), 24.

42. Perry, "Interview: Motomichi Anno Sensei," trans. Heiny and Holiday, Aikido Today Magazine. (The last three paragraphs of the section "The Meaning of Ukemi" have been adapted from the interview.)

43. Morihei Ueshiba, *The Secret Teachings of Aikido*, translated by John Stevens (Tokyo: Kodansha International, 2007), 108.

44. Hideo Takahashi, ed., *Take Musu Aiki: Lectures of Morihei Ueshiba Sensei* (Chiba-ken: Byakko Shinko Kai, 1976), 112. "The second opening of the stone door" was a frequent reference in O-Sensei's teachings.

45. A *do-ka* poem by O-Sensei; with my translation (see Endnote #1, above).

46. Morihei Ueshiba, *Excerpts from the Writings and Transcribed Lectures of the Founder, Morihei Ueshiba*, compiled by Morihiro Saito, translator unknown (pamphlet published with permission of Aikido Hombu Dojo in Tokyo, 1982), section 1.

47. Takahashi, *Take Musu Aiki*, 48; with my translation of this excerpt.

48. Ueshiba, *The Secret Teachings of Aikido*, 112.

49. Saotome, *Aikido and the Harmony of Nature*, 66.

50. Herbert, *Shinto: The Fountainhead of Japan*, "The Genesis of the Universe—The Pre-Material Stages," 234–251, and "The Birth of the Land," 252–268.

51. Ueshiba, *The Secret Teachings of Aikido*, 112.

52. A *do-ka* poem by O-Sensei; with my translation (see Endnote #1, above).

53. Perry, "Interview: Motomichi Anno Sensei," trans. Heiny and Holiday, *Aikido Today Magazine*. (The last three paragraphs of the section "Kototama: Words of Spirit" have been adapted from the interview.)

54. Ueshiba, *Aikido* (1957), 199. Translated by Pranin and Terasawa, *Aikido Journal*.

55. Morihei Ueshiba, *The Art of Peace*, translated and edited by John Stevens (Boston: Shambhala Publications, Inc., 2002), 21.

56. Stevens, *Abundant Peace*, 101.

57. A *do-ka* poem by O-Sensei; with my translation (see Endnote #1, above).

58. Takahashi, *Take Musu Aiki*, 47; with my translation of this excerpt.

59. Takahashi, *Take Musu Aiki*, 38; with my translation.

60. Stevens, *Abundant Peace*, 108.

CREDITS

Sincere thanks to all of the people who have provided the images in *Journey to the Heart of Aikido*.

Photograph of O-Sensei on page 14 courtesy of Moriteru Ueshiba, Aikido Doshu, used with permission.

Unless otherwise noted, the historical Aikido photos of O-Sensei, as well as Hikitsuchi Sensei, Anno Sensei, and others in the Kumano region are courtesy of Motomichi Anno, Minako Hikitsuchi, and the Kumano Juku Dojo photo archive.

Photographs in the first color insert are © Tanabe City Kumano Tourism Bureau (page 2) and Linda Holiday (page 3). Photographs in the second color insert are © Dan Caslin (page 1); Koji Kusumoto (page 2); Motomichi Anno (page 3); Nico Secunda (page 4, upper); Nathaniel McCully (page 4, lower); Katsuya Nakao (page 5, upper); Michael Smith (page 5, lower); Larry Colen (page 8, lower; page 11, upper); and Jan Nevelius (page 10). All other photographs in the two color inserts are © Beau Saunders, used with permission.

Photos on pages 10 (right), 41, 90, 135, 151, 170, 172, 176, 178, 182, 187, 190, 192, 195, 198, 203, 208, 213, 216, 272, 276, 279, 288, 294, and 302–310 are © Beau Saunders, used with permission. Beau Saunders also restored and archived the historical photographs from Kumano and prepared all the photos in the book for publication.

Photographs on the following pages are © the photographers listed below, used with permission: Dan Caslin (37); David W. Christie (5, 44, 96, 153, 159, 184); Larry Colen (265, 283); David Gross (25, 49); Garth Jones (55); Alan Holiday (28); Linda Holiday (74, 241, 261); Alexander Kolbasov (197); Jean-Pierre Kunzi (274); Mark MacDougall (212); Nathaniel McCully (94); Katsuya Nakao (223, 225, 227, 229, 233); Geoffrey Nix (138, 167); Nico Secunda (10, lower left); and Tosh Tanaka (267).

Photographs on the following pages are courtesy of these sources: Aikido Journal (218, 221); Robert Frager (7); Linda Holiday (31, 37, 49); Danielle Smith (93); Noel Tendick (146); and Jack Wada (32).

CREDITS

Photographs of O-Sensei's calligraphy courtesy of Ryoichi Kinoshita (100, 106, 132, 236, 262); Motomichi Anno (x); and Aikido of Santa Cruz (149).

ACKNOWLEDGMENTS

The first day I stepped onto the Aikido mat in 1970, I learned to express gratitude and respect in the form of a simple bow. In the course of an Aikido class, we bow many times to the people we practice with, as well as to the art of Aikido and its founder.

The journey of creating this book has spanned the last fourteen years, but in a real sense it began that first day on the mat. The support I have received over the many years since then, from my teachers, colleagues, students, and dear friends, has enabled me to bring this book into being. With a full heart I offer, to one and all, a sincere bow of deepest gratitude and respect.

To O-Sensei, for his profound gift of Aikido to the world.

To O-Sensei's son Kisshomaru Ueshiba Doshu, and to his son, the current Doshu, Moriteru Ueshiba, for their lifelong devotion to the leadership of Aikido.

To all my teachers in the Kumano Juku Dojo in Japan, especially the late chief instructor Michio Hikitsuchi, the late Yasushi Tojima, and Motoichi Yanase.

To the pioneering Aikido instructors in California, who inspire me still: Robert Frager, Frank Doran, Robert Nadeau, Bill Witt, and Stanley Pranin.

To Mitsugi Saotome, the late Terry Dobson, and the late Hiroshi Kato, all of whom have influenced me deeply with their instruction.

To Mary Heiny, lifelong friend and generous *senpai*, who introduced me to my teachers in Kumano and has supported my dojo over all the years.

To Jack Wada, a true friend and inspired colleague since our early years training together in Kumano.

To Richard Revoir, whose casual comment to me in 1972, "I think I'll go to Japan to study Aikido," started the whole adventure.

To Glen Kimoto, for nearly forty years of co-teaching, collaboration on the dojo, and consistent support.

ACKNOWLEDGMENTS

To all the students and teachers at my dojo, Aikido of Santa Cruz, who have inspired me with their sincere training, strength of community, and dedicated work to support Anno Sensei's many visits to the United States.

I am deeply thankful for the many friends, colleagues, and students who have contributed to this book in a myriad of ways, providing logistical support, translation advice, research assistance, editorial review and feedback, and personal support and encouragement: including Dan Caslin, Scott Evans, Richard Strozzi Heckler, Laurin Herr, Alan Holiday, Jerilyn Munyon, Neville and Jane Nason, Jan Nevelius, Susan Perry, Stanley Pranin, Brant and Nico Secunda, Casey Silvey, Danielle and Michael Smith, and Laurie Talcott, among others.

I am especially grateful for the personal support I have received over all the years of this project from my close friend, longtime student, and colleague in San Francisco, Penny Sablove.

Beau Saunders has worked tirelessly for more than a year to collect, archive, restore, and edit the photographs in *Journey to the Heart of Aikido.* His own photographs grace many pages of the book, along with the generous contributions of nearly twenty other photographers. I sincerely thank Beau for his devoted and excellent work.

Carolyn Brigit Flynn has been the mainstay of my support on this book for several years. She is herself an author, poet, and teacher, whose deep perception and keen editorial eye helped me to shape the complex material into a book with a clear vision. I cannot thank Carolyn enough for her dedication to the birth of this book, her constant faith in me, and her enduring friendship.

I thank my agent, Steve Scholl, for his enthusiastic expertise as he guided my first foray into the world of publishing. North Atlantic Books has been wonderful to work with, especially my editor, Erin Wiegand, whose patient support and cheerful encouragement made it all possible.

What a deep joy it is to share the profound path of Aikido with my son, Nathan Holiday. He has watched me work on this book for most of the years of his life, and cheered me on. May he and others of his generation love Aikido as much as I do, and be moved to carry it forward into the future.

ACKNOWLEDGMENTS

With the deepest respect and a lifetime of gratitude, I acknowledge my teacher Motomichi Anno Sensei, whose wisdom, sincerity, and dedication to the heart of Aikido is a shining light in my life.

To all of you, I bow.

—LINDA HOLIDAY

ABOUT THE AUTHOR

Photo credit: Beau Saunders

LINDA HOLIDAY is a senior American Aikido teacher who began her practice of Aikido in California over forty years ago. In 1973 she moved to Japan for several years to receive instruction from the generation of Japanese Aikido teachers who had studied directly with the founder, Morihei Ueshiba. Holiday was one of the first Westerners to undertake intensive training at the Kumano Juku Dojo. It was during this time that she met Motomichi Anno Sensei and began to study with him.

Holding a sixth-degree black belt awarded by the Aikikai Foundation in Japan, Linda Holiday has devoted over three decades to teaching Aikido in her native California as well as leading seminars in the United States and Europe. Complementing her training in Japan with academic study in the West, she received a BA in Japanese and Chinese Studies from the University of California, Santa Cruz, in 1979, and a master's degree in East Asian Studies from Stanford University in 1983. She has served as an interpreter for numerous Japanese Aikido teachers.

In 1982 Linda Holiday founded Aikido of Santa Cruz (North Bay Aikido, Inc.), a nonprofit educational organization and dojo, where she serves as executive director and teaches regularly as chief instructor. Traveling nationally and internationally, she leads and co-teaches Aikido events that draw together teachers and students from a wide variety of affiliations.

ABOUT MOTOMICHI ANNO SENSEI

MOTOMICHI ANNO is one of the highest-level teachers of Aikido in the world today. An eighth-degree black belt since 1978, he is one of the few remaining Japanese master-teachers who received direct instruction and inspiration from the founder of Aikido. In 2009, Anno Sensei received the prestigious Distinguished Service Award from the Japan Martial Arts Association for his lifetime dedication to teaching Aikido.

Photo credit: Beau Saunders

Anno Sensei was born in 1931 in the Kumano region of Japan, where many traditions and spiritual practices of Japan have been kept alive. When he was twenty-three years old, Anno Sensei met the founder of Aikido; he has been dedicated to the practice of the art ever since. For over four decades, Anno Sensei served as a senior instructor at the historic Kumano Juku Dojo in Shingu, Japan. He also founded his own school, Matsubara Dojo, in Kumano City in 1969. In 2004, he succeeded the late Michio Hikitsuchi Sensei to serve for nine years as the chief instructor of the Kumano Juku Dojo.

Deeply rooted in traditional Japan, Anno Sensei has a remarkable ability to convey the heart of Aikido to people of different cultures. Now in his eighties, he has traveled many times to teach in the United States and Europe. Anno Sensei lives with his wife on his family homestead in the countryside of western Japan.